I0428836

Author:
Bodo Dietrich
E-mail:
bodo.dietrich.buch@web.de

Available at:
amazon.com
amazon.de

First English Edition February 2016

My Successful Way Out Of Burnout.

"Come on Amygdala, let's dance…"

Dedication:

This book is dedicated to:

My wife Marliese because, with her love and help, she gave me hope and courage during this time that everything would be fine and because she carried a large part of the burden, which my situation introduced into the family life.

Our 2 children so that they learn from my mistakes.

My mother because we (and especially I) have a lot to thank her for. She was always there for us and lived for us.

During my second visit to Carolabad (this time as a guest) I had another idea.

I also dedicate this book of my own personal experiences to the **doctors** and **therapists,** especially my then therapist, our doctor at home where I live, GP and the medical team at the Rehabilitation Clinic, who save the lives of patients or give them back their will to live, vitality and courage every day. That is certainly not often an easy thing to do and it also is not always successful, but when it is, it does an infinite amount of good.

Maybe they do not really know anymore how valuable this work and their daily efforts are.

Even when it is "only" their normal job: THANK YOU!

Contents

Chapter   Page

Short comments from readers of this manuscript   004

Foreword by Dr. Thomas Schell   006

Comments by K. M., Psychotherapist   011

1.) Introduction: Why am I writing this book?   012

2.) The beginning: The time with my six "Pressure Points"   018

3.) The 23.11.2011. My personal 09/11   030

4.) The Rehabilitation Clinic   062

4.1) The first day in the Rehabilitation Clinic   067

4.2) The first morning meeting   069

4.3) Sports Course 1   072

4.4) 2.5-week bed rest with an infection!!!! So annoying!   079

4.5) "My Therapist and me"   084

4.6) "Who or what is the most important person or thing

   in your life?"   086

4.7) Organization, timetable and breaks   091

4.8) Working on the core problem at work   095

4.9) Helper syndrome: say NO   103

4.10) The "Fear" Group   107

4.11) My friend Amygdala   114

4.12) A lecture by my therapist   124

4.13) The "Thinking Trap"   127

4.14) Social competence   128

4.15) Health care behavior   132

4.16) The creative area. Painting, pottery etc.   136

4.17) Bio Feedback   139

4.18) Relaxation therapy   144

4.19) Social therapist: Reintegration   152

4.20) Group therapy   153

4.21) Social Network + Diagram   159

4.22) Family visit   169

4.23) A difficult goodbye   173

5.) Reintegration   174

6.) Back to work   183

7.) The old and the new boss   189

8.) Letter to a friend   199

9.) My Therapist   206

10.) Return to the Rehabilitation Clinic
      (21 months after the 11.06.2012)   209

11.) What have I changed?   214

12.) My personal conclusion   227

13.) What do I have to do with God?   233

14.) Thanks   238

15.) List of references   244

16.) Appendix   245

Short comments from "first-time readers", who read the manuscript of this book in advance:

"With this book you give the reader a very personal insight into the circumstances which led to your burnout and show how you can overcome the misery by yourself. I can see the particular value of this for a reader who is possibly confronted with a similar situation."
(H.-U.K.)

"I am the managing director of a company and, as such, I have a lot of responsibility for my employees. I read the book and recommended it to an employee affected by this as well as her department"
(M.G. from H.)

"Thanks for this open and honest book!!!
I think that it should not only be read by people at risk of burnout, but also by their partners and relatives".
(A.U. from R.)

"This book really got under my skin. The fears, anxiety and doubt are very easy to understand. Above all, it is brilliantly successful at describing how quickly a person can get to such a point. "I'll manage it", "It has to work now", "It's bound to get better soon" - most people know these thoughts! All the more valuable is a book that makes it clear that you need to be CAREFUL – listen to your body! The experiences in this book can help in a burnout situation, and for that, thank you very much!"
(I.M. from N.)

"Wow!! I am speechless (doesn't happen so often!) Very brave und "brutally" open in the description of your own situation!"
(R.R. from O.)

"The beginning of the book didn't really benefit me, but I found the letter to a friend really good."
(T.D. from M.)

"I found it very interesting how the stressful situations were described and how the physical reactions were successfully dealt with in order to be able to control them"
(K.U. from R.)

"I'm sorry, but I was never in such a situation and it is hard for me to put myself in your shoes. I would have reacted differently, sooner so that it

wouldn't have gone so far. Therefore, I personally cannot really relate to the described feelings and emotions"
(Anonymous, known to the author)

"It isn't easy to write such a profound book about yourself "
(anonymous, known to the author)

"As a person who has been affected, I couldn't put this book down. I am deeply impressed by how intensively and openly the situations have been described"

(I.R. from A.)

Foreword

These days when we open newspapers and magazines, surf on the Internet or sit in front of the television, we could get the impression that it is being reported more and more often about the incidences of a condition, which almost nobody knew anything about a few years ago, never mind being mentioned in the media: "Burnout." The question is, what kind of condition is it, which has seemingly spread like an epidemic, under which those affected often suffer, but which some experts say does not exist?

What is burnout, and what are the symptoms? Most of those affected, especially those in the advanced stages, report distinct feelings of exhaustion, a loss of interest and motivation, insomnia and difficulties in making decisions – symptoms we know from depressive disorders. That is why Burnout Syndrome is often equated with depression and there are, without doubt, clear overlaps. Even the physical symptoms, which can accompany Burnout Syndrome, often also occur with depressive conditions.

While the expression "depression" does not explain the cause of the condition (genes, external stress factors and/or a person's own personal attitudes could all play a role), the expression "burnout" gives some clues to the reasons behind the symptoms: the person is "burned out", is totally spent, has become overly committed to achieve a goal or a task, has demanded more of himself than he can actually give. It involves people who show particular dedication, but who do not consider their own limitations. Originally, the expression "burnout" was reserved for people in the care profession, as this was where "over-commitment" was often observed (so-called "Helper Syndrome").

So the question is why "burnout" has become even more important in the media these days. Depression has been around for 50 years and there have always been people who are strongly or too strongly committed to things. There are 2 factors playing an important role here:

First of all, we live in a society in which performance levels have been given enormous meaning. There seems to be more focus on performance in schools than on developing social competence, creativity, spontaneity or emotionality. We should make ourselves available to the job market as early as possible with optimal schooling and excellent grades. Those who achieve these goals receive recognition, which initially seems to reinforce our self-worth. In an age, which is all about constant optimization and growth, there is also an intensification of work: we are expected to achieve more in less time and with fewer resources. In this situation, it is often those who are especially committed who try to compensate.

As an example, when the number of care givers and medical personnel is reduced in some hospitals, but at the same time more treatments are expected to happen in order to increase profits and returns, experience shows that the most conscientious people commit themselves even more to their work so that the patients do not suffer. However, the management of the hospitals only sees that everything continues to work despite cutting jobs and could then feel the need for further "optimization measures". People who have a high commitment to performance and distinct conscientiousness are especially at risk, as they want to fulfill expectations with ever increasing levels of performance. They work themselves into the ground and eventually "burn out".

Another factor why "burnout" is mentioned more often in the media could be the fact that our society has become increasingly more open about this topic and about psychological conditions in general. A person who has a heart attack can typically handle it: the colleagues often show understanding and the relatives sympathy. Unfortunately, the reactions are more often than not completely different when it comes to depression. People often cannot understand the condition. They think, "someone is not pulling himself or herself together", believe the person suffering from depression is just "lazy" or think that he is just "crazy" and so on. In reality however, the line between full health and depression is very fine. An ECG cannot detect depression, but, it is an illness of the human body like every other illness and it should be taken very seriously – like a heart attack – as a deep depression can also end in death through suicide.

Fortunately, more and more people are open to the topic of "depression", firstly because they are confronted with it through acquaintances, relatives, colleagues or work and spend time dealing with it. Secondly, the stigmas attached to the topic are disappearing thanks to it being in the media more frequently. Even doctors outside of the psychiatric-psychosomatic field are becoming more open and are also better trained in how to deal with it. Nowadays if you would like to become a GP, you generally have to complete a course in, for example, "Basic Psychosomatic Care". Due to these developments in society and the medical field, conditions can often be recognized and treated earlier.

Whereas a few years ago those affected did not know or did not dare to say that they suffered from depressive symptoms, but would, for example, be more likely to visit the doctor with the physical, accompanying symptoms, today psychological conditions are more likely to be recognized and named as such. This development, which is very welcome, accounts for the fact that psychological conditions are more frequently diagnosed today than in the past.

I am very grateful for the emergence of the expression "burnout" and the discussions surrounding it in the media despite all the scientific inaccuracies: To suffer from "burnout" seems to be by far more acceptable to people than to have depression. I have often spoken to patients, who at first attach great importance to suffering from "burnout" than from depression, even though depressive symptoms were clearly in evidence and the criteria for depression were undoubtedly fulfilled. In therapy however, this was a "door", a possibility to discover the real problems and to then create an effective treatment for the good of the patients.

With that, I come finally to the book, for which the author has asked me to write a forward. From the beginning, I thought the idea to write the book was fantastic. Firstly because the author is once again confronted with the experiences of his illness and return to health, and secondly because he can use this book to share these experiences and knowledge with others. It seems very important to me to share information about depression and burnout with relatives and, above all, those affected by it, but at the same time to give them legitimate hope that, with frankness and willingness, a successful treatment with a return to a high quality of life can be reckoned with. Who could portray this better than someone who has been affected by this condition, who has been through all the highs and lows, who can report on all the pitfalls which can be encountered, who, after a lot of hard work (including the use of therapy), proactivity as well as the necessary patience, made a successful recovery?

Unfortunately, therapy is a lot of hard work, especially for the patient. In the initial phases, the Therapist will contribute to relieving the burden and a stabilization in the condition. As it continues, the patient will only profit from the therapy in the long-term if he is confronted with his own attitudes and behaviors and scrutinizes, at least partly, his previous view of the world and himself so that the right steps can be taken and the patient can find a suitable path to recovery for himself. If the patient is only told in therapy that everything is terrible, everyone else is to blame and he is the victim, most will, at first, feel understood and relieved, but he will potentially have difficulties in the future accepting personal responsibility or actively contributing to making the necessary changes.

I have respect for anyone who is prepared to seek support and make use of psychotherapy. This requires openness, courage and a willingness to scrutinize and work on yourself, as well as patience and trust. Whoever decides on this route and commits themselves to it can, in my opinion, be proud of themselves and has already taken an important step towards recovery.

The author realistically portrays the stages on his own route as well as the factors, which accompanied and influenced him in the development of his burnout and on the road to his recovery. It is not only our own attitudes and behaviors which can influence our feelings, thoughts and actions or which could have an effect on the development of psychological conditions, but also the prevailing circumstances and interaction with others.

Within the framework of the therapy, we first need to understand what the problem actually is, which symptoms do we have, why do we have them and how have they developed. It is all about self-awareness and acceptance and, later on in the therapy, also about defining new goals ("Who am I? How should I shape my future?") as well as how to put this knowledge into practice. During the implementation phase, it is often important to integrate the social environment, which is normally only indirectly involved in the one-on-one conversations, in order to receive greater support.

The author is a very good example of a person, who suffered under an increasing number of symptoms of burnout, recognized it himself and accepted it and who finally summoned up the courage, openness and willingness to commit himself to support and therapy. In this way, he himself contributed considerably to overcoming the crisis as well as to the recovery of his health and quality of life. By portraying his personal experiences, he would like to help others who are affected, as well as their relatives, by giving them information and some encouragement.

I hope that this book allows as many readers as possible to reflect on the topic of "burnout" and other psychological conditions and will also encourage discussions. Even though there is no definition of "burnout" accepted by everyone and there will always be different opinions of the symptoms and the use of therapy, I believe that it is very important to keep a dialogue going about it, to take it seriously and to support those affected in the best way we can.

I wish all readers a lot of joy when reading as well as fruitful conversations about the topic afterwards. To those reading this book who have been affected, I hope that you find valuable tips and motivation and, if necessary, that you will commit to therapeutic help.

Finally, I wish the author and his family all the best for their future lives and a lot of success with this book.

Dr. Thomas Schell
Heidelberg, July 2014

"For me, this book is a very successful "closing" to a particular chapter in your life as well as a great new start for you. As your former therapist in Carolabad, it is also a new and interesting experience for me to read about the effects of therapy (and especially of my words) from a patient's point of view. It is a valuable tool for me to gain knowledge. In my opinion, you find the right words and write with heart and soul, which is sure to touch other people."

(K. M. from J., Psychotherapist)

1.) Introduction: Why am I writing this book?

I am a simple person. One of you.

Someone who has put burnout behind me.

I have a very loving and understanding wife and the best two girls in the world (in my eyes) are my children.

I am 53 years old, speak 3 languages, weigh 82kg, am 1.79m tall, have grey hair although I am balding, 2 crooked teeth and no six-pack.

I do not smoke and generally take care about what I eat.

I like travelling with my family.

I have run 2 marathons and have varicose veins on my left calf.

I was never a high achiever in German. At school I always read the books at the last minute.

I am a mechanical engineer, a technician, not an author.

I plan warehouses and conveyance systems and put them into operation.

I give presentations, lead project meetings, create RFQ and technical contract documents, write project specifications and compare offers.

In my job I sometimes make people unemployed, but also contribute to the competitiveness of the company and, therefore, save jobs. When we build new warehouses, we also create work.

I have a large circle of friends and very good colleagues. The atmosphere at work and the relationship to my boss were and are both very good.

Together with my wife, I buried my mother's ashes.

I hardly read any books, but I collect Mickey Mouse (for the children of course).

I ignored all the signs of burnout, and there were enough of them.

I was in hospital because of burnout and massive heart problems. I was unable to work for 9 months and was in rehab for 7 weeks.

I am quite good at listening, sympathizing and at putting myself in other people's shoes, but that is all. I do not suffer with them anymore.

I have just managed to put the most difficult part of my life behind me.

Why am I burdening myself with this book?

Why am I reliving the last 3 years?

Why am I baring my soul?

Why am I not using this time for my family and myself?

Why do I not just lie in the sun, go to the sauna or to the cinema with my wife and children?

Because I experienced and learned a lot before, during and after my burnout.

Because my life has changed and improved.

Because this book is helping me to draw a line under things. It is bringing closure.

Because I met people during and after rehab who are going through the same or something worse.

Because I realized that it is so good when somebody says that they understand you, that they have been through the same, that they had felt the same or something similar…

Because I want to share my experiences and help others by doing so.

Because I believe I can give courage to at least some of you.

Because this book should be a warning to take the danger signs seriously so as not to gamble with your long-term health or even with your life.

Because I do not want that this whole time and all my experiences were for nothing and do not help other people.

Because while I was studying, a professor said to me (after I had failed a test), "Mr. Dietrich, if you want to progress or if you have a problem, you should use all the resources available to you in life". I now see this time, in which I experienced such a lot, as a "resource". If this hadn't happened, I never would have had these experiences. I had a host of guardian angels, and so I am going to try and get something out of it and a part of that is this book.

Because I have the courage to talk about my feelings.

Because I am not afraid to talk about myself if it could help others, even if some people see me as a wimp afterwards.

Because I realized how much it has helped me to have understanding and support.

Because I know there are a hell of a lot of people like me out there. With almost every new project I meet people who had exactly the same experience or who are in a similar position as I am.

Because I know that some people are desperate and don't dare to do anything more in life.

Because, should this book ever be printed and sold, I will donate 50% of my personal proceeds (whatever the publisher leaves!) to the treatment of psychological illnesses or to the children of the Katutura slum in Windhoek Namibia. 1 Euro is enough to feed 1 child per day. Current status 15th of December 2014: This book already collected 1 year for 1 child. Thanks to all readers, who bought this book.

And so I have a request, if you find this book helpful: please recommend this book and help me! The book also helps in Africa.

Because I have experienced that there are far too few psychiatrists and therapists. (Warning: this book is not a therapy guide. That would be arrogant and wrong. It is only a description of my personal feelings!)

Because a psychological illness should not be a taboo subject and it is a mistake to label a person who has been affected by burnout as, for example, crazy, a wimp or weak. With external help, it is possible to return to a "normal" life and to perform a good level of work. This is something that is different depending on the individual and their environment.

Because I want to show that it is possible to "get out of the hole".

Because it will have been worth my time if this book helps just one of you out of a hole.

Is that enough for you?

It is enough for me!

In this book, I am going to speak to you the reader (I hope there are some ☺). That is what we all did as patients in rehab. Our education, origins, profession, bank balance, car, horse, yacht etc. were not taken into consideration. We were all reduced to the basics – a human being, a person with the feelings and problems we had there. That was all and that was the most important. Nothing else played any role at all.

You'll notice that this will be neither an advanced literary book, a scientific paper nor a doctoral thesis. My language is simple and honest, like me. The exception is when I borrow from books that I have read or want to pass on experiences from them.

Everything I have written about happened. I have changed names and locations so that nobody feels I have trodden on anyone's toes, especially those who don't want to be personally named. I have tried to describe all causes and reasons for me becoming overburdened as objectively as possible. Despite that, there are of course some subjective, personal assessments. That also includes private, family and voluntary activities.

In case someone feels they have been unfavorably portrayed, I should make it absolutely clear that this was definitely not my intention. This book and the descriptions within it are used to portray the circumstances and situations, which led to certain developments and results, as realistically as possible. My hope is that this will make things more understandable for you. This should in no way be seen as me accusing anyone of anything.

If anyone made a mistake in the end, it was me. My mistake was not being strict and resolute because I was afraid to change things. I would handle things differently today. I simply ask for understanding and leniency. Whatever is behind you is no longer important as it cannot be changed. You can however learn from it for whatever lies ahead. You can do things better than before and avoid making mistakes.

I have only written about my personal experiences and thoughts. I haven't read any psychosomatic literature. I haven't done that on purpose because I don't want to publish any incorrect theories or conclusions based on my own personal, superficial knowledge. If I had wanted that, I would have studied Psychology.

Everybody reacts differently. That is why this book isn't a guide but a personal report on my experiences and can, at most, give examples of how I was feeling. These experiences should act as encouragement.

It is possible that this book will contribute to an increase in understanding among those in a person's immediate environment, so that they can assess such an incident differently and better understand the situation of their colleague who has had burnout. Mutual understanding and a willingness to talk are the basic requirements for this.

This book should act as encouragement to get out of this difficult period. Everyone has to find his own way. Some people choose isolation while others change their lives completely. Everyone has to make his or her own decision. I have also made some changes and prioritized other things than I previously did.

This book definitely won't trivialize burnout with the idea that "everything will be fine given time". Burnout is a serious condition and its symptoms can lead to permanent psychological and physical problems with serious consequences including strokes and heart attacks. The results could be fatal. I don't want to panic anyone, but it is important to know.

A business partner once told me "impatience is a very bad counsel". And he is right! I know from my circle of acquaintances that things haven't ended well for them at all.

I also describe feelings clearly. If I was feeling "shit", I will write, "shit" if that is the best way to describe the situation. Everyone knows these emotional releases and they are authentic.

Some people will think this book is good. Others will think it isn't. Some will understand the feelings. Others won't. Some will thing the book is honest and brave, while others will see it as nonsense and a waste of paper. This book is written for those who want it to be the beginning of something, who are affected themselves and who will hopefully get some kind of use out of it.

For your information:

Text written in italics is comments from the time of writing.

The small number of pictures are very simple. They are used to help get across some information. All I did was to take photographs of the things I created myself on the flipchart or created some qualitative diagrams in PowerPoint.

There is one thing I'd like to say before I start. There are a lot of books and publications, which try and define burnout using a clinical picture and symptoms etc. They try and say that there is no such thing as burnout, but it is only something like depression. This does not help people who are affected.

I can only say one thing to this: I had burnout. It didn't matter to me whether it was called burnout, a depressive phase or an anxiety syndrome. The only thing I wanted was help to get out of the cycle and the people from rehab were the same. Even if you can't completely understand the feelings and situation of other people (nobody expects that), you can still believe and accept them. That is what we should expect.

I began writing this on the 26.06.2013. I only write when I am motivated to do so. No stress. I'll need about a year for it. Time isn't important.

Oh yes, I have a request: I have (with the help of Mr. Bill Gates!) done my best to write a text, which is at least partway respectable. If, however, you do find a spelling mistake, I ask for your understanding.

On 11.06.2014, exactly 2 years to the day when I began rehab, I'll have the first bound copy of the book in my hand. It will be a great feeling.

Right! Let's begin…

2.) The beginning: The time with my 6 "Pressure Points"

Hindsight is a beautiful thing. Everybody knows that. It is also the case here. When I look back, I can see that there were signs over many years of the condition developing, which intensified as time went on. I noticed these signs, but didn't assess them correctly.

I made the biggest mistake because, quite simply, I was ignorant. Thoughts like "That won't happen to me. It happens to others, but not to me. I do sport to balance my life and, to some extent, pay attention to my diet. I'm not a high-risk patient and have been physically fit for the last few years. How could I be susceptible? I've run two marathons and five half marathons. I know what I can achieve. I know my limits. What's more I don't let my colleagues down. We are all in the same boot in the department and I'm not the first one to give up. The years before were all fine so why should something happen now when I have a lot more experience and can work more quickly and efficiently than before. That means I can achieve more."

That's what you think, but that can be very dangerous. Everyone has his or her own individual limits.

How did it all come about and what were the causes looking at it in retrospect?

From today's perspective, I know this: it was the result of six "problem areas" in my private and professional life, which for many years had run very well in parallel. Then something went wrong in one of these "areas", which I was to blame for and which increased the stress on myself, negatively affecting the other areas. This was the start of a chain reaction.

First Pressure Point: The workplace

I work as a planning engineer for conveyance systems and warehouses in the logistics industry. My field of responsibility includes surveying current setups; planning, implementation and start up. Own employees – none. We carry out all necessary work in the team as project leaders.

We always have a lot to do the department. It is definitely not boring. I'm sure most of you reading this know that situation. On top of all the work, we also have to go on business trips at particular times during projects or, at the end, for the project implementation. This is something we have experience with and it doesn't really pose any problems. As a general rule, every one of us has up to 10 projects on the go at the same time. Depending on the size and phase of the project that can mean a lot or a little work. Of these 10, 2 are normally large projects, which are the main focus of the work; 3-4 medium sized and then "odds and ends".

Things became more difficult in the last 2 years. Our manager had planned to get us some support in the form of new colleagues. 2 new colleagues HAD started in the department, but during the trial period, or shortly after, both decided that their focus lay elsewhere. We couldn't understand that, as a few years earlier, another colleague had started to work with us and settled in without any problems. This colleague is still with us today. Together with our manager, we had tried to teach the two exactly as we had with the colleague previously. While I was in rehab, another colleague joined the department, who has now several years of experience working with us.

This had a big effect on us in the department. We had spent a year doing the additional work of training both new colleagues, but in the end it was for nothing. That wasn't really very motivating. It was just bad luck.

Second Pressure Point: Volunteering in the parish

I had been on the Council of Elders in the parish for 15 years. At the beginning, this was a really lovely time. It needed me to invest a lot of energy, but it was worth it. The whole family gained a lot of positive experiences from it and we don't want to do without, even today. Then, as everywhere else, came the period of money saving. This affected every parish in our area. A lot of difficult decisions had to be made. Unpleasant decisions - sell the Parish Hall, renovate the church. The savings began in 2004 and the projects with the Parish Hall and church have been dragging on since 2008, the reasons for which the parish isn't responsible.

Third Pressure Point: Nursing my mother and great-grandmother

In 2005 my mother was diagnosed with dementia. For the first couple of years, we took care of her in our own home. In the final stages, this became extremely stressful, especially emotionally. Stressful for her because, at the beginning, she herself noticed that not everything was OK in her head and she knew what was to come. I had flipped out several times out of fear that something would happen to her, because she had often unconsciously gotten herself into dangerous situations e.g. on the street. Her powers of recall simply weren't there anymore. She forgot even more frequently what she had just done, what we had just discussed or what a lot of things were used for. And then one morning we found her unconscious on the floor after a fall during the night on her way to the bathroom. Suddenly, alarm bells were ringing. On this day, we went to our GP, organized a referral for a care home, enquired at 6 in the area, packed her things and moved her. We couldn't take care of her anymore. The dangers were too big. I had always promised her that she wouldn't have to go into a home. The next day I had to go abroad to oversee the start-up of a project, which I "couldn't" postpone, and so I ran away for a week. Three companies had been coordinated for this week, the warehouse had been rearranged and everything would have had to be rearranged and there would have been delays. So, cancel or not?

Everything was organized with Mother. Everything worked out and, even though it was very stressful, she was in good hands. Everything had been discussed with the manager. If something critical had happened with Mother, I could have cancelled the trip at any time. So, the choice was not to cancel. My wife took care of the rest, kept me up-to-date and the week went very well.

For a year, we always visited Mother in the care home and supported her with everything that was necessary. When a person close to you slowly disintegrates and, at the end, doesn't know what to do with the spoon in his or her hand and the soup bowl, it is extremely hard to comprehend and come to terms with. My mother died in 2008 in hospital. While this episode took place before my burnout, it did take a lot of energy and it isn't possible to simply erase the pictures and experiences from the mind. That takes time. I'm sure a lot of you know this as well.

Fourth Pressure Point: Converting my parent's house - Accessibility

I had promised Mother that I would build an extension to the ground floor of my parent's house so that she didn't have to use the steep stairs to get up to her bedroom. There wasn't really any equity to pay for it, and so I basically did everything myself - excavation for the foundations, formwork, concreting, laying bricks, putting up the wooden beams for the ceiling, plastering, laying the electrical cables. We only paid a carpenter, roofer and tiler. The construction work was in two stages and began in 2005 just as we noticed that Mother wasn't as spry as she had used to be. Her dementia was faster than I was with the construction. It wasn't ready in time. Only the ground floor was ready to be moved into, but the upper floor remained a building site until after her death. In total, including delays when taking care of my mother, I had worked for 5 years on the project. I had thought that I would be able to manage. It wasn't the case. What actually happened was that I slowly started to lose energy. This all happened a few years before, but it had taken up an immense amount of energy. At that point, this was the hardest time of my life.

Fifth Pressure Point: My family

Oh yes, as well as all this there is also the family with two children. That means that there is also a family life and a circle of friends. I want to do something for my fitness. In order to make it through the daily madness, you go on holiday. Something comes up every now and again in the school etc. etc. etc. etc. etc. You know what I mean.

Sixth Pressure Point: Holiday home in St. Peter Ording

We bought a small holiday home in St. Peter Ording in 2006. It had been built in 1975 and was in need of renovation. The basic structure could be left as it was and could therefore be rented out as a holiday home straight away. At this point in time, we had no idea about the situation of my mother. I would be taking care of the "small" renovations (painting, new flooring and furniture), and these jobs could be spread over 5 years. That was doable. The "bigger" jobs such as the work on the roof, in the bathrooms and on the doors we would have done by professionals. The house was a little secluded, but therefore good value for money and we planned to make the mortgage repayments using the rent that we earned. This was the plan and everything started well. Of course, this meant that holidays were not only for enjoying the beach, but it was so much fun to see how the house slowly came together and the work didn't bother me at all. It was physically demanding work, but we didn't have any fears that it wouldn't wok out and we always drove home in a positive frame of mind. It is a provision for the future and the time after retirement.

In January 2011 a water pipe broke and a bathroom needed to be completely redone. This meant cancelling rentals and unexpected, additional renovation costs. The insurance only covered half of the costs and we suddenly had to dip into our savings, which hadn't been planned. Nothing else could go wrong

All of these "Pressure Points" were easy to deal with as long as things didn't go wrong all at the same time. For more than 5 years, everything had gone well, as it had for 10 years before that in the company and when we had built our house. We had a lot of fun at this time (otherwise we wouldn't have done any of it) and we had been able to enjoy a lot of holidays, especially when we had been skiing.

Ultimately everything was part of a plan for the future - for our children and our twilight years.

2011 wasn't a good year at work and, together with the other pressure points in the parish etc., I noticed how my resilience was diminishing and I developed a fear that, because of all the personal and business pressures, things would really start to fall apart at the company. I mean with projects worth 10-50 thousand Euros. I always try to do my job well, just like I'm sure each of you does. In doing so, you get even more bogged down with things and that takes up a lot of time. If you have a lot of projects running simultaneously, it could happen that problems suddenly crop up in several areas. You end up running around, trying to patch things up to save them while dealing with deadline pressures. At some point it just isn't possible anymore and it's impossible to keep your head above water. Maybe you know that feeling. As I said before, everyone knew the situation and our manager was trying to change things. Unfortunately, he was unsuccessful at the time.

There is another important factor that shouldn't be overlooked. It might sound stupid, but we are getting older. I still notice that a person with many years of work experience is valuable as they can avoid the mistakes of those just starting out in their career, which could end up costing a lot of money. These are often the same mistakes you made yourself and that's of course why you know have the experience! It is also a fact that a person can handle multiple roles much better until they reach a certain age (this age can of course vary). We arrange our lives including our work, family and social life in such a way that we can manage it all. As time goes on, it becomes even more stressful to maintain everything at a certain level. You really don't want to have to do without anything because they are all fun, but it's just that they are very energy consuming. I hadn't taken the opportunity to end my involvement in many things because they had become too much. When it came to my time as a Church Elder, for example, I had just thought that I'd done it for 14 years already. There were only another 3 to go and I didn't want to let people down especially not with the church renovations coming up.

Things become more difficult when you can't stop thinking about your problems. You have the feeling that the pressure is growing and you can't find a solution, you can't sleep at night, you write yourself notes and emails and wake up soaked with sweat. You drink more and more Coke and coffee just to keep yourself awake. These are warning signs. Everyone can handle different amounts of stress. One person might have reached his limit while another would be able to continue with a smile on his face. This is where care is needed. Burnout can affect anyone. In the company I had already had 8 managers and I had seen how some, who you would consider to be as hard as nails, had been toppled. One more thing: One of the biggest causes of death in Germany is suicide. Are you as surprised as I was? It is reported in newspapers that 30% of employees are suffering from symptoms connected to being overloaded or having burnout. This is not without reason. This isn't scaremongering. I just want to say: be careful and don't just blindly carry on, but think about how you can stop and go back to how things were. You don't want to end up throwing everything away (that isn't a solution), but if it's too much, then it's too much and if the people around you are good and responsible, they will understand that. Everyone reacts differently and individual breaking points are also variable.

In the end, what happened wasn't the result of one pressure point, but was down to a combination of all the pressures together. Nobody else is to blame but you. There are of course some individual circumstances to consider. I remember my childhood when my parents had to scrape together every cent (or pfennig as it was back then), because at the end of the money there is always so much month left. However nothing is more important than your health. We take a lot of things for granted and you normally only recognize how important and valuable they are when you don't have them anymore. This can happen from one day to the next.

My former running partner once told me about a situation in a department in his company. A colleague there had a heart attack. Dead. Just like that. No second chance. Not there anymore. A wife and two children were left behind. He was always such a laid back person and liked to take things easy. Everyone was stunned. There was a big funeral service with all the trappings and a lot of tributes were paid. Sadly he didn't get anything out of it and neither did his family. I know exactly how good things are for me - I'm still here and writing this book. I hope that you will get something out of this.

It seems I've gone off topic of the pressure points.

The only thing that is missing is what, for me, was the major catalyst for my decline.

My situation at the time can be illustrated schematically and is shown on the following page. Everything closes in around you and you have the feeling that you can't escape from these responsibilities. Saying "no" doesn't always work

Maybe you will be able to identify with at least some of these things.

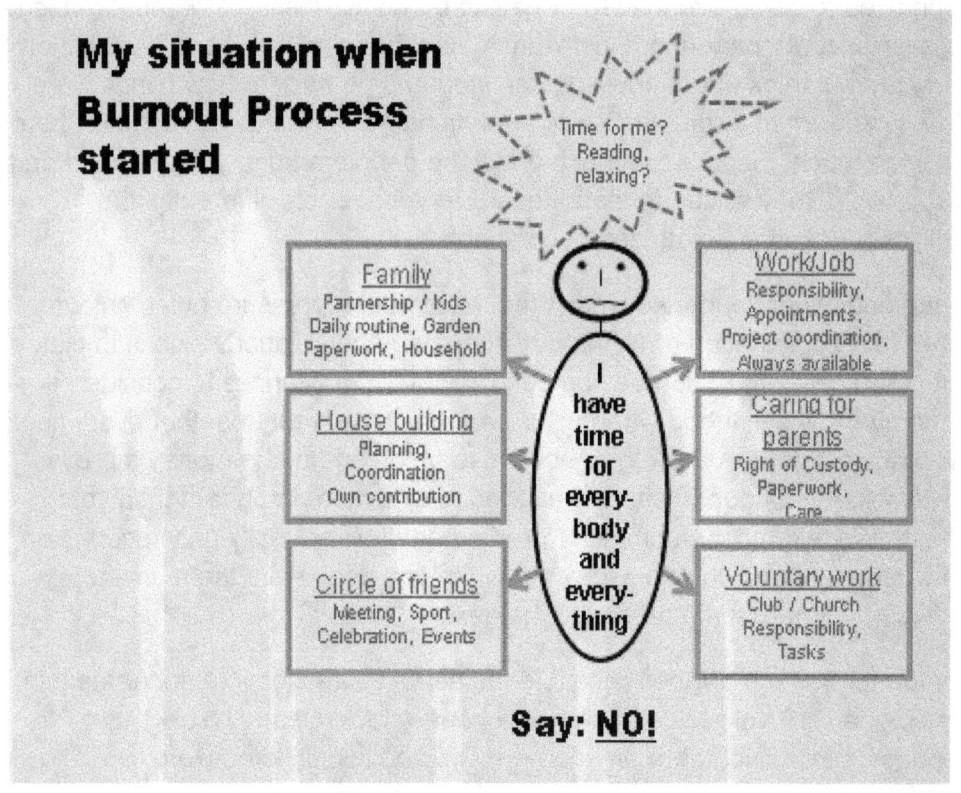

All aboard. Close the doors and fasten your seatbelts. The rollercoaster ride is about to begin:

At the end of 2010, just like at the end of every year, we did the budget plan for the following year. In this year, I had projects with some loose ends because a few had been delayed and others were still ongoing. I couldn't really focus on the detailed planning for the upcoming projects because the ones, which were already running, were simply more important. In the next year I had a very big and complex renovation project to deal with. The project had a budget of just over €5 million, was divided into several stages and would take almost 2 years to complete, but would be carried out while daily operations continued. There would be testing at the weekends before normal work continued on Monday. On top of that were two medium-sized projects worth around €3 million and €1 million, one of which was abroad, plus the standard odds and ends and the ongoing projects.

The Board of Directors had approved all of the projects and I was able to start work on them from February 2011. In the spring, I noticed that an error with the dimensions had crept in during the planning stage of one of the projects. The entire concept and planning were now in doubt. I drove to the site, measured everything again and came up with a solution, which was similar to the original. The whole thing dragged on until May. Parallel to this, I was involved in the detailed planning for the 2-year project, with which there was a long-running issue with a static calculation of a mezzanine, which needed to be checked. Then there was the project abroad. Problems with the roof of the building there had been discovered and, if necessary, the entire branch would have had to be redesigned in a new location. Up until this point, only I had been responsible for the projects in this country.

It was in May that the sleepless nights began. I had a notebook next to the bed. My wife asked what was going on and if I was crazy. My reply: "If I can write things down, I can sleep because I don't have to constantly think about them". The detailed planning for the renovation project was in full swing in June and July and the first weekend tests took place in September. There were 10 in total with a break now and again. (I often asked myself how the sub-contractor's technicians coped with it, but realized that they only had to deal with one project at a time instead of 5 to 10)

The damn static calculation of this mezzanine still wasn't finished and time was running out. If we had had to reinforce something, there wouldn't have been enough time for the deliveries and the entire schedule would have gone out of the window.

Bad news then came in July. I had asked for some photos to be sent to me of the location where the renovation project was taking place. Damn it! The smoke vents in the ceiling were exactly where we wanted to do the installation work. I'd totally overlooked about them what with all the measurement checks and coming up with alternative solutions. Completely overlooked them. 2x6m vents I hadn't noticed. I thought we would have a big enough gap to the ceiling so that it wouldn't be important. That would've been the case if the original height dimensions had been correct. When correcting the measurements, I had simply forgotten the vents. The solution I had found was now unworkable.

9 months of planning had been for nothing. A part of the assembly section had already been ordered. Contracts had to be cancelled. Shit! I'd never made such a mistake. One million Euros squandered. Ok, the money wasn't lost, but one year of work was and the contractors were angry. This is when the night sweats began and I sometimes woke up in the mornings completely soaked, but it wasn't because of the heat of the summer. I also developed stomach problems: Mucositis, stomach problems caused by stress. Facial tics also became more frequent.

Understandably, my boss wasn't exactly over the moon, but he reacted very rationally and together we tried to find a viable option out of the situation. There was no pressure and no reprisals. That wasn't his style. That's different in a lot of companies.

Our summer holiday came, but I couldn't switch off and, after 2 weeks I went back home, leaving the family behind. The test weekends for another renovation project were pending when I got back. The tests for the first big phase went well. There were no great problems and the collaboration with the colleagues on site and the contractors was perfect. Finally, a ray of hope. The 9 weekends were, however, exhausting. I had made a mistake. I wanted to save my leave and hadn't taken any time off in the meantime. This mistake had severe consequences.

Everything was taking its toll. Test work on the weekend before our planned holiday in St Peter Ording was postponed by a week. Originally, I had wanted to travel with the family on the Saturday for our autumn break at the North Sea, but had to let them go without me and then join them on the

Monday. After operations on site had successfully restarted on Monday, I drove directly to St Peter Ording. The weather was bad on this day and I was on the road for around 9 hours. When I arrived, I went straight to bed and had a lie-in the next day. Things were much better then and even though I could still feel the exertions in my bones, I was able to switch off a bit.

St. Peter Ording (SPO) Holiday: The holiday was OK. Due to the implementation phase at work, only a few small repairs had been planned, but there were also a lot of walks along the beach, scores of cakes to eat (SPO has the best cakes I have ever eaten!), and stiff breezes to clear my head. It did a lot of good. After 5 days of holiday, we had to go home. The next implementation phase was due and after that had been done, the first stage was complete and I was so relieved. Made it!

My head wasn't clear though. Planning for the next year was already well underway. There were so many projects abroad. Somehow it looked like there were even more than before. I had barely made it through 2011! Now I was really on the ropes. Nights were restive and I sometimes had those stupid night sweats, and in the morning I woke up to a mountain of work. I had messed up the project in July. What if it happened again?

The fear increased. Things were different than the year before. We had always had a lot of work, but it had always been manageable. Now for the first time, I was afraid. It didn't matter what I did. I couldn't stop it. Distracting myself from it didn't help. The sleepless nights meant the downward spiral continued. I couldn't concentrate anymore and I needed twice as long for some jobs as I had before. The number of notes increased exorbitantly. Sometimes I had written the same thing down in three different places. I had lost perspective and I didn't know how I could get out of the situation by myself. All of my colleagues were under pressure, and so I couldn't pass anything on to them. Having said that, things weren't quite as chaotic with them as it had become with me.

At the beginning of November, it was the boss' birthday and, as is usual in our department, we celebrated with a drink. He had told us 2 years previously that he had decided to retire in the next year. We hadn't expected that. Of course it was a shame, but at that point, none of us really thought any more about it. However, the closer the time came, the more the uncertainty grew about what would happen afterwards. On the other hand, we were a great team. We would deal with it.

On the 19th November 2011, my wife and I had our combined 100th birthday. We celebrated together with friends, family and colleagues; around 80 people in total.

Party planning, room, catering, seating, salads, drinks and all the other organization. I noticed how much I was deteriorating. On the Friday evening, a friend and I set up the table and chairs in the church hall we had rented. I couldn't think clearly and didn't have any plan. My friend asked, "What's wrong with you?" "I don't feel very well. I only slept 4 hours last night. Hopefully everything will be OK tomorrow." What I actually meant was that I hoped I would be able to see it through. The night before the party I slept almost exactly 3 hours. I just hoped I wouldn't run out of steam at, of all events, our party. I already felt so old. The stress grew in the afternoon until the caterer had delivered everything – the table decorations, drinks etc. Everything had worked out.

On the morning of the party I just hoped that everything would go OK. I was running on empty.

I was able to get my head down for an hour just before the guests arrived at 7pm. That helped a little.

The party went very well. Everyone was in a good mood and we were given a lovely surprise present from my colleagues, which really suited me – a breezeblock which they had filled with 5€ notes and then covered with mortar. I had to break it into pieces and I knew that would be fun!

Another present, which would prove to be a very big help for me later on, was a picture of Donald and Daisy. The cheerfulness of the picture would help me get through some difficult times.

The celebrations with my wife, children and the "hard core" few continued until 2:30am. I actually felt quite good. It wasn't until the Sunday that I realized that I had been running on fumes the whole time; but that the party hadn't been the first time that had happened.

I was totally run down on the Sunday when tidying up after the party.

I felt blessed, though. "Hey;" I said to my wife. "We did it. The party was great and I think the guests enjoyed themselves too".

The following 2 days were too much for me.

On the Monday, I wanted to go to the office to save some emails. I couldn't find the target directory anymore and needed an eternity to figure out which emails belonged to which project. I couldn't concentrate. I felt unwell and had to take a break, but things didn't get better. In the afternoon, I explained a couple of points to a new colleague for his project and then I drove home. Exhausted. Not tired, but completely jaded.

The next day was exactly the same. I couldn't do anything properly and there were a few queries. At 4pm I realized that I was near mental collapse. I couldn't think anymore, and so I went home earlier than usual and went straight to bed. "Marliese, I'm tired. I don't feel very good and I have to go and lie down." And off I went. It is 22.11.2011. I hardly slept. I woke up several times drenched in sweat.

My mind was racing.

Today, more than 2 years after my breakdown, I have to say that I underestimated the situation at the time. I couldn't imagine that this was the final straw. Of course you don't know what's going to happen before it does, and you can't imagine how it is going to happen and what effects it will have. That's why I hadn't realized that I was standing on the edge of a precipice. I also hadn't known what the consequences were, and so I had tried to carry on. This is also what people who had been affected told me later on.

Even if I am doing much better now, there are still some limitations on what I can do as compared to the past. I can deal with these well and seem to have them under control in such a way that I can work again etc. However, I wouldn't have these limitations if I had slowed down or applied the brakes. Even if that had had consequences for me (which thankfully wasn't the case!), nothing is more important than your health.

3.) Wednesday, 23.11.2011. My personal 09/11:

Marliese had a bad headache that morning, and so she asked me "Could you deal with Sara this morning? It feels like my head is about to explode." OK. I could deal with that somehow. I had hardly slept, I felt ill and I was dizzy.

"Sara, can you get yourself ready and have breakfast. I'm going to take you to the bus today." "Yes, OK." I dozed a little and took a deep breath to relax myself and then we went to the bus stop. The fresh air helped a little. "I'm not going to go all the way with you because I don't feel very good." "OK. Bye Dad. Get well soon." I turned around and staggered the 500 meters home. I lay down straight away. I was so completely exhausted, but I couldn't sleep. My mind was racing. I was always thinking about something. I couldn't find any peace. I tossed and turned. I was soaked in sweat and felt ill. My heart started beating faster. I was agitated. Something was wrong. I was afraid! What was I afraid of? Not being able to control myself anymore? My heart beat faster until it felt like it was thumping in my neck. Something was going on! I didn't have any control anymore. I had to go to the doctor. I stood up and staggered to the phone, dialed the number for my GP and reached his assistant. "How can I help?" "My name is Dietrich. I feel really unwell. When can I get an appointment?" "As soon as the doctor is here at 8am." "Ok. I'll be there."

I lay down for another 45 minutes. It didn't get better despite the certainty of the doctor's appointment. I couldn't relax and I began to panic, because I didn't understand what was happening to me. I couldn't lie down anymore. I feared that it would just get worse. I had to go to the doctor. Now! I got up and got dressed 30 minutes earlier than planned. I let Marliese know. I took it slowly. I was dizzy. My stomach was turning. I had indigestion. I concentrated on my breathing. Slowly. In and out. "Concentrate! Do you hear me? Concentrate! In and out." I stayed standing. Half of the distance had been covered. I was still dizzy. "Keep going. Come on, keep going." Nobody else is on the street. I was alone. If I had passed out here, nobody would have found me for a while. Come on. Keep going! I continued slowly, breathing in and out. I began to shake. I made it to the corner and, from there, there were only 100 meters to the Doctor's surgery. Just up the stairs and then I'd be there. I carried on more quickly. "Control yourself and breath slowly you idiot. Come on, what's wrong with you? You've already run 2 marathons, so you know what to do when you've hit the wall but have to keep going. Pull yourself together!" 50 meters and the shaking got worse in my arms. My breathing was irregular. I was nearly there. The door downstairs was open, thank God! Up the stairs I went. I rang the bell. My whole body was shaking and I was agitated. My breathing and my racing heart meant I stuttered my words. "I, I, I can't take it anymore. I don't know what's wrong with me. Help!" I collapsed into the arms of the assistant. She tried to support me and called for the doctor.

"Mr. Dietrich, come and lie down in the ECG room. Can you hear me? Do you understand?" "What? Yes. ECG room", I stuttered and I staggered in and fell onto the bed. I was on the bed, but I wasn't really lying down. My whole body was still shaking – my arms and legs, too. I couldn't control them anymore. "What's happening?" The doctor had run into the room. "Mr. Dietrich? Mr. Dietrich can you hear me?" He shouted at me: "Can you hear me?" During this, his assistant took my blood pressure, pulse and tried to hook up the ECG. "Yes, I ca…can hear you. What's happening to me?" I was still shaking. It just wouldn't stop. Shit, shit, shit! "Mr. Dietrich, you aren't having a heart attack, do you understand? It isn't a heart attack, understand?" "Yyyes- nnn no heart attack". "Your heart is beating irregularly. You have an arrhythmia. Your pulse and blood pressure are all over the place, but it isn't a heart attack. OK?" "Yyy...yes. O..OK." "Try and calm down. Calm down!" "I, I, I've been ttttt…trying!" "We are going to give you something to help you calm down. It works very quickly". The nurse gave me some drops. She couldn't give me an injection because I was shaking so much. I swallowed the drops. She tipped it all into my mouth. "We've called an ambulance. It will be here in 15 minutes. You'll be taken straight to the Cardiology Unit at the hospital." The medication did work quickly. Before the paramedics arrived, there was time for an ECG. "You have an arrhythmia, an irregular heartbeat. Do you understand?" "Yy...yes, bbb...but why?" "The nerves and sinus nodes are all over the place, but it isn't a heart attack. Did you hear? It isn't a heart attack and it will be OK, do you hear?" As the medication worked I started to calm down. The shaking started to relent. I could speak without stuttering again. My heart was still beating hard. I looked at the strange lines on the monitor. It was something I couldn't understand, something that I had never had before. I had this eerie feeling of nervousness. Maybe it was the irregular heartbeat, I didn't know. I just didn't know. What the hell was going on!?

The sedative relaxed me somewhat.

The paramedics arrived and my GP explained everything, giving them the ECG and my records. "Everything is fine," one of the paramedics said. He had absolutely no idea, I thought.

"We'll call your wife Mr. Dietrich," said the nurse. "Is that OK?" "Yes, definitely. Please," I shouted from the ground floor back up through the stairwell.

The 15 minutes it took to get to the hospital seemed to take an eternity. It was the first time in my life I'd been driven with the blue lights on, but at least the sirens weren't being used. When I had travelled like this with my mother, I had always been sitting. This time I was "allowed" to lie down. Great.

I felt a bit calmer. Physically at least. Everything still felt very unsettled in my chest, though and my mind was still racing. "What's wrong? Where has this come from? I've never had anything like this before! Thank God I went to the Doctor's. At least I'm now under observation."

The paramedic spoke again. " Everything will be fine. Just stay calm." I just wanted him to shut up. He wanted to kill me with kindness, but I just had….fear!!!

The eternal journey was finally over and we arrived at the Emergency Department. Straight inside, cannula in, blood-thinning medication given and hooked up to the monitor to check my heart.

Even I could see the irregularities and the differences in my heartbeat. It wasn't exactly reassuring. It's a horrible feeling when you can see that there is something wrong. Things had always been OK before. I slowly started to calm down because I thought nothing else could happen. Cardiology had been called and someone quickly arrived.

He looked at my file and the ECG and note from my GP. I explained to him everything that happened earlier in the morning. "Yeah, and now I am here!"

"Right, Mr. Dietrich. We can see the irregular heartbeat on the monitor and we can diagnose an atrial fibrillation by considering your pulse and low blood pressure. When the atria of the heart fibrillate, they are not working in rhythm with the heart and this means your heart can only work at 20-30% of its normal level. When this happens to a person, who is normally healthy, it isn't usually life threatening because the body can cope with this for a short time until the person recovers. It is still critical though, because a result of this could be that blood clots could form on the heart valves due to the blood swirling around slowly in the atria. If these clots end up in the brain, they can cause a stroke. That's why we have given you some medication to thin your blood and some drops for your blood pressure. In most cases, the heart corrects itself within a day or 2, it returns to its normal rhythm and the fibrillation disappears. If this doesn't happen, we can help using medication. There is also the option that we can stop your heart while you are under anesthetic and we can then "restart" it using a defibrillator. That means your heart will be back in a regular rhythm. So, you can see we have a lot of options here to get everything back to normal. Most people don't even notice that they have atrial fibrillation until they are under some kind of pressure."

That was the information from the Consultant Cardiologist. "Super", I thought. "Just stop my heart. It's not so bad. Just stay calm. I couldn't help thinking about the film "Flatliners". I asked if it could happen again. The answer was yes. Great. I'd really hit the jackpot. So, it could be that I don't notice that I have another atrial fibrillation, but if things go badly, it could cause a stroke. It doesn't matter though. I can always take blood-thinning drugs and in an emergency, all I will need is a quick pit stop where everything can be put right using electricity. Isn't modern medicine great?" I'm sure the Consultant was trying to put my mind at rest by giving me this comprehensive information. Maybe he had just done me a huge favor. Whatever he meant to do, my feeling of calm disappeared.

Do you know what is great? I had completely suppressed all memories of this, one of the worst days of my life. I was nervous about having to relive it, but I managed to do it without getting upset. That is a great feeling!

I'll continue with the "highlights" of what happened at the hospital so that I don't bore you.

What had actually happened to me?

Clearly, I had spent too long operating at dangerous levels. All of the stressful situations had become too much for me and so all additional strains had made the situation worse. I found out later in rehab that it is possible to illustrate the connections qualitatively as I have done in the following diagram.

As you get older, you train your tolerances and your breaking point rises. This starts to decrease at a certain age, but the external demands and burdens, which have been building up over the years, remain. If you have a lot of pressure points, you become more sensitive to your situation because you can't plan a long time in advance. At some point, you reach the "red zone".

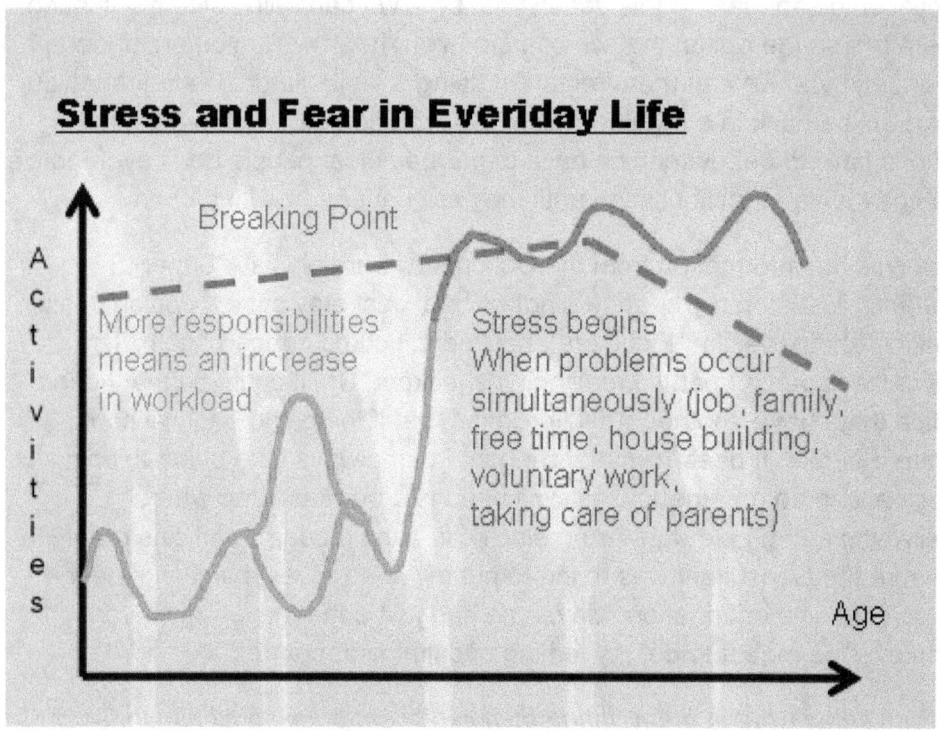

So, let's continue with the actual "treatment".

I spent 3 hours hooked up to a monitor in the Emergency Department until a bed became free in the Cardiology Unit. It was around midday when I was moved, but the free bed turned out to be a trolley in a corridor because everything else was completely full. Wonderful! But what could I do. At least it was at the end of the corridor, so I had some peace and peace was really what I needed. I tried to sleep, but of course that wasn't really possible in the corridor. There were people constantly walking past or beds being moved around. Time crawled by and the evening came. Blood was taken and I was booked in, but I had to spend the night in the corridor. I asked if it would at least be possible to turn off the lights, but of course it wasn't because it was essential that the emergency lighting stayed on. Thankfully, every second light of the emergency lighting was off. Of course, the one diagonally across from my bed was on. The Night Sister found a screen from somewhere and put it in front of my bed so that the light wasn't shining directly in my face. I thought I would be able to enjoy some sort of peace during that night, but that wasn't to be the case.

First of all, the Night Sister would cross the corridor every half an hour or so to attend to some patient or other, and then the lights did become annoying. As coincidence would have it, across from me was an elderly man with dementia who called out at least 10 times that night for help. By the following morning, I had managed to sleep around 4-5 hours and that had only been in fits and starts. I was dog-tired and that was on top of what had happened the day before. I requested to be given a room. Just not one with the elderly man. I wouldn't have been able to cope with that!

Despite my complaint, I spent the rest of the day in the corridor. I was told that patients were being moved around (from one room to another) in order to create a space for me. I ended up in the room next to the man with dementia. (Of course, he couldn't do anything about it and I'd had enough by then anyway). The following night I noticed that the 30 year old sound proofing in the walls wasn't especially good. At least there didn't seem to be a difference in noise levels between my place in the corridor and in that room. The only positive was that the light was turned off, but at least that was a small improvement. My condition didn't really improve because I was so exhausted, but still couldn't really get any sleep at night. During the day I had cardiac echo tests, ECGs and visits. I spent all the time lying in bed, feeling tired. I even started to break out in sweat again and I could feel my heart racing. I still couldn't sleep, though and I started to become quite aggressive. I called to the nurse and had an ECG right there. No change. Marliese and the children visited me often and at least that brought some kind of variety to the day. I was, in the course of the following days, also visited by colleagues, a neighbor and our priest, (who was visiting as a friend and not because I was close to death!) There was definitely no lack of support and I would like to take this opportunity to thank those people for that. I stayed in this room and the elderly man next door was sent back to the Care Home he'd come from. Great, I thought. My "room mate" also changed and I was joined by a friendly guy, who worked shifts in an Aldi warehouse, but who was suffering from stress and had been brought in with a blood pressure of 250! None of the standard treatments and medication helped until he was given triple the normal dose and then it dropped to 160.

He never had anything positive to say in the time that I was awake and receptive. I was sure the next night would be wonderful...

I settled down to sleep, but was woken up quite abruptly 30 minutes later. Next to me, it sounded as if someone was using a chainsaw to chop down trees in the nearby forest. My nice, 198cm tall, 140kg roommate made such a noise snoring that I actually longed for the elderly man to come back. Nothing helped. Not pillows over my ears or calling out during the snores. My last hope was to call the nurse: "Hello. I need earplugs and sleeping tablets or I'm going to go mad from not sleeping for the third night in a row. You know my diagnosis, and the situation here isn't exactly helping the recovery process." "Yes, I understand, but we don't have any other space. We are completely full."

The sleeping tablets worked for 5 hours. The earplugs weren't enough. In the morning I was close to totally losing the plot. I was becoming more and more exhausted. This wasn't normal tiredness anymore, where you can sleep for 10 hours and then be ready to go again. It was something much deeper than that. Despite exhaustion, you can't sleep. Your body is dog tired, but your mind is racing and you can't find any kind of peace to recover. You start to go crazy. I had some good news on that day, though. During the ECG that morning, it was discovered that my heart had corrected itself and was beating regularly. Yay! I couldn't really get excited about though because of the exhaustion. I spent the day tossing and turning in my bed, as my roommate's visitors were annoying. I wasn't hungry. I asked the nurse if I could have some more sleeping pills. "No problem," she said. The nurse that evening said that I'd had enough to knock out an elephant. Before dinner I had the feeling that my heart was racing again and I also started sweating. I shouted for the nurse and the doctors came as well. I was shaking as I had the ECG, but the diagnosis was negative. Everything was normal. I didn't understand. It was exactly he same feeling as I'd had the morning before I went to my GP. Despite that, I was given the all clear. Well, that's what they said, but I knew I wasn't crazy.

That evening I spoke to the nurse. I was afraid and knew I couldn't put up with another night sleeping next to the chainsaw guy. It was a very one-sided conversation:

"Nurse. I can't take this anymore. I am physically and mentally exhausted. I'm under a lot of stress and I'm here because of an irregular heartbeat, but I haven't been able to sleep the last 3 nights. I may as well be sleeping under a railway bridge. I know that the unit is full, but I don't give a damn. I need a room tonight for me alone. I don't care where and I don't care how big it is. I'm sure that you have a bathroom, a cleaning cupboard or something else somewhere which is empty at night and in which a bed can be put."

"No, I can't do that. You have to stay in this room."

"Yes, you can do it. What if I sleep somewhere else at my own risk? Anywhere would be better than where I am now. I can't take it anymore. Do you understand? Let's call the Consultant. I know that there is a bathroom for disabled patients out there. I had a look this afternoon."

"Yes, but there isn't any room in there at the moment. That's where all the wheelchairs are."

"Yes, but they can be folded up and put in the corner. During the day I'll be back in here."

"If you are sure, maybe we could see."

"Yes, please do."

We looked at the room together. It was ideal and it even had a disabled toilet and it would be mine for the night. "I'm going to have to check this with the Night Sister first. If something happens in the night and we need the room, that will mean that you have to get out." "Fine. Then just push me out into the corridor and then back in again afterwards."

Everything was sorted, but I took no chances. I had my earplugs and a sleeping tablet. I just couldn't take it anymore. Sleep didn't have any noteworthy effect.

The following two nights I managed to sleep 6 hours with a sleeping tablet. It didn't really improve my exhausted condition, but at least it reduced my increasing levels of aggression and I got through the days with normal feelings of tiredness. It wasn't a recovery.

I didn't understand it. Why couldn't I sleep? And when I do sleep, why didn't I feel any better afterwards?

All further tests and ECGs were OK, as were the blood test results. Despite that, I had other episodes where I felt my heart racing and I was soaked in sweat. Whenever it happened, I panicked that the same thing would happen as before. Once I even shouted at the Consultant: "You can see I'm exhausted. I don't know what is wrong. Are you sure you can't see anything on the ECG? Why aren't I getting better? Why can't I sleep even though I'm so tired?" It was a false alarm. The ECG was completely normal once again.

All following examinations were OK, which meant that, "mechanically" at least, my heart was fine. I had to do a Stress-ECG on the bicycle that afternoon and then I was to be discharged the next day.

In my head I thought, "You're all stupid." (Sorry, but that was my spontaneous reaction to the situation at that time) I hadn't been able to sleep since I'd been there, I was running on empty, had just suffered a serious heart problem, my colleagues wanted to temporarily "put me out to roost" and now they wanted me to jump on bike to do a Stress-ECG. Just like that. I supposed that there were enough doctors there in case something should happen.

It was on this day that one of the doctors spoke to me for the first time about the chance of there being a psychosomatic cause. It was a possibility. I was going to be put into the care of the hospital psychologists. They were specialized in addiction, but they had a broad range of experience in other areas.

So, to the ECG: I had a sip of water beforehand, got a towel and then climbed on the machine, foot on the pedals, all hooked up. "The machine automatically turns up by 50 Watts every 2 minutes. As soon as it gets too much, let us know." "Yes, I know that," I answered a bit annoyed. I started, pushing slowly on the pedals. I guessed that the stress would somehow cause my to panic again and I'd start trembling, but as I said, the Armada of helpers was near by. I started at 100 Watts – comfortable pace. 150 Watts – slight increase in the breathing rate, but everything was fine. 200 Watts – sweat, heavy breathing. It was becoming difficult. I was thinking that this was the beginning of the dangerous phase. 250 Watts – I was working hard, dripping with sweat, my lungs were burning and my breathing heavy. I was gasping in the oxygen as if I were climbing a mountain. "You've done 1 minute at this level. Are you OK to continue?" "Yes." I wanted to know. "Then I'm going to reduce the time of the levels by half." 275 Watts – I'm drenched with sweat. I can feel how my legs are starting to struggle just like they had done before when I had overexerted myself and my muscles were battling against it. It was no wonder really. It had been such a long time since I had done any exercise and I had spent the last week lying down, plus I was psychologically and, in terms of sleep, at the end of my tether. "It's going to happen. It's going to happen, " I thought. I was finally rescued by the sound of the end of the level. I'd had enough. I breathed deeply in and out and recovered myself. "That was good for someone in your condition. The ECG was good even under stress. I'm almost satisfied. There was only one point where there might be some concern, but I'll have to show that to the Consultant." Wow, I thought. Should I be pleased? I felt like shit and nobody could tell me why and the next day I would be discharged as "mechanically healthy". Super. It really was a good result. The doctors had done everything they could from a cardiology point of view, and that was OK. I wasn't making any accusations because of that. Today I know exactly the huge role the mind can play – thoughts, feelings of anxiety, panic. It doesn't have to, but it can. Unfortunately, you can't always understand that by using normal diagnostic machinery, as it turned out to be in my case.

There was one positive thing that had stayed in my head: "we can stop your heart and then "restart" it." Nothing came of that, though.

I talked intensively with a therapist in the Psychological Advice Center for Addictions. I noticed during this that I constantly stopped. I always had to take a break and it was incredibly stressful to talk about the time before – what had happened, all my pressure points, everything that had gone wrong at work, the problems we had had looking after my mother, the construction project which wasn't finished, the voluntary work in the parish, how all of this stress was affecting the family and so on and so on. It made me choke up.

The result: I was discharged from the department as requiring no further treatment, without medication, but with the following advice: "Go to the mental health clinic in Mannheim and find yourself a psychotherapist. The one thing with the Stress-ECG is nothing to worry about. It's understandable after what has happened. It will subside after a while." It seemed that I was perfectly fine, although I didn't really feel like it.

On 29.11.11, 6 days after my 9/11, Marliese picked me up. I was really frustrated and felt as if I'd just been pushed out, but "mechanically", nothing more could be done for me.

The next day I went to my GP. He was really very good and I see that now. When it comes down to it, he really just wanted to help me as much as he can. " You need psychological help and, without doubt, some rehabilitation in a clinic." "Doctor, I'll do anything to get over this." "I can understand that and I know it. We'll send an urgent request to your insurance company in the coming days. I got all the information together, all the medical certificates, hospital records form this year and last plus your own description of the current situation and what led up to it." The doctor did everything else and wrote in red pen in the top left corner "URGENT". "That normally works."

Going home:

The 2 weeks before my appointment with a neurologist were a psychological catastrophe.
I was at home. Thank God. I was looking forward to finally being able to have a lie in. Finally! I couldn't do it though! Why not? Why was I waking up after 2 hours sleep, soaked in sweat and shaking? I was wide-awake. I spent the nights walking around. After 2 nights of this, I "moved" upstairs so that my wife could at least get a decent night's sleep. I would go to the fridge or drink something. I felt completely exhausted, but I still couldn't get a wink of sleep. I became aggressive and lost my temper. "Damn it! What's wrong?! This has never happened before. I've got peace and quiet here. Why isn't that helping? It was understandable in the hospital, but now?" After about 1 week, the insomnia improved a little. I had around 4-5 hours of sleep and the sweating became less often.

In this situation, I made a deal with the Man Upstairs. I know you can't negotiate with him, but it's possible to ask for something and hope that it works, so I did what a lot of other people do – I prayed. I very rarely pray for things for myself because I'm actually relatively happy, but at this time, I prayed for my life. It's not a bad thing to do and it doesn't hurt. Even for a man. Since then, I have also prayed for other people. It's possible that the situations for which I prayed would have turned out well, even without my prayers, but it didn't do any harm - to me or to the other people.

By the way, it is amazing how many people pray, if only for a moment, when they find themselves in very critical situations, looking for help.

The search for a neurologist and a psychotherapist was grueling. The referrals from one doctor to another, being advised of the long waiting lists and searching by myself for a neurologist and a conversational therapist were very frustrating and added to the stress I was under. I felt helpless and alone because I couldn't see any improvement or progress in my situation. Due to their workload, the Call Center for the Allocation of Therapy Places for Psychosomatic Conditions fobbed me off until after the Christmas holidays. If I were lucky, there might be a space on a therapist's list, but I would have to wait 5 weeks. I told them on the phone that wouldn't work for me. I couldn't take it anymore. Even emptying the dishwasher was a massive undertaking, but I wouldn't get any medical support for 5 weeks?! "Unfortunately, I can't do anything. Have a nice Christmas." That was just great. If I have a scratch on my finger, I can go to my GP. Even if I sneeze, I get an appointment. If I have toothache, I can get to see the Dentist the same day without having to wait. With a psychological problem, I have to wait 5 weeks! That meant nothing was as bad as I thought. I thought I would turn up and find out that I was actually completely healthy. Yes, that was what was going to happen!

You would even get an appointment quicker than I did if it was for your dog or cat. Maybe some cases solve themselves in this waiting period.

I was definitely shocked by this. I'm sure it wasn't the fault of the therapist. Psychological treatment requires a lot of time and there just aren't enough doctors. Having said that, something has to be changed. There is considerable danger that depression can become chronic after more than 6 months. That means that treatment BEFORE this time is crucial to its success. Due to this, the resulting costs, never mind the number of patients who don't find a way out of their depression shouldn't be a surprise to us. It is exactly these people I want to give courage to.

So, I was looking for a therapist for psychosomatic conditions

I laboriously searched the phone book, Yellow Pages and the Internet. In between times I had a break and tried to get some sleep during the day. The time just before Christmas is bad. Everyone was busy or already on holiday. There was just one more number on my list and that call went straight to answer phone. I left a message at about 9:30, but didn't have any hopes that it would come to something. At 11am I got a call back. "Hello, Mr. Dietrich. I listened to your message and wanted to let you know that my appointment at 12:40 has been canceled. You can jump in then if you like and then we can decide if we should continue meeting." Wow. That was lucky! Good. And it was even for today! She didn't tell me how long the appointment would last, but that I should take my health insurance card with me.

I arrived at 12:30 and knocked. She came out and said, "I'm just talking to someone at the moment. Have a seat in the waiting room and I'll call you in when I'm finished." "Thanks." At 12:45 I heard the door opening and the goodbyes and then "Mr. Dietrich, please." "Yes, I'm coming."

I will never forget what happened in the next 15 minutes!

"Have you brought your insurance card with you? The first introductory and counseling sessions always last around 15 minutes. Please take a seat over there. So, have you thought about whether you want a short or long-term therapy?" I was still rummaging around for my card and was, at first, a little bit surprised by this question, because I had expected her to answer that question for me. "Here is my card." She stood up and went to the computer. "You can carry on talking. I'm just going to enter your details. I am listening to you!" She began to type. "I don't know. This is the first time I've been in such a situation and I can't really assess it. I wanted to find that out with your help."

"Well, I don't offer short-term therapy. It's not really worth it because of the health insurance companies' points-for-payment system (they were her actual words), and that's why I only do long-term therapy. I also offer relaxation courses and they normally last 12 weeks, meeting once a week. A course started 4 weeks ago, so you could only join that one in March or there is another one starting in February. What exactly is your problem?"

The printer rattled into life. I didn't say anything for a moment because I thought it was outrageous that I should be talked to in such a way. After about 10 minutes had passed, she sat herself opposite me with a clipboard and the printout in the second, round, pink-leather armchair.

I didn't think about the time. I thought I finally had the opportunity to talk to a therapist and get my problems off my chest and to get a few pieces of advice. I started and explained to her about what happened on the 23.11.11, the situation at work as well as the different pressure points. She made a few crosses on the printout. When the 15 minutes were over, of which I felt I had only had 5 to explain my situation, she stood up and said, "Mr. Dietrich, in my opinion, it seems that a short-term therapy would be the best for you. I'll give you my diagnosis sheet (the paper with the crosses). Here is a brochure of the courses I told you about before. If there is anything that could be suitable for you, please get in touch. Thank you very much, but unfortunately I have another appointment now."

I stood in front of the door for a while and then plodded crestfallen to the car. It was only when I got home that I realized what had just happened. I had just been the gap-filler for another billable appointment. Introductory appointments with other therapists all lasted at least 50 minutes. In some cases, I had 3 sessions to begin with. (The health insurance company allows you to choose from up to 5 different therapists. It would be unwise to commit to someone if there was no mutual trust.) I'd really hit the jackpot with my first appointment. Congratulations, I thought to myself. I was now really frustrated. I needed help and then that had happened. I must say that only happened the first time. All others were exactly how you would expect them to be when you visit a therapist. I certainly don't want to generalize the experience I had.

I also want to encourage you, not to give up, if the first try is not successful. You are free to "test" up to 5 Therapists in Germany to be sure to find the one you like to tell also your confidential personel secrets.

I will briefly describe what happened next in order to illustrate what happened in the time up until Rehab and also so as not to bore you too much.

Since 2011, despite being at home signed off sick, there were more incidents at frequent intervals, for example:

- Beginning of December 2011: We were invited by friends to a birthday party. I couldn't sleep the night before, and so was exhausted the whole day and went to bed at 5pm. I couldn't take the anxiety and exhaustion anymore and had to get out. My wife couldn't understand why I didn't stay at home if I was so tired and we had an argument. I just couldn't stay at home anymore. The music at the party was loud and I tried to ignore things and to celebrate like I had always been able to do. I was done in afterwards and needed 2 days to recover.

- Middle of December 2011: After a lot of telephoning and many conversations explaining with despair to doctors' receptionists that I couldn't take it much longer, I finally got an appointment with a neurologist. The call center for appointment allocation for people with psychosomatic conditions made a referral for me 4 weeks later in the New Year!!

- The neurologist prescribed me a low dose of Mirtazapine. At last I was able to sleep for at least 5-6 hours in one go. Slowly, some kind of recovery started to take place so that from the middle of December, I once again had a structure to my day. That was the first time in 4 weeks. Power levels: 1 out of 10.

- 20.12.11: I was very anxious and agitated. I had a tingling sensation on the left side of my chest and down the whole of my left arm. I almost hyperventilated (a physical reaction) in a similar way to 23.11.11 and took a sedative.

- 29.12.11: At last I had an appointment with the therapist the neurologist had recommended. Thank God, a slot had just become available. The first meeting seemed to be promising and the chemistry between us seemed to be correct.

- Between Christmas and New Year 2011 I contacted the pension insurance company (DRV) to see if they had received the urgent request from my GP. Yes, they said. It was there, but it hadn't been marked as being urgent.
"But I saw my doctor write "urgent" in the top left corner with red pen."

"Yes, "urgent" is written on it, but that doesn't mean it has been given that status. There is a cross missing in the relevant box on page 2 of the form from the health insurance company."

"Yes, but that is how they sent the forms to me."

" That is why it hasn't been classed as an urgent case."

"And how do I make sure it becomes that?"

"It's not possible to change it now. The case is already being processed."

"Yes, but only because a cross has inadvertently been forgotten? The doctor marked it in red for a reason!"

"I'm going to have to clarify this, but if it is possible to change, it will only be possible from the side of the health insurance company."

"Could you call them for me. I'll give you my details."

"No, the insurance company makes the application and has to contact us."

"Please give me your phone number. I'll call them myself and then they can contact you directly."

He gave me his number or rather, that of the responsible department. I called the insurance company. The employee there was very helpful and contacted the pensions company. 30 minutes later I got the feedback that the cross had been added. Urgent case. Finally! So much bureaucracy!

On the 4th January 2012, I received a letter from the DRV and, full of expectation, I ripped the envelope open. I held the letter refusing my application for rehabilitation care in my hands. What the hell was this? Are they crazy? I was desperate and felt completely wiped out. Did they think I was playing games? I had been paying my contributions for 20 years and I all I got was that!

Result: Symptoms on the left side of my body. Nervousness, tension, tingling, insomnia, sweating, brooding (what's going to happen if I don't get the OK?), anxiousness. My GP also didn't understand the decision. "That has to be a mistake in the processing over the holidays. Normally an application including symptoms like yours is approved straight away," he said. "We'll appeal against the decision." We did that as quickly as possible and the DRV confirmed that they had received my appeal before the end of the month.

- 14.01.12: Agitation with nervous symptoms on my left side when picking up my crying daughter from the bus stop (This was the start of Sara being bullied in school). In the past I had always hidden away such things or calmed her down and allayed her fears. Now however, it really affected me. Suddenly I had become vulnerable to even the smallest things.

- 21.01.12: High blood pressure according to my portable monitor. Broke out in a sweat in the morning and very anxious and restive. 2h hours previously I had had my blood pressure measured at the GP's – the result was normal. Everything had been OK.

- From 02.02.12: Stopped taken Mirtazapine as a test.

- 05.02.12: Similar symptoms during the farewell service with the church elders.

- 07.02.12: Woke up soaked in sweat after a bad dream.

- 12.02.12: Nervous tension and the same symptoms after a sleepless night after watching a movie on TV with my daughter, Viktoria.

- 14.02.12: Woke up at 5:30 feeling nervous and tingling. Had increasing fear of an escalation of my situation, as there was no sign of any progress and the cause was still unknown. Took a sedative and visited my GP. After that I started to take Mirtazapine regularly again. I couldn't manage without it. I felt like I was dependent on it even though the instruction leaflet said that wouldn't be the case.

- 25.02.12: Symptoms of anxiousness after a 2 hour meeting with the church elders (although I was only taking the minutes of the meeting because I had wanted to very slowly start taking on more responsibility again). I had to abandon the meeting, so that hadn't worked out at all! I wasn't ready. Even with relaxation, I couldn't control the symptoms, which kept reappearing, and had to take a sedative.

- After 3 months, I still hadn't reached a point, which would allow me to work regularly and I started to panic. Why, why? I was still waiting to get into a rehabilitation clinic and it had become very wearing. I had gotten used to the idea that nothing would be like it had been before. I felt the fear growing inside me and that was a fear of what the future would bring.

- I never would have guessed that my character and my thoughts, which were the things that had given me my zest for life and had made me into a friendly and fun-loving person (that's how some of my friends have described me anyway) would change. I suddenly had some very strange thoughts like:
  What would the future be like if things didn't go back to how they were before? I support the family and earn the cash, so what's going to happen? Can I take responsibility for the family? How are we going to have change?
  They weren't so bad, just normal questions that get asked sometimes.

- The next level of questioning came a few weeks later and was even harder:
  Will I be a burden on the family? Are my children going to have to go without things? Can I, or we, still provide them with the education they want? Will Marliese have to work and, if yes, how much? To what extent will this affect the family?

- Level 2 became a little dangerous: I had the nightmare that my 3 girls were left alone. I saw them from below, just like one of those photos when you put the camera on the floor, stand in a circle and look down smiling. Only they weren't smiling. They were crying. And then sand fell into my eyes…

For God's sake, what is happening to me!

I caught myself starting to drink 1 or 2 beers in the evenings so that I could switch off more easily and then sleep better. I thought that it wasn't much, so it couldn't be that bad. The huge difference was that in the past, I had treated myself to a drink as a reward for something or just because I enjoyed it. At this point I was drinking out of fear that I wouldn't be able to sleep. That was unbelievable!

For a third night I woke up from this stupid dream. I was nervous. I was shaking. I stood up and tried to relax. I calmed myself down. I was tired, but, thank God, it worked.

Of course I discussed all of this with my therapist, without whom my rollercoaster ride would have been much more dramatic. He always picked me up again and together, we focused on the things, which had gone well in the week and we analyzed and alleviated a lot of my fears. However, once a week wasn't enough and the basic problem remained the same: I didn't know the reason why I wasn't making any progress, even though I was off work and at home the whole time.

- I then made a decision: I had to get myself out of this situation. I had to get out!

  This stuff had started to change my thoughts. It had started to change me!

  I couldn't let that happen! I would find a way, but I wouldn't let this happen. I was going to fight for this damn rehab. I was going to fight for my family! I was going to fight for myself! I didn't know who exactly I was going to fight against, but I wasn't just going to sit in the corner and wait.

- I needed external help, advice from doctors, to hear experiences from people who had also been affected. I needed to get out of this. I needed to talk about it with my friends. That's what friends are for! If needs be, I would have had to Google or read up on it. This wasn't a broken leg or a cut, which would heal by itself because of the body's own defense system.

  I knew if I bottled it up, it would eat me up. Anyone who laughed or talked about me then would be people I couldn't count on anyway. It would only have been pretense. I thought that I might not be able maintain all of these relationships in the future anyway, so it was better to concentrate on those that were serious. Empty promises such as "Yeah, I'll call you and we can meet up every 3 months for a chat" and then nothing happens were not going to help me. I didn't have anything left to give other people. I needed all my power for myself.

When talking to people, it is astonishing how many of them have had to deal with stress. It is possible to read in the newspapers and magazines all about burnout and the 30% of the working population with symptoms of stress, as well as those under great pressure to perform well. This pressure begins in the schools and is something that many pupils and young people have to deal with. With hindsight, it is possible to see all the warning signs, which most people just completely ignore. Allow me to give you an example of a Worst Case Scenario:

1. Think about what is the worst thing that could happen.
2. Think of a solution, which will avoid this situation or help you overcome it.
3. Act accordingly

Sounds easy.

My problem was always with Point 1! I didn't want to accept a worst-case scenario and I was afraid of it happening.

This meant that I was going to have to really face up to the things that had been demoralizing me. If I wanted to escape from this, if I wanted to rid myself of my fears, I was going to have to start dealing with it.

What was the "Horror Scenario?"

That is easy:

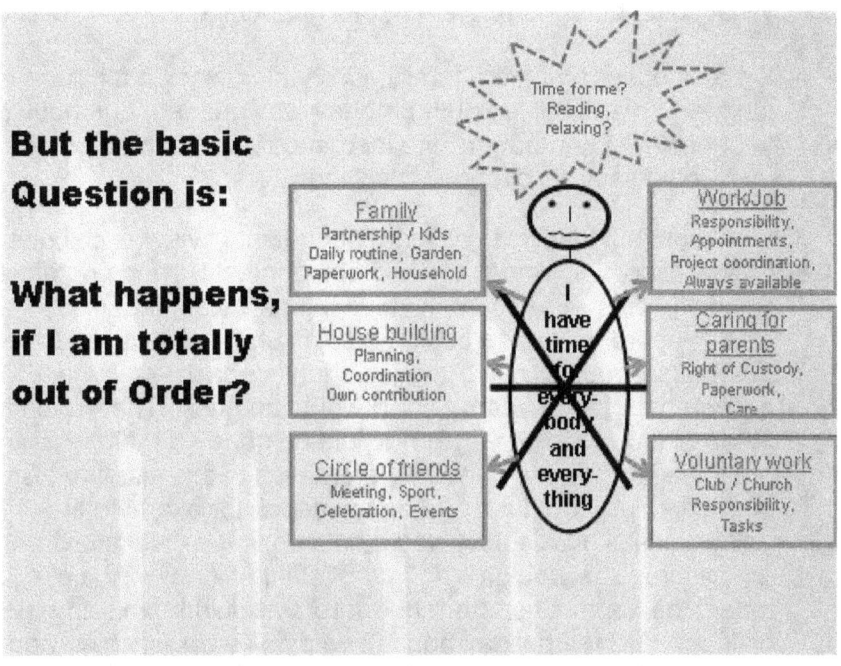

This can lead to several different scenarios:
Firstly, I have a complete mental breakdown and am unable to get out o fit. If that happens, I'll need a Plan B.
Secondly, I have heart problems again and this leads to a stroke. I wanted to counter this by doing regular sport so that I would become more physically resilient and so that I would have way to clear my head.
I definitely wanted to avoid that because if I didn't, I would have some real problems. It wouldn't only affect me, but my family and everyone around us as well. I had to be careful! Also when the time came and I was back at work.
And so to my Plan B:

I wouldn't be able to bounce back from this and then I would lose my job because I wouldn't be able to do it as I once had. Full stop. I would lose my job, not because my boss threw me out, but simply because I couldn't do it. Just like if someone had worked as a postal worker before an accident left him or her in a wheelchair. In an attempt to make the situation better, I supposed that I wouldn't have to leave the company, but that I might be able to do something else

51

there instead. I calculated however, that my salary would be reduced by around 50% if that happened.

What could be done to prevent this happening?

Discuss options with the family: Everything was up for negotiation. A long-term plan until my 60th birthday was needed, but that was 10 years away! After that, my life insurance was due to be paid out and that would save us over the following years.

I am a project leader. I calculate budgets. Now I was calculating for my own survival. Things change sometimes! Savings potential: A car (running costs were scarcely anything as it was already 15 years old), my parents' house could be sold (Shit, this was really painful!). The house would provide a good chunk of cash – around 1000€ every month for 10 years, which would be great. That would however mean that our "extra pension" would be gone and that wasn't good, but there really wasn't another alternative in this situation. Club memberships would have to be canceled, for example the children's riding classes. Our eldest would have to find casual jobs to fund her education. (She would've done that a little bit anyway, but it just meant the contribution from her parents would be missing). Forget holidays. Sell the holiday house (we didn't earn anything from it, but we were also going to use it for our retirement. The risks of keeping it were too big). Household expenses and running costs would have to be reduced.

Over all, these things didn't quite reach the 50% target, but we were pretty close to it.

At a push, Marliese would work part time. I didn't really like the idea because she had always been there to support our youngest with her schoolwork and this wasn't going to be an easy time for her what with exams coming up. If that was the only way, though, that is what we were going to have to do. It wasn't a problem for her. This is normal in a lot of other families because it isn't possible to live on the salary of only one person. We would have to deal with it.

What did the plan achieve?

Basically, the plan had 2 very important consequences:

1.) We could appreciate for the first time all the things we had been able to afford along the way. The things that people get used to because they are enjoyable and they are so important to our lives. The things that we have because other people have them, but are things that, when it comes down to it, we don't really need, but could cost money. We also noticed that, materialistically, we were actually pretty well off. There were things we could do without if we needed to and we had spare money, which other people didn't have. What would they do in such a situation? They would definitely be more frugal.

There was also a change in the way we viewed people, who for example, are disabled or ill, or who have to come to terms with lasting problems after an accident. If these people are able to remain optimistic and not give up despite being restricted somehow, this deserves the upmost respect! In the meantime, I also know what I will do as a doddery old man with my zimmer frame (as long as I still have the mental capacity to do things). I will be the grandfather reading fairy tales at the kindergarten with my wife once or twice a week. It is so easy to make children happy and grandparents are the best at doing it.

So, the first effect was: "You know what, you can do something. You aren't totally helpless. What you need is a roof over your head, something to eat and a job, which allows you to have these things. And anyway, you have additional resources."

We know a family in our circle of friends who don't have these extra resources. Both parents had a normal job. She used to be a secretary and he worked in a warehouse. She became unemployed because the small company she worked for went bankrupt. He lost his job because his company was making savings. Both were over 50, and so they were both pushed down the pecking order when looking for a new position. They could only find temporary work for the minimum wage and after 5 years of that, they couldn't find a way out despite writing numerous applications.

2.) The fear for my own existence was gone! There was a solution, a way out! Ok, we had to give up a lot and our later years would be different to how we had planned, but at least we had a future. I was still a little bit fuddled in the head, but life goes on! We were just like those who don't have their parent's house or 2 cars and who can't afford a holiday. I remember as a child how my mother had to go out to do some cleaning just to keep us afloat. There was nothing else to do. So: don't give up! And anyway, we were nowhere near that point yet.

Let's continue with the developments:

- 08.03.12: Was exhausted and haggard after several days of doing little jobs around the house. Had worked around 3 hours every day. Had been invited to a birthday party that evening during which I suffered some symptoms of stress, increasing in severity afterwards.

- 10.03.12: Spent some time doing some work on the lawn. Experienced the same symptoms as the previous day. Took a sedative and 1 Mirtazapine in the evening.

- 11.03.12: Became extremely nervous during a church service. Became anxious and uneasy and had tingling sensations all down my left side and arm. I had the feeling I was about to hyperventilate. I could only relax by forcing myself to concentrate on relaxation and breathing techniques. This was a setback and I felt exactly as I had done 8 weeks before. I had a lot of feelings of doubt that I could ever be 100% fit again. I began to think again about what would happen to the family.

  I discussed this event, as I had the others before it, intensively with my therapist. I tried not to pay as much attention to my symptoms when they appeared, but despite that I also tried to react accordingly to them when they did.

- 20-24.03.12: I experienced the same symptoms once again while renewing the antivirus software subscription on our 2 laptops. The problems with my arm meant that I had to stop what I was doing and in the end, it was only completed after working on it in stages over several days. I couldn't concentrate for long periods of time and that is why I needed a long time to compile this report.

- 14.04.12: Meeting of the Council of Elders in the parish (I had already said that I wouldn't take such an active part in the discussions because of my situation.)
  During these discussions I experienced the same physical symptoms twice. As every time there were the feelings of anxiety and tingling sensations. I had to take a break to try and relieve these symptoms using breathing techniques, exercise (gentle jogging) and "release" techniques (aggression). This worked both times and I was so happy about that. I was then totally exhausted on the Monday, and so had a "recovery day". On Tuesday, I went for an 8km run. Wednesday I went for a bike ride and to the dentist. On Thursday I was completely exhausted again and stayed in bed until around 3pm. The recovery took until Saturday.

- On 26.04.12 I found out from a colleague, who had called that evening, that a new manager was going to start on 01.11.2012. We already knew the date, but didn't know if someone would be found by then and how his or her appointment and way of working would affect us.
  All this uncertainty! We also talked about the current projects, the stress on the other colleagues and how I was doing. That night I woke up at 2am and 6am. On both occasions I was soaked in sweat and found it very hard to go back to sleep. I took a sedative to help.

- I experienced the same physical symptoms at the funeral of the father of a good friend on 04.05.12. I had to leave after the service, meaning I couldn't go the burial.

- 06.05.12: I was beginning to feel as if I was being pushed from pillar to post… On 02.05.12 the pensions insurance company (DRV) said they hadn't received a report they needed from an assessor. The assessor had sent it on the 10.04.12, though.
  The previous day, I had thought a lot about why this report hadn't made it to DRV yet. On the morning of the 6th I woke up at 5am after a dream in which I was sliding down some kind of funnel with smooth sides and couldn't get out. At the bottom was a millstone rotating slowly.

- 07.05.12: My wife had bad stomach pains. I had been awake since 4:30am and couldn't get back to sleep. I got the children ready at 6am, feeling uneasy. My wife's pain slowly improved. It was a tiring day, but I found it difficult to fall asleep. I was tense and ended up taking 2 tablets of some herbal medicine to help me relax.

- 08.05.12: Woke up at 5am feeling very uneasy. I got up, had breakfast and thought about the assessment. I sorted out the children again, but then couldn't go back to sleep so I relaxed on the sofa and calmed myself down with my breathing exercises. I rode my bike to an appointment in the city. I was tired afterwards, but I didn't feel as tense anymore. I still had stomach problems though and took something for that. However, they didn't really improve and so I just had something light to eat that evening.
  No TV anymore.

- I wrote a letter to the DRV because I didn't know what to do anymore:

Dear Sir or Madam,

I would like to ask for your understanding, but I just don't know what else I should do. What was an urgent request for rehabilitation in December 2011 has been dragged out to last over 5 months and still hasn't been resolved today.

I received an immediate rejection to the request, but I then had to wait 8 weeks for an answer from you after I had appealed against the decision. After these 8 weeks, I received a letter informing me that I needed to be assessed. After selecting someone to do this, I then had to wait a further 4 weeks for an appointment with Dr. Assessor. The examination took place on the 4th April 2012 in Mannheim after which the doctor told me that he was going to immediately send the report and that the DRV would contact me.

Due to the fact that I still hadn't heard anything after a further 4 weeks of waiting, I called the DRV on the 2nd May 2012 and was told by Mrs. XY that Dr. Assessor had sent no assessment report.

I contacted Dr. Assessor and he told me that he had sent the complete report on 10th April 2012 to the DRV. That means 3-4 weeks previously. That means that the report had been lying on a desk somewhere at the DRV, but hadn't been read or filed.

Please understand the situation I am in. My therapist had already given the opinion in a report on the 4th January 2012 that this was an urgent case. I understand why you require an independent assessment, but this has now been dragging on for an eternity and nothing has improved in that time. I feel like I'm not being taken seriously and that people see me as a time waster or someone who can just be ignored.

Meeting with my therapist for 1 hour every week isn't enough. I wrote Dr. Assessor a letter describing my situation in detail as well as the how my condition developed. I am sure that he took this and notes that he made during our discussions into account when writing his assessment.

I now feel completely helpless and increasingly dispirited and I really don't know what else I can do. So much time has gone by without intensive treatment. At every stage of this process I have done what I can to push it forward. I only have the possibility to discuss my problems with my therapist once a week. We haven't really had any time to discuss what lies ahead for me. Most of the time, we talk about and deal with problems, which have just cropped up (physical symptoms, my youngest daughter being bullied at school, the exam stress of my eldest daughter, distancing myself from the voluntary work I do in the parish, calls from work etc.)

Every answer I have received from you has made me feel very low because, every time, things haven't worked out as I thought they would. I like working together with people and am also cooperative, but this delay is causing me a lot of stress. I have been unable to work since 23rd November 2011. My GP told me that in such situations, cases are given preferential treatment in order to allow people to quickly get back to work.

I feel like I'm being pushed from pillar to post. Yesterday, I thought a lot about why Dr. Assessor's report hasn't been received by you yet and this morning, I woke up at 5am after a dream in which I was sliding down some kind of funnel with smooth sides and couldn't get out. At the bottom was a millstone rotating slowly. I couldn't get back to sleep after that, so I got up and started making notes for this letter in order to try and get these thoughts out of my head and try and process them.

The longer this goes on, the more I worry about how things are going to develop with work when I return as well as with the family. Will I be able to work full time? What's going to happen with my children's education and our house if things don't work out?

For the last 2 days I've had terrible stomach problems again.

I understand that I am not the only person to make an application, and I'm sure that you have a lot to do, but I'm asking for your understanding and your help. What would you do in my position? What do other people do when they are stuck "on hold"?

I regularly do sport because my doctor advised me that it was good for my heart. I feel good doing it, but I can also feel that, physically, I am making progress, but mentally, stress is still a problem. These days I find myself becoming uncontrollably anxious, uneasy and under pressure in what were always everyday situations. I then experience physical symptoms such as tingling sensations in my left shoulder and all the way down my left arm as well.

I would appreciate it if you could give me some information regarding how much longer this could potentially go on for. How long do I still have to wait for a response? Will there then be a waiting list for the Clinic etc.? My company and colleagues have been asking for this information.

Thank you very much. I'm looking forward to your prompt answer.

Best regards.

- 09.05.12: Bad night. Took a tablet to help me sleep. Had stomach problems again. Slept between 11pm and 2am and then was awake for 2 hours feeling uneasy and sweating. Slept between 4am and 7am. Still felt uneasy in the morning and had stomach problems. Canceled an appointment at the dentist's.
  This bad phase had lasted since 02.05.12: Causes: problems and delays with the assessment, constant back and forth, waiting times, having to take care of everything myself. I had felt better for about 2-3 weeks before, even without Mirtazapine.

- 10.05.12: Slept about 6 hours. Felt nervous again in the morning. Still wasn't taking Mirtazapine, stomach problems, and indigestion. I took something to calm down and something else for meals. Considerably less resilient than the week before. Felt a little better after a sauna. While I was out, someone said to me, "No-one would know there was a problem from looking at you. You really don't look so bad." Of course I tried to act as normally as possible otherwise everything would be so much worse. Actually though, things couldn't be more different. I was trying to suppress things because I didn't want to be like that and I wanted to fight against it and I didn't understand why things were not getting better.

- 11.05.12: Slept from 11pm to 4am and woke up with whistling noises in my right ear. Also had stomach problems because of nervousness. Got up at 5am feeling completely exhausted. Rested in bed between 7am and 11:30am. I still wasn't stable without medication I had a feeling that ants were crawling over my body. I telephoned my health insurance company to ask if there was the possibility of a direct admission because I couldn't take much more of this.
  I went to my GP and he told me that the DRV wouldn't ask for the assessment themselves anymore (he had called and asked). I had to do that for them. I got very annoyed about this, after all, it was the DRV who had demanded the assessment. It wasn't my fault that it had got lost. I asked the doctor about a direct admission, but he

recommended waiting for the reply from the DRV because it really shouldn't be much longer before it came through. He gave me another prescription for Mirtazapine and Pantoprazole, which is used to help prevent Mucositis and stomach ulcers by reducing stomach acid.

I then wrote to the assessor and asked him to send the assessment he had already sent 3 weeks previously to the DRV.

IF I HADN'T ASKED, I WOULD HAVE JUST CONTINUED TO WASTE AWAY AT HOME.

At this point, I felt like I had done back in January. The physical symptoms were the same: uneasiness, nervousness, insomnia, finding it difficult to fall asleep, sweating, shaking, tossing and turning at night etc. Since then I only drink still water because of the carbonation.

- 12.05.12: First good night with a sedative and Pantoprazole. Didn't feel as exhausted, but still wasn't very resilient. I still had a stomachache, but the indigestion improved. I was still sleeping alone so as not to wake up my wife and children when restless, but also so that I was undisturbed.

- Until 17.05.12: Similar to 12.05. Slow improvement thanks to the medication, but still careful and delicate. Was nervous and tetchy during the day.

- 22.05.12: Had an appointment with the psychotherapist. He told me that he hadn't had the time to fill in the information requested by the insurance company. His priority was to treat patients. I told him that I understood that, but who else could evaluate my condition. We had a tense discussion about that and, after around 15 minutes, I had to draw it to a close because I was getting tense and nervous. I was afraid that I would lose control. I went to the window and started my breathing and relaxation exercises.
  15 minutes later, we continued the appointment and changed the topic. It showed me that even here, when it came to difficult conversations about things that were important to me, I was unable to remain strong.

- 24.05.12: Swim and sauna day. It was good. Relaxing. On the way home I went to visit a colleague. He was still at work and his wife sent me away saying that it wasn't a good time.

I started to worry (completely unnecessarily) that her reaction had something to do with me because I had been unable to work for such a long time and was at home while my colleague had to take over some of my projects. This was despite the fact that he had ridden over to visit me 2 weeks before.

I was unsure and brooding. Everything was cleared up 5 days later when another colleague telephoned me about something else and told me that colleague 1 had been packing for his holiday the next day. (This was a topic for discussion at my next appointment.) It had been a false alarm. I never would have had these thoughts before all of this started.

- Otherwise, up to 06.06.12, my stomach problems continued to improve slowly with Pantoprazole and Iberogast (drops und Maaloxan for the stomach acid.) When it came to sport I felt stronger. I was slowly returning to the state of health I had had at the end of April.

- Until 09.06.12: Packed my case, filled out questionnaires and anticipated rehab.

- The physical symptoms that I had never had before 23.11.11 (tingling, anxiety, pressure in my shoulder and arm, nervousness) continued as before. They came everyday in different situations. Sometimes only mildly, but other times very severe. It made me fear that this would become chronic stress because of all the setbacks I have described.

- A lot of my therapy was taken up with dealing with problems which had arisen during the previous week. An hour a week was too little. I found that my situation seemed to stagnate, but I was still a very long way from reaching my previous levels of performance.

I had FEAR and PANIC that I wouldn't be able to break free of this loop and that I would never be the person I had been again. I feared that everything would collapse around me.

Summary of my condition before rehab:

- I was clearly still not as strong as I had been before 23.11.11. I noticed this in normal, everyday situations. (See examples above).

- Even at home I didn't feel like I was improving anymore.

- On some days I couldn't deal with answering the phone. I just didn't really want to talk to anyone, and so I would give it to my wife to deal with.

- Coffee and tea could also cause stress, and so I went without them or drank only decaffeinated coffee so as to spare my already delicate stomach. I also drank only still water, but the majority of the time I drank chamomile tea.

- Since the end of December I had always carried sedative drops with me in case of emergency because such situations were always a possibility (see above).

- My situation was also creating strain at home because my family was feeling my problems too. This then put even more pressure on me. (My youngest daughter was sad because I was ill and my eldest daughter had exam stress.)

- I tried twice to come off Mirtazapine (mild sedative which had sleep-inducing effects). I wasn't successful. If I didn't take this medication, I slept very badly at night, woke up several times, and was constantly exhausted and less able to cope with pressure. After consulting my therapist, I had started to take it regularly again.

- I was afraid of how things would work out for me professionally, as I have already written about above. There wasn't a problem with this period of illness because I had supplementary insurance for occupational disability, sick pay as well as additional payments from my company. What would happen, though if I couldn't manage to do my job anymore?

- At this time I couldn't imagine being able to go back to work because the anxious feelings and other symptoms would still crop up unexpectedly even after 5 months. I could usually only deal with them during long periods of relaxation (breathing techniques) or movement and sport (to reduce the feelings of stress). This wouldn't be possible at work. That's why I was hoping to make progress in rehab and was determined to cooperate as much as possible.
- My goal was, and I hoped for, a period of reintegration, which would take place in stages after rehab in order to get as close as possible

to my previous performance at work.

- I could still see potential problems, which I would have to face gradually. This was especially the case with project discussions, tasks that included contact with external customers and presentations, during which it is always possible that unexpected problems and stressful situations will arise. I was confident, though. After all I had done all of these things in the past often enough and sometimes I'd even had to do it in English or French.

- In November of this year, our department head was going to retire. This was something that caused me quite a headache. What would the new boss think of me? Would it be possible for me to stay in the department after being reintegrated or will they try and find an "alternative" for me?

- I worked voluntarily as Deputy Chairman in the parish and that meant I was often asked questions about, for example, the rebuild of the church. I had largely delegated my responsibilities. I needed a break in order to switch off. I was going to resign.

- On 11.03.12 I once again felt anxious and had physical symptoms during the church service before my announcement. The symptoms down my left side were so severe that I was almost unable to control it. A nurse I knew had sat down next to me.
  This incident and the other 2 due to the assessment frustrated and frightened me after such a long time of being at home.
  I asked myself what else we could do. I had hoped for a speedy admission to a treatment at a health resort with all necessary medical specialists so that I could avoid setbacks and mistakes.
  Unfortunately, this didn't happen.

- I always discussed the problems as they occurred and that helped me a lot. We worked a lot on reviewing and evaluating situations as well as on different options for how I should deal with them.

- In the past I had always been a person and a colleague, who had supported others, who volunteered, who had always been active with a large circle of friends and was also quite sporty.

It depressed me that my family was suffering and that my already over-stressed colleagues were having to now take on some of my work or postpone some projects. (In doing so, mistakes are made, appointments are delayed and there are also additional costs etc.)

1.5 year after my reintegration, when I look back at this time I have to say that I was relatively unprepared and uninformed when I entered rehab. If it happened today, I would try to find out more background information about burnout, psychological stress and physical reactions. Back then, being in a situation, which was unknown to me and in which nothing was working like it used to or how I wanted it to, made me feel completely helpless.

I made basic realizations about personal changes in my life, firstly with my therapist and then really consolidated them during the therapy sessions in the clinic and through conversations with the other patients. I have given some book recommendations for background information in the chapters.

A good start would be, for example a lecture by Dr. Poppelreuter: "Burnout, Avoidance, Recognition, Understanding, Treatment." It can be downloaded free on the Internet. Another book, which studied in great detail the situation and everyday stresses in the workplace, is: "Psychological Stress in the Workplace. Causes, Effects, Possible Treatments". (Poppelreuter/Mierke) The book gives very good examples of different stresses, analyzing them in terms of the risks and alternative treatment possibilities and also gives practical advice. In my case, I was able to find a lot of points in this book, which I could identify with.

In my experience, when considering the factors, which can lead to burnout, I would add the circle of friends and family to the list.

I would also like to mention the paper by Business and Management Coach Ramona Meinhardt on the topic: "Burnout Prevention Is Better Than Cure." It includes some good basic information on the causes as well as a lot of good suggestions on how to examine your own behavior and slow down in your private life.

4.) The stay in the Rehabilitation Clinic (RC):

Today is the 27.06.13, 7:45pm. I'm sitting on a plane on the way back from a business trip. I'm a little bit tired, but I'm pleased about starting this chapter because this period changed my life and my health considerably.

11.06.2011. The journey to RC:

My wife took me to the station in the morning. I was so happy to finally be able to go. I had put so much hope in rehab after my condition hadn't improved over the previous 3 months and the mistakes made by the DRV had dragged me down. Finally, finally, finally!! Of course I knew that others still hadn't found a place and had also been waiting for a long time.

We said goodbye and Marliese hugged me tightly, saying "Good luck. I'm going to keep my fingers crossed for you. Let me know when you arrive. We'll come and visit. Take care of yourself."

Both of us had a few tears in our eyes and then I got on the train.

We pulled out of the station and I went to look for my seat. I couldn't remember which one it was because, for some reason, I was feeling very nervous. I had to change trains twice and I hoped that I wouldn't miss one of the connections. What was my seat number again? Which carriage was I supposed to be in? Ok, so the carriage was number 7. That meant I had to go along 3 more carriages. Off I went…

OK. So I found the carriage. Now for the seat. The number on the ticket said 143, which was at the other end of the carriage. There were some people sitting and I made my way along the aisle. This damn seat number! Why couldn't I remember it? Which pocket did I put the ticket in? Ok. Right. 143. It was empty and it was also a seat by itself at the end of the carriage, which meant there was space for my luggage.

I had to change in Fulda, but what time? In 2 and a half hours. Time to change trains: about 20 minutes. That had to be OK. I was pleased.

I read a magazine. The time passed. I went to the on board restaurant for a bit.

There were only another 15 minutes until we arrived in Fulda. Which platform did I have to go to next? OK. Where was the ticket? Oh yes, platform 4 and I was going to arrive on platform 2. It wasn't so far. I wasn't going to have any problems making that connection. Despite that, I started to get a little bit nervous and tense. The train stopped, I got out, went down the steps from the platform, went back up to platform 4, was out of breath, but it was OK. There were still another 15 minutes before the next train was due to leave. God, what was wrong with me? Why the rush? Nothing would have gone wrong. I had the ticket out of my pocket until I made it to my next seat.

Oh damn. I had to change again in Leipzig. Platform 22. God! That was a bigger problem. I was going to arrive on platform 5. Time to change trains: 11 minutes. Shit. What if something went wrong? I was becoming nervous. In the 90 minutes on the train I probably looked at the ticket 3 times: Platform 22, 11 minutes. Platform 22, 11 minutes.

The train stopped. I was standing right at the door. I got out, turned right and followed the sign for platforms 6-24. I was running. By the time I got to platform 18, I couldn't run anymore. The sign was pointing out of the station building. I looked at my watch: 6 minutes. Damn it, where was platform 22? Was I in a Harry Potter Movie?

I was standing in front of the station, looking around me. There was no sign. I asked someone. Answer. " Oh yes, those platforms are in the Regional Station and that is over there, over the crossing". Time to go: 4 minutes, shit. Time to panic. The light was red, but I didn't care, and so I crossed anyway, dragging my wheeled suitcase behind me. I ran into the Regional Station. Platform 22 was straight ahead. I was running but I was getting out of breath. I couldn't do much more and that was even though I had once run 2 marathons! Time to go: 2 minutes. In a corner I could see a sign: Platforms 20-24. I carried on, around the corner. Damn it. It was a long corridor. I pushed my way past the people. I had a stitch. I reached the end of the corridor at the scheduled departure time. I could see the train. I could see the train and I ran, the suitcase rattling along behind me. I ran and got on the train, the door closing behind me.

I was coughing, was completely out of breath and also very nervous. I felt like I was going to start shaking. What the hell was wrong with me?

I didn't know. I just didn't know!

I tried to calm myself down and collect my thoughts. I looked out of the window and tried to find a seat. I looked once again at the ticket. I wouldn't have been surprised if it had started to wear thin with all the looking at it! The train was going to the last station on the line – a suburb of Chemnitz where I was going to be picked up. I had made it. Good.

Another 45 minutes and then everything would be OK. Stay calm. Everything was going to be OK.

I arrived, but this time without any panic. A car was going to be waiting, OK. It was a small station with only 2 platforms so I wasn't going to get lost. I went through the underpass and saw a waiting car. A friendly looking young man said, "Are you Mr. Dietrich?" "Yes." "I'm going to take you to Carolabad." "Great. Thank you." I was feeling happy.

I arrived at the Clinic 15 minutes later. This was going to be my home for the next 5 weeks of my approved stay in rehab. As I said, I had put a lot of faith in this time. I expected so much and didn't know how it would work out in such a short period of time when I had been trying for 7 months (!) to sort myself out and I couldn't do anymore. What would happen if it didn't work? What then?

It didn't matter. I was now there and I would take everything I could from this. EVERYTHING. I wanted to be the old me again. I wanted to be able to empty a dishwasher and do the shopping without starting to panic. I wanted to get out of this hole! Hey God, did you hear me? I wanted to get out!!!

I went inside. The young man helped me with my suitcase. A friendly young woman spoke to me: "You must be Mr. Dietrich." "Yes." "Welcome to Carolabad. I would like to go through the admission process with you and then show you your room, and then you can settle yourself in in peace. Later when the other patients have arrived, we can do a tour together and I'll show you everything that'll be important for the first days so that you can get your bearings."

"Great. Thank you." It all sounded very relaxed and well organized. Admission, personal details, medical documents, a few questions about my medication and 30 minutes later I was a full member of the "crew" of RC. My room was on the ground floor and nice and cozy with a table and 2 chairs, a comfortable bed and a nice bathroom. Thankfully there wasn't a TV. At that time I could only sometimes listen to music. There was a telephone, but if I wanted an outside connection, I had to ask and pay for it. As I found out afterwards, I would make very few calls. I enjoyed the peace and quiet and sometimes even the loneliness. It was strange, as I had always enjoyed being among friends. I only had to think about the Parish parties over the past 15 years!

There was still a bit of time until the tour, and so I went to the big entrance hall to see who else was arriving. It was still nearly empty. I sat next to a man I'll call Günter and we started to chat. He explained some things to me, which I had already forgotten since the admission process – the first week was for arriving and getting to know people and that the doctors put in a lot of work. It wasn't a hotel and sometimes it was going to be stressful.

Slowly the other leather sofas filled up with people after their admissions and it wasn't long before we were complete. It was an interesting group of people - another 9 women and a man all around the age of 40. They were all very nice and didn't really seem at all depressed. We quickly fell into conversation with each other. The other man, who I'll call Frank, was also suffering from burnout, and I would go on to play a lot of table tennis with him. There were a lot of different characters in the group – people exhausted due to professional reasons, a woman who had lost her son, nurses who were overworked or just couldn't cope with their working conditions anymore etc. etc. etc.

I quickly connected with Frank. We talked about the sport we liked and swapped room numbers. Time flew by and it was soon time for the tour.

Tour: It was great to see everything they had there. The Internet hadn't been lying. In various wings, the Clinic had around 100 patients. There was Occupational Therapy, Hydrotherapy, a sports hall, therapy rooms, opportunities for cooking, arts and crafts, pottery, painting, basket weaving, Exercise Therapy, Yoga, Tai Chi, PMR and breathing exercises. Everything was there. It looked good.

Every patient had his or her own therapist and counselor. The therapist was responsible for the psychological care and suggested therapy sessions while the counselor took part in the sessions and created a timetable for the week. This was the contact person for all organizational questions and the therapist was for all emotional issues.

All sessions we attended had to be confirmed by a signature. Everyone was given a folder with a list of the various sessions in the first week. We were given a new list every week. I was given my folder after the tour.

My God, there was so much on the list already! I looked more closely at it when I got back to my room. Where were all these rooms again? And the Medical Center? Oh yes, in the corridor next to the Therapy Rooms in Block 1. What about Counselor's Room? I didn't have any idea!

The timetable seemed to be pretty full already. 2 blocks in the morning and then 2 more in the afternoons of doctor's appointments, therapy sessions etc. etc.

While I had been at home I had struggled with having 2 or 3 things to do every day and now I had such a full week. According to Günter the first week was easy, things would start to pick up in Week 2 and in Week 3, the appointments would double. How was I going to manage that in such a short period of time? I'd only just managed to survive the train trip! I tried to stay calm. Maybe the others were feeling the same. We would see.

I unpacked and arranged everything and organized what I would need for the next day. I set the alarm and put the timetable out on the side. Oh yes, I had to fill out the questionnaire about illnesses and conditions, how I'd got there, etc.

I found it quite stressful as I started on some of the questions and couldn't really concentrate anymore. I gave up and decided to do the rest in the morning. We had until the day after to hand it in.

<u>4.1) The first day in Carolabad (CB):</u>

Don't worry. I'm not going to bore you with my CB diary and describe every day in minute detail.

I'm going to limit it to the most important things that happened during my time there.

In the morning was my first breakfast in the dining hall, but I forgot to say that we had to make sure we registered ourselves there before 11am so that they knew everything was OK. Otherwise they would have come to check the room for safety reasons. I thought that was good. You never know what problems new patients could have. There must be house rules for our own safety. What's more there was also a complete ban on alcohol. If you broke the rules, the rehab would be ended and the worst-case scenario would be that you would have to pay for everything up to that point out of your own pocket.

Of course, I forgot all about the registration on the first day and had to go to the Medical Center after breakfast to confirm that I was OK.

The schedule of appointments then came into effect. First of all, that morning was the medical examination necessary at the beginning of the rehab. It was the usual thing – weight, blood, urine, medication etc. Then followed meetings with the doctor, the senior consultant and the therapist. The conversation with the therapist was tough. I had to go over the whole story again. I noticed how much I stuttered, how often my throat tightened and I had to stop. I was still getting upset about all these things. I didn't have it under control at all.

The therapist made some suggestions for the first workshops and relaxation courses and, with this list, I had to go to the counselor the next day so that she could create a timetable for the first week.

That afternoon I went to the block where the creative workshops were located to see what things they had for painting.

There was no one there. The room was open, so I went in and looked around, but couldn't see anyone. There were some brushes on the shelf.

"Hello. Can I help you?" A young, friendly looking woman smiled at me.

"Oh. I'm sorry for just walking in like that. I would like to paint something in the creative workshop, and so I wanted to have a look at the things you have here."

"Watercolors, acrylic or textile paints, brushes, canvas. We have everything. You just have to say what you need. You can even do silk painting."

"Oh that sounds good. Do you have stretcher frames? 100 x 80cm?"

"No, I'm sorry. We don't have them in that size. The biggest we have is 30 x 40cm, but I can give you the address of a shop in the area if you like and you could go and buy a larger frame yourself."

"That would be great. I might paint a picture for an acquaintance of mine!"

She gave me the address. Yes! That had worked out well. My first success!

4.2) The first morning meeting:

For some reason I felt quite nervous. I was also late and, when I arrived, everyone else was already there. I had got lost on the way to the room. They had kept a seat free for me, next to a person, who (I would find out later) had similar symptoms and diagnosis to me.

This was an introductory session. That meant that every time a new patient joined the group, the others introduced themselves, explaining a little bit about themselves and giving their own tips for the daily routine. This morning meeting was also intended to be a place to talk about important experiences and results from the previous day and, if necessary, we could also make extra appointments with the therapist.

Everyone was very friendly and talked about how well they were being taken care of, described the different activities we could take part in and explained the things we needed to be aware of. Some of them found it difficult to talk about themselves and there were some tears, while others had to break off completely.

It was getting close to being my turn. I was the third last. It wouldn't be so bad. I would just tell them everything I had already told the therapist at home, the neurologist and the DRV assessor. I thought it would be easy, but the tension and my pulse rate began to rise the closer it got to being my turn.

It was finally my turn. Name, profession, age, my family, happily married with 2 kids. That was all fine. I wanted to briefly talk about 23.11.11, what had led up to it and what had happened afterwards until I finally made it to CB. I started to stutter. I became very nervous. My voice was shaking. My breathing was heavy. I tried to concentrate, to speak slowly and it got better, but I had to really force myself. It was quiet in the room. Very quiet. I could sense that everyone was listening to me. About half way through what I wanted to say I heard a hasty, "That's enough for today" coming from my own mouth and I stopped. The therapist thanked and reassured me. "If you want to say more tomorrow, you are more than welcome to. If not, then that's also OK." The person next time had already been there for 2 weeks and knew what it was like. He worked as a police officer and he gave me dozens of really good tips and, over the course of the next 3 or 4 weeks, we had a lot of contact with each other, e.g. playing table tennis! "It's normal to be nervous at the beginning. You'll feel more at home after a week so don't panic."

Wow. What happened there? What was that? What was wrong with me? I'm a project leader and I've introduced myself to new customers thousands of times over the last 23 years. I run meetings and give presentations in 3 languages. What the hell was wrong in this meeting? I couldn't understand. Just talking about my burnout and its development made me break out into a sweat and meant I couldn't continue. Shit. Shit. Shit! The 5 weeks in CB were never going to help. It wasn't going to be enough. Damn it!

I was so tired and frustrated and it was only the first day! Shit.

After the morning meeting I had to go for the physical examination – blood pressure, ECG, blood count.

My blood pressure was a little high at around 140/100. I also had a uric acid level which was too high. Both would have to be checked every morning. Everything else was fine. It took a week before everything was normal again. The high blood pressure was probably because of general tension. I had never had a problem with it before.

We did the same thing after lunch, but this time it was in a one-on-one conversation. Just the therapist and me. "You can take a break if you start to get upset. Breathe slowly while you are talking. When you need to take a break, just look out of the window and think about something, which is fun for you." OK. Thanks for the tips. I still found it very difficult and I stuttered a couple of times, but I got through it. Of course, there were fewer people listening and this therapist was a person I could trust.

With time, and the more often I spoke to the others, things became easier. After some time, I realized why that had been the case.

After talking for the first time about my problems as much as possible in one hour, my therapist recommended different seminars, workshops, courses and relaxation methods.

The following day saw my first meeting with my counselor. Together we created a timetable for the recommended courses. This certainly wasn't a holiday! The first 2 or 3 days weren't so busy and we could check out all areas of the building, but after that, the work really began. I calculated that every day had 5-7 hours of planned activities. There was 1 hour for lunch and a 30-minute coffee break. Of course there were some relaxation or creative courses included in that, but there was no time for slacking.

The leader of every course had to sign that I had attended it. There was no opportunity to skip any classes. If for some reason I couldn't take part in something, I had to let the course leader know. The people were very understanding, but it wasn't acceptable to just not turn up. The courses and the timetable changed a little after every week and then the patients met with the same counselor to create a new timetable for the following week, based on the courses that should be attended. The counselor then checked that everything had been included. The old timetables with the signatures had to be handed in every week.

I had huge problems in the first week with the frequency of the courses. Most of the time I arrived late because I had overlooked something or simply because I had needed to take a break in my room where no one could disturb me. I found the sports and relaxation courses were very good from the start because I was able to switch off and clear my head.

4.3) Sports course 1:

All patients, who didn't have circulation problems, took part in Sport 1. I wasn't allowed to take part in the first week because of my high blood pressure. I was, of course, quite annoyed about that because I had been a marathon runner and they had volleyball once a week. I had played volleyball for 12 years and had been looking forward to it. During the second session of the week the focus was on circulation, and so this often involved circuit endurance training lasting 45 minutes or more. We were really getting down to the nitty-gritty now.

I found it good that we were free to use the sports hall whenever we wanted to if there were no courses taking place. After a few days, we had managed to organize some extra times, once a week in the evenings to play volleyball and table tennis among other things. Almost every evening, as soon as the hall became free, in one half, people played table tennis, while in the other there was badminton. We found we could use this time to really let off steam and we also had some really good chats, which was good to do outside of the therapy sessions. I got a lot out of these conversations, which mostly took place while playing table tennis or volleyball – experiences, other perspectives and also ideas. We also talked about things that helped me assess my situation. It was incredibly important for me to be open about my problems so that I wouldn't shut myself away. Others also experienced the same thing. Most of the people showed total understanding straightaway, and not only within the sports group, but also within the creative groups. There was no need to be afraid of being classified as "incapable" or "second class". We were all in the same boat and had the same goal – the boat needed to find a safe harbor so that we could all get our feet on firm ground again. None of the people, who I got to know during this time wanted to slack off. None of them!

On most Fridays in the afternoon, there were talks. The topics were varied and comprehensive, covering burnout, health precautions, lifestyle, relaxation methods etc.

I have listed the key messages when it comes to the topic of burnout, which have stayed in my mind. I've also added some things I found in daily newspapers and journals, which are connected to the topic

- Burnout (BO) can affect anybody and that was clear from looking at the kinds of people with me in the Clinic.

- BO is an exhaustive process, which is characterized by psychological and emotional involvement in work. This can eventually lead to physical symptoms or a defined illness such as depression, heart attack or chronic pain. (Spiegel 2012)

- Stages of Burnout Syndrome (according to my own experience): Physical symptoms in the early stages – as already described – decreasing levels of commitment, emotional reactions (excessive feelings of tension and irritability), diminishing levels of concentration and performance, scaling back of social and spiritual life, physical reactions, feelings of doubt (I compiled this together with my therapist at home)

- Levels of fatigue: pain, tension, lack of energy, insomnia, brooding Physical changes: irritability, aggression, feelings of guilt, social withdrawal, overtime, memory problems, reduction in performance and vitality, total exhaustion.
  The final stage: suicidal thoughts, agonizing levels of anxiety, depression. Every 7th severely depressed patient can have suicidal thoughts and that is why it is so important to prevent chronic depression.

- An estimated 30% of all workers in Germany have experienced serious symptoms of or suffered from burnout (confirmed by an article in our local daily newspaper as well as in "Spiegel" magazine).

- The consequences of burnout can be very different. This is something I found out during conversations with the other patients. They range from a total inability to work to being able to work to a certain extent, but with some limitations. In some situations it is necessary to change the working environment or to do some kind of retraining. This very much depends on the parameters of the work - stress, conflict, psychological pressure, hopeless situations. The more often a person suffers from burnout, the lower the chances of recovery and that is why it needs to be treated slowly and with a lot a patience to ensure the best possible success.

If you search Wikipedia for "suicide" or "suicide rates", you'll be able to find the following information:

In 2007, suicide made up for 30.7% of all deaths caused by external factors (As a comparison: accidents - 60.4% of which falls 25.2%, traffic accidents 16.9%).[destatis 1][destatis 2] An increase of around 9% in the suicide rate since 2007 corresponds to the large increase in the number of psychological problems, especially depression, which affect men more than women.[14]

The percentage of deaths due to suicide hits a peak when considering young adults, as these are less likely to die due to illness.

One in 6 people (16.5%) aged between 15 and 35 died as a result of taking their own lives. In total, 5.7 women and 17.4 men per 100,000 inhabitants committed suicide. Of the 9402 suicides in this year, 7009 (74.5%) of them were men. This is a growing trend due to the fact that the rate among women is decreasing [destatis 1][destatis 2]

In comparison to "successful" suicides, the number of attempted suicides is 10 to 15 times as high, which means there are around 100,000 to 150,000.

I would never have guessed that there are twice as many deaths due to suicide as there are because of road traffic accidents or that there are 10 to 15 times as many attempts at suicide.

- The danger of developing permanent, chronic depression increases after 3-6 months of suffering from a depressive phase brought on by illness or other causes. This is why it is so important to help people who are experiencing depression due to a change in their situation (e.g. due to an accident, illness, loss of a partner, relative, child etc.). When I think about my experience - waiting such a long time for psychological care because of under capacity – and combine it with the possible causes of suicide I read about on Wikipedia which can be the result of such a long wait, I feel sick.
There is of course a problem with recognizing depression and then the person affected letting themselves be treated for it because it is still an absolutely taboo topic. This was also my experience at the beginning. There is the fear that people will think that you are crazy or incapable if you are in therapy. First of all there are the feelings of negativity. The longer it goes on for, the less hope there is that the situation can be changed. That is what I experienced. Dreams and thoughts changed and somehow I became different even though I didn't want to.
Now I was being quite open about the topic and had searched for professional help. This is normal behavior – something you would do with every other illness too. It's a mistake for this topic to be made taboo in society because it can affect absolutely anyone. I got to know people from all kinds of professions while I was in the clinic:

doctors, nurses, teachers, police officers, priests, bankers and other employees who had had problems at work, with the family or within their social group.

And it's true. Later, when I started to talk about my problems, it was amazing how many people in my circle of friends or on project trips admitted to me that they were affected. Suddenly after rehab, a lot of people came to me and asked what my experience had been. It was just like how things had been in rehab. Just 2 weeks ago I spoke with a colleague at a software company about a project. He had retrained and now has another position within the company instead of in Project Management, which saw him working on site. He experienced the same symptoms for the same reasons.

In my opinion, there is a big advantage for people if they talk about it openly. If you can at least manage to admit you have a problem, there is no need to have any fear about what people might think or even about if someone knows, guesses or heard something. This also takes the pressure off and you notice who you can really count as a friend.

- A human being isn't a computer or any other kind of machine. He can only do parts of several tasks at once, but every one of those tasks then has to be reworked one after another. That means that you find yourself jumping between different tasks and that leads to stress. It's impossible to concentrate on one thing. The probability that mistakes will be made increases. Most of the time it makes more sense to focus on 1 or 2 tasks. That means you can go into problems in more detail and find better solutions to them. What's more, these things are more likely to stay in your long-term memory if you can work more intensively on them.

- Important basics for action against burnout:
Improvement in health, positive attitude, take mistakes seriously but don't overrate them.
Important: No taboo topics (this is from my own experience because then you aren't always thinking about what other people think about you, or how to avoid people finding things out about you), early recognition (this is something else I experienced during my long wait, which I have already described), relaxation, recovery, healthy eating, sport and movement.

In reality it never pays to be under pressure or have stress as work, neither for the employer, nor for the employee. (There is of course positive stress and, when it isn't too much, can lead to success, praise, recognition etc. This is OK and can even "give you wings").

In many cases working conditions as well as dealings with people in the office are crucial elements that can lead to psychological pressure. This doesn't just affect the relationship between manager and employee, but also between colleagues (bullying).

Nobody is helped by the kinds of working conditions in Aldi, Lidl and other companies, which were recently reported on in the press. A former divisional director of Aldi wrote a detailed book about this.

When an employee feels good in his/her job and can draw motivation from the recognition they receive and the success they experience, they are then more hard working and innovative and are also prepared to do more than asked out of fear for their jobs or their existence, but they stay healthy. An unwell employee is more expensive for the company than a healthy one. It also costs a lot of money to change employees and this is especially true in professions, in which experience plays an important role, as it isn't possible to replace an employee with many years of experience at short notice. It's normal for new employees to make some mistakes and they are often the same things that we got wrong when we first started! They need some time to be trained. In some professions, practical experience is a necessity especially when there is a lot of interaction with other people. Everybody knows how important contact with the customer and relationship building is in a Sales Department, but these things need time to develop.

About 30% of project work and management depends on communicating with partners. If everyone involved works together as a team, results can be achieved in half the time. If everyone tries to pass the buck and nobody makes decisions or takes responsibility, everybody knows what the result will be. This has a lot to do with interpersonal relations, conflict management and communication. I know this isn't anything new, but I just wanted to mention it because it fits here. This is also social competence and it is possible to find a lot of literature about it on the Internet. (Leadership, motivation and training seminars, management seminars etc.)

"The most important part of a company is its motivated and hard working employees." I remember reading this somewhere once.

Motivation is also something very important. A person either enjoys his job, is happy to do it and is motivated by recognition and success, or he can't be bothered and only does what he has to. Salary and pressure, special conditions etc. are often secondary factors. I normally look for a job, which I know I will also enjoy doing. After all, I'm going to spend 30-40% of my life doing it. If the basic conditions aren't right, I can always change employers (as far as my situation allows me to).

Multi-Tasking:

The constant change between different tasks, and the stress which results from it, is interesting to think about, when you think that things tend to remain in your memory only after a person has worked on it for about 20 minutes. The converse argument is that the probability that a person will make a mistake is higher when several things are done at the same time. You can become more forgetful if you jump from one thing to another and back again. This means that you have to concentrate even more and you fall into a vicious circle. This theory was proved in my situation and illustrated by the ever-increasing number of notes and moans I had in the half year before 23.11.11. In the end, everything was totally chaotic.

Being constantly available is also a factor. It can be a very good thing. Customer service is important and absolutely necessary when there are serious problems. If there is a problem, which could cost not only money, but also time, it is important that something is done. This also means that manpower has to be available too. I've often seen how technicians, fitters and suppliers at building sites sometimes are when things become too much. These are no longer isolated cases. Going back quickly to my circle of acquaintances: A colleague in the IT department in another company was always available, had too many things to do at the same time, 45 years old, suffered a massive burnout and has been off work for 3 months waiting for a place in a clinic.

Unfortunately, in many cases working conditions have developed in such a way that we are unable to deal with them in the long term. We just aren't "built" for that (Not my words!) It might be worth thinking about this as the costs of this stress for society are enormous and are growing, as are those for employees who are unable to work. This isn't a topic for this book, though as I don't have the detailed information about it. It would be interesting to see the connections though. Maybe there has already been some research into it and I don't know anything about it because I'm too lazy to read. I still feel quite good despite that!

4.4) 2.5-week bed rest with an infection!!!! So annoying!

When the opportunity for canvas painting was perfect and the therapist in the creative group had given me the information about the source for the stretcher frames, I got started. It was agreed that I could take everything I needed to paint with me to my room so that I could work on the picture whenever I felt like it. I bought a frame 100 x 100cm and first drew 2 figures with a pencil. I didn't have an easel in the room, and so I put the frame on my dresser. It worked quite well and, after 3 evenings, the pencil outlines were finished. It required another kind of concentration and, after I had finished for the evening, I was always really tired and fell straight to sleep. This wasn't, however, exhaustion which made me anxious or on edge as had happened in the past. It was strange, but interesting at the same time and this was the reason why I could work on it relatively regularly.

Unfortunately, my project was interrupted.

In the first evenings of drawing, and because of the height of the dresser, I had had to kneel on the floor so that I was level with the bottom section of the frame. This wasn't a problem for the first 2 evenings, but later I noticed a red mark on my left knee, but I didn't really pay any attention to it. This became a little inflamed and it developed into a spot. Nothing terrible. And what does everybody do when they have a spot? That's right. Give it a good squeeze between your fingers and then it is gone! And it was, but not completely. The area became more inflamed and the spot came back. Of course, this happened at the weekend and I didn't want to have to call the doctor about a normal skin infection. Instead, I went to the nurse in the Medical Center on the Saturday and we did what we could with various anti-inflammatory creams and bandages. It didn't help. The weather was so nice, I decided to sit myself in the sun that afternoon and rest my knee. This was also a mistake because the warmth actually made it worse. The infection spread and so did the pain. The nurse then correctly decided to send me to the nearest hospital the following day. It was only 2km away, and so I walked, not wanting to call a taxi for the short distance. In the meantime, the inflammation had improved slightly, and so it was OK to do that. However, the infected area had grown and was now almost as big as a hand. I had to wait for 30 minutes in the Emergency Room before it was my turn to be seen. The doctor working that day seemed to know what she was doing, but she looked immediately concerned. "When was the last time you took Penicillin?" "About 9 months ago." "Do you have an allergy to it?" "No." "OK.

You have Erysipelas. That's an infection, which can spread very quickly under the skin and, when it has spread a certain amount it becomes dangerous." If I understood her correctly, it could lead to blood poisoning. "Right, so you need to keep your leg still and raised and cool the infected area. You need to do it all day so that it doesn't spread any more. You should take 2 x 500mg Penicillin tablets everyday for at least 10 days." As far as I knew, the normal dose was 1 x 500mg for 5 days. "After that, we'll see how things are. If things don't seem to have completely improved by then, we'll have to extend the treatment." "What do you mean exactly when you say I should keep it still?" "Don't bend your knee, walk as little as possible, but when you do walk, make sure that your leg stays straight. You shouldn't do any kind of sport at all. Keep the leg raised and make sure that it is always being cooled. How did you get here?" "I walked. It's not far - only 2km. It's OK." "Wow. And in this heat, too. It's no wonder that the infection has spread so much. You'll have to take a taxi back and make sure you start taking the Penicillin straight away. Come back in 10 days time."

Great. That was absolutely brilliant. I was in rehab. I had finally worked out that sport and movement were the things that helped me and I had access to the best training facilities and now this! 2 weeks without moving. Nothing. No sport. Not even yoga or tai chi to relax. 2 weeks completely down the drain. On top of that, I would have to always carry cooling pads with me to the other courses AND put my foot up while I was there. I'd waited 7 months for rehab and now this! How many times had I dealt with a spot like that before? And of all the times it had to happen, it was now! Congratulations! I had really landed in the shit now!

At that point I was pretty upset about it, but it wasn't as if I could change it. So, the alternative was to think about what I could possibly do in this time. Read? I don't really like reading. Wait, I still had all the painting stuff in my room so I could finish that picture first. It worked pretty well with me lying down. The frame wasn't particularly heavy, so I could hold the frame in the corner with my left hand, sit in my bed, supporting it on my thigh and painting with my right.

It went well. I always had a break every 30 minutes to rest my arms and then carried on. As I was painting, I had my favorite CD playing and the picture was finished after a week. By the third day I recognized that, even though I had to concentrate, it worked much better than when reading a long text. I didn't have to remember any contents. I even did some relaxation exercises while painting – trying to coordinate my breathing with the strokes of the brush. It was a little bit like alternative relaxation therapy. By the end of the painting I was able to work on it for 4-5 hours with breaks. That was definitely progress, but it was something I didn't notice straight away. I hadn't been able to work on something for such along period of time. This gave me motivation. I discussed it with my therapist and then ordered all of the 40 x 40 cm frames available in the Creative Group. The infection wasn't healed yet after all.

During my enforced break, I managed to paint around 15 of these smaller frames with pictures of Mickey and Minnie Mouse. They were for the children at home, for goodbye gifts for colleagues etc. I got the nickname "the Mouse Painter". The check-up 2 weeks later showed that the infection still hadn't gone. The whole procedure had to carry on for a whole other week. Shit!

My therapist helped me out. We requested that the rehab be extended by 2 weeks, as I couldn't take part in the therapies and exercises, especially the relaxation exercises and hydrotherapy. The 2 weeks were approved and that meant I was going to be at the Clinic for 7 not 5 weeks. It was good, but annoying at the same time because the others I had got to know were out much more often doing things, while I was lying in my bed, but there was nothing I could do about it.

After the third week, the infection seemed to have abated a little and I started annoying the sports therapist about being able to take part again. She wasn't having any of it: "Mr. Dietrich, as long as the infection isn't completely gone, there is no chance!" "OK, but I want it to be checked regularly." 3 days later and the infection was gone. And the doctor gave me the green light. 1 hour later I was standing in front of the therapist to ask if I could start back doing sport that afternoon. "What about the infection?" "Gone. I was at the Doctor's this morning and got the OK." "I need to see that confirmation myself, but once I do, you can take part this afternoon. How mobile are you? You haven't moved your knee for the last 2 weeks." She was clever. I could only bend it around 10-20° and that definitely wasn't enough for sport. "I'll do as much as I can and I'll be careful. I promise." "We're doing circuit training today so you can decide what you can and can't do." That was perfect. From then on I did my daily physical therapy to improve mobility and muscle strength as often as I could – going up stairs, walking, yoga, in my room and after a week of this, I could bend my knee 90° again, even if it did hurt! It was a lot of hard work, but I managed it and 2 weeks later I was able to walk around completely freely. There was a positive effect to all of this. I had discovered an alternative way to relax during this time – I had the sport and the painting also worked really well and I had been able to train my relaxation techniques while doing it. That meant that painting was a way for me to relax.

I spent most of those 3 weeks in bed and, because of that, I didn't really have any contact with the others during the day or at the weekend and, when I was fit again, most of them had already gone home. There seemed to be some kind of "generational change" and I became the oldest at the morning meetings. We were a group of only 3 by the time we had had 2 very nice and funny leaving parties.

I started to think of a plan. My goal was to try and get as much out of rehab as possible. I had the best support there. The further I managed to get there, the easier it would be when I got home. I decided to give myself some kind of task that I could focus on over the next 2 weeks of my stay there. It had to be something that was fun: painting!

I spoke to my therapist about the idea:

"There is a projector in the clinic, which is used for lectures in the sports hall. I want to paint a big motif of the Disney characters. It could be done in different ways: either on a wall or on a canvas frame. I'd project the picture onto it and then trace the outline. I could then do the larger areas during the day without the projector. If someone is interested, maybe we could turn this into some kind of group work. Would that be possible?"

My therapist asked if I had the belief in myself to be able to do that. "Yes, and if it doesn't get finished, then it doesn't get finished. I'll just do as much as I can." "OK. You'll have to ask the caretaker about the projector. If you want to do some kind of group work, then you'd better talk to the leader of the creative group to see when the rooms are available outside of the normal course times. You could put a sign up on the notice board asking if anyone is interested." "OK, I'll try it." I found the caretaker and got the projector the same day and in the afternoon I went back to the shop I had previously bought the canvas frames in. The sales woman remembered me. "I need 3 more stretcher frames. 80 x 100cm, 100 x 100cm, 120 x 100cm." "Ah. So you've got something else up your sleeve. Let's have a look……" "Could you bring them over to me after work?" I asked, waving a 5€ note in her direction. "Put your money away. Of course I will."

The only thing missing now was the motif. It was going to be a triptych – a picture split between 3 frames. There was a simple reason for doing this: I'd definitely be able to get one frame finished and the others I could use as some kind of therapy, depending on how everything else went. That meant it would be totally stress free. And the picture? Well, 10 years ago at home I had painted a picture on the wall of our garage, which was made up of 22 Disney characters from 7 covers of the Mickey Mouse series of books. I would just ask Viky to take several photos of them and email them to me at the clinic and then I would be able to begin. I had my laptop with me, so that wasn't a problem.

It worked out pretty well. OK, the response wasn't that overwhelming and I painted all 3 frames myself, but I managed to do them all and the entire picture with all the figures was finished on the very last day of my stay in the clinic. That was a great success for me and I was really happy about it.

And then came the cherry on the cake on the last day in the morning meeting. Someone had the idea that the 3 pictures should be donated to the Children's hospital in Chemnitz. That was a real bonus for me. All the work had been worth it. Thank you! My therapist told me that she was happy to deal with organizing it and promised to keep me up-to-date. Everything worked out really well and, one week after returning home, I got an email from the director of the hospital, thanking me for the donation. Perfect. All the hard work had paid off – for the hospital and also for me.

<u>4.5) "My therapist and me":</u>

(I've rewritten the dialogue to make it relevant to the various topics rather than recording word for word what was discussed.)

My therapist is a very friendly person. She wanted to help me, but she only gave me support. "You have to do the work yourself. In the conversations with me, you have to find out what problems you have, what the causes of them are, what you can do about them and what changes are necessary. There isn't a universal cure because everybody is different." She was tough. Really tough. She pushed me to the edge. She supported me in finding the root cause of the problem and never let up. I couldn't run and hide. "If we don't find a solution in this session, we can try again in the next. We'll definitely find one before you leave." She never left me on my own. She always saw when I wasn't making any progress by myself and then offered me her support. She was experienced.

She was good. Really good. At least I can say that she was for me. Thank you! Without her it never would have worked out for me or for this book. This is an example of a typical chain reaction. Sometimes it only takes something small to get the ball really rolling.

The first session was pretty unspectacular. She asked how I had got to the clinic, how I was feeling, if I had already met some of the other patients, if I liked my room and if the food in the canteen was OK.

She knew that the results of all the tests I had had when I arrived weren't that great. My blood pressure was a little high and my Uric acid level was definitely too high. She said it was probably because of first day nerves and it would get better, but that we would have to keep an eye on the Uric acid level. She asked about my diet. "I mostly eat wholemeal things. I don't really eat so much meat, but I do like fruit and vegetables. I have a bottle of beer 1-3 evenings a week." She said that was fine, but that we should keep an eye on those levels. She reminded me that the clinic was an alcohol free zone.

Afterwards I told her everything I had already told my GP, the neurologist, my therapist back home and the assessor. It was OK though. She just wanted to hear it directly from the horse's mouth. It's better than just reading the notes. Although I'm quite sure that she had read the notes as well, but there might have been some things, which had changed in the meantime. I told her all about the "pressure points" I had simultaneously at work and at home, the pressures in the job, which had become too much and about the project I had totally messed up on.

She made suggestions for the courses I could take and explained why I should take part in them. I met my counselor the next morning and she created a timetable of the courses for me.

One of the courses I attended was called "Fear". I asked why was I going to a group about fear? She told me that they did really interesting things, She thought it would help me and that I shouldn't be afraid of going. It was fine for me to go, but I was a little curious.

I haven't reported every session here because firstly I can't really remember all the details about them anymore, only the things that were the most important for me.

<u>4.6) "Who or what is the most important person or thing in your life?"</u>

She asked me this in one of our sessions.

"My children, Sara and Viktoria, and my wife," I answered like a shot. "And then?" "Well, then that would be my job because we have to live somehow and I'm the one who earns the money. Then would be our close relatives, good friends I can rely on and who we sometimes go on holiday with etc." This was pretty much the second part of the answer.

"Ah-ha. That's the answer of around 95% of all men who are fathers and have no problems with the family. How do you think a single person might answer that question?"

"I've no idea. It's hard to say how a single person would think. My wife and I really love having our 2 children, having a family. It would be so boring without them! Of course it can be really stressful sometimes and there are different problems to deal with depending on their age, but it's great. It's incredibly enriching all the feelings, fun, joy and appreciation you get in return. It would be as if a part of our lives was missing. We can take all trips and other holidays later on. But anyway, back to your question. I think he wouldn't list the children, but he would definitely say his current partner, then his job and so on.

"Mr. Dietrich, has your life ever been in danger?"

"Um. I don't really understand the connection. I suppose we are always a little bit in danger when driving or flying, but I don't stay at home because of it. If I did, I would be really depressed and I want to work on making myself normal again"

"In our first sessions, you explained in great detail the background and events leading up to your stay in hospital and what happened after that until you came here. Did you ever think then that your life was in danger?"

I thought again about it.

"I suppose I was pretty afraid at the beginning because of the problems with my heart, but I was relieved when my doctor told me that it wasn't a heart attack. Then I thought that somehow everything would be OK. Then they told me in the hospital that the fibrillation I was having could cause blood clots and they could lead to a stroke, but that most people don't even notice when they have a problem (they just feel a little tired). I was really afraid when they told me that it could happen again. I just assumed that things would get better quickly and that my body would be able to deal with it itself, just like with other illnesses. That isn't what happened. That's probably why I was afraid that it could happen again and subconsciously I guess I was scared that things wouldn't work out as well the next time. Something similar happened to someone at work. He worked in a department in my company. I know that the treatment was different, but in the end, it seems his heart problems were caused by stress, worry and generally being under too much pressure. He didn't get a second chance. He died in the passenger seat of their car, next to his wife on the motorway on the way home. That was it. He left a wife and 2 kids.

Since then I've been afraid and react to things differently. I'm more focused on safety. It's quite often that I have the same symptoms I had before my "meltdown". That makes me nervous and sensitive because I know what the consequences could be and it has already happened once. I didn't know that before, but now I do.

"So, you are afraid that if the same thing happens again, it could mean serious consequences for your health or even death?"

"Yes:"

"And you are also afraid at the moment that there won't be any progress in your recovery, and you will continue having the symptoms you mentioned if you find yourself in situations that are stressful or tense. That means that it could happen again and you are still feeling very "precarious"."

"Yes, at the moment I don't feel up to dealing with the stresses of my job at all – the arguments, discussions or negotiations. I wouldn't be able to control my reactions. My ability to deal with stress is still far too bad." My hands were becoming quite sweaty with the whole discussion.

"What would be the worst that could happen for your wife and children if the same thing happened again, but this time worse?"

"Well, our family life would be completely changed if they had to care for me. I wouldn't be able to be there for my wife and kids anymore. We wouldn't be able to play together or go skiing, for example. Maybe I would have to lie in bed and I wouldn't be able to do anything with my 3 girls. There is also the financial situation to consider – we would have to give up a lot of things. Everything is different when a member of the close family suddenly becomes extremely ill. I suddenly thought about all the examples from our group of friends and acquaintances (but I'm not going to mention them here.) I started to sweat.

"So if I've understood correctly, your biggest fear is that a repeat of what happened before could, as a worst case scenario, lead to your death."

Silence.

She watched me.

I was nervous and clenched my fists. I was also sweating.

I was mentally preparing myself.

I took a breath.

"Yes!!" I managed to shout out.

"Yes, I'm so afraid that it'll happen again and it won't end well. I don't know how to get out of this stupid cycle I'm stuck in. Before I came here to the clinic, I always tried relaxation techniques at home. I don't know. Maybe I'm doing something wrong. I've no idea. The problem is there are always emotional situations that are too much for me to handle and I can't handle them normally. Then I take Baldrian and, in the evenings, Mirtazapine. I want to be able to control things by myself though. I don't want to be or become dependent on medication. The body manages to deal with all other things, even big operations, transplants, new joints etc. So why is it that these damn symptoms won't go away. Why do a shake, have these feelings of tension and the tingling down my left side? I haven't worked for 8 months, so why isn't it any better?"

Silence again.

"How are you feeling now?"

"I feel tense, but you've noticed that anyway," I told her a little aggressively. "Now that it's out in the open, I feel better even if I did seem to be a little upset before."

"Should we take a break?"

"Yes, please." I drank a glass of water and was able to calm down again.

"Is it OK for you to carry on or would you prefer to stop for today?"

"No. Let's try and carry on. I have to try if I want to beat this. And you're here anyway"

"Good. I won't pressure you, but let me know if it's getting too much for you. Today's opening question was: What is the most important thing for you? It wasn't "who means the most to you?"

After everything that you've just said, how would you answer that question now. Think about it. Don't answer straight away. Take your time."

The right answer was so easy, but why hadn't I considered it from the very beginning? Why did I need someone to steer me in the right direction?

I knew the answer. It was because I had always assumed that I would be OK, that I wouldn't have an accident and that I was capable of dealing with every situation. If I couldn't, then there was always the hospital, the doctor and the insurance company. Things can always be worked out. Nothing really bad had happened in the last 50 years, so why had it happened now? It's not as if I lived a particularly risky life. I didn't do bungee jumping or other extreme sports, didn't smoke, regularly did sport, ate healthy, had never had an affair, drank a moderate amount of alcohol, so why should it all go so wrong?

The problem is that it did. I hadn't listened to my body because I thought I had known better. I had been afraid of being a failure and I didn't want to say: "I can't do it anymore" because everyone else was going through the same. The new colleagues we were supposed to get had quit of their own accord (See chapter: The Beginning) and then came the warning shot from my body. It wanted me to stop, and as I wasn't prepared to listen to it, it "engaged the emergency brake" for me. Thankfully, I had remained physically "intact". I was just having problems with my "control system."

"You're right", I began the second answer to her question. "The most important thing is me and my health even if it sounds egotistical to say that. If I'm not OK, then I will very quickly become a burden to my 3 girls and that would be a lot worse for me. I don't want them to be crying over me in my coffin.

That's why I have to do whatever I can to recover, so that I can be my normal self again. Even if, along the way, there are some things, which I just don't have the strength to do, my girls will understand. And if there is someone, who doesn't understand, then that's not my problem anymore. My only goal at the moment is to do whatever I can in this clinic to make my condition and my situation better. With the help of you and your colleagues, I have to try and find a way to permanently get out of this hole.

It might also be helpful if I could understand what is happening when I have all of these physical symptoms."

"Mr. Dietrich. You haven't been here very long and these things don't just happen over night. You have to take your time and have some patience. You've already achieved so much. Do you remember that first morning meeting and what you could tell the others? Now compare that with what we have talked about here today. You are making progress, but you have to see this progress too. This isn't a cut, which you can just stick a plaster on and everything will be OK. It needs time and, like I said, you have achieved so much today. Maybe you don't realize that, but you should believe me. I think that's enough for today."

"Great. Thanks. I feel a bit better, but that was really stressful and at one point I really felt like giving up and leaving. It was better to let it all out than to run away, though. I'm totally exhausted but relieved. I think I'm really going to give everything during sport this afternoon."

"OK. Then have fun!"

"Thanks."

Oh my God. I'm 50 years old and I told all of that crap to a woman who could be my daughter. Who would've thought it? She was very clever, though. All she did was ask the right questions. Nothing else. I think she did a very good job, but I would find out later that she could do even better.

We played volleyball that afternoon. I hadn't played so well in over 20 years! (I had given up playing 30 years previously.)

4.7) Organization, timetable and breaks:

We now had a new topic of discussion:

"Mr. Dietrich, how have your days been organized up until now?" In the previous session, she had given me an empty timetable, and I had to fill it in with everything I did during my normal working week. "I've done my homework," I told her. This was also part of the therapy. Now and again, we were given a few tasks to do outside of the courses, which we were expected to do by ourselves. These were mostly small things, but they were used to see how we dealt with them.

We looked through my timetable together. There was nothing unusual included in it: work, time with the family, weekends spent in the garden, house or the building site at my parents' house, meeting with friends, voluntary work in the parish, doing homework with the children some evenings, paperwork, jogging once at the weekend if I had the time.

"Do you have any hobbies?"

"Sport."

"Is that all?"

"Yes. During a normal working day, I never really had any time for myself anyway, and so I was pleased that I could do something for my health by doing sport. I'm pretty lazy when it comes to reading, but I like to do craft things. There is always some kind of work to be done – either at the house, in the garden, on the car and right now with the building work on my parents' house. During the time I couldn't work, I went swimming once a week with my wife and then we went to the sauna. That was really good and very relaxing. It was almost like "pulling out the plug to reset the system". When I got home afterwards, I felt physically tired, but I had a clear head. Unfortunately, I don't normally have time for things like that.

"Take a close look at your weekly schedule again. Do you notice anything in particular?" I looked at it again. "I've no idea what you mean."

"Where is the time that you have set aside for yourself? I mean for you alone, not for the family, the children or the friends. Not private time you have with others, but the time for yourself. A hobby that you have, which you can do without worrying about what everyone else is doing."

I looked at the plan again. Hmm. She was right. "There isn't any time for that anywhere," I answered. "But the things I do with the family and the children are also fun and they let me think about other things than work." I was trying to defend myself.

"What's the difference between coming home after being at the sauna and coming home after doing something with friends or family?" she asked.

"Like I said, at the sauna I feel like I have a clear head. I'm relaxed. I can just sit in there and I don't have to think about anything. When I sweat, I feel like all the stress is leaving my body. It's almost like the internal memory has been deleted, but not the hard drive because that would mean all the programs and basic data would be lost," I tried to joke.

"And when you are with your friends and family?"

"Well, it's not as if I think about the work at the company unless I'm talking about it anyway. We also discuss private plans and problems, but it's not possible to have a totally clear head. It's more about having a change from the ordinary without any time pressure.

"Do you always look forward to these get-togethers?"

"Yes. We have a very big group of friends, especially because of the voluntary work my wife and I do in the parish. She helps out once a week with coffee, I'm on the Council of Elders and she is still part of the team that helps during the services. It can sometimes be a lot of work. You look at the calendar and see that the next 5-6 weeks are completely full of appointments and the weekends are also really busy. You end up having to make appointments for our free time activities! But like I said, these are things that are also a lot of fun and it would be a shame to have to cancel on a friend especially if we haven't seen them for a long time."

"Do the expectations of the people around you to see them after a long time put you under pressure?"

"Not really, but when it starts to get a bit too much, you do tend to think "wouldn't it be nice to have some free time now, but the get together is going to be fun and the last one was a while ago and that was also really nice.""

"How were things directly before you entered rehab? Did you use all your free time to do things everyday?"

"Hardly. I mean we sometimes went to birthday parties to the city or the cinema, but most of the time I needed to have my peace and quiet between these things. Sometimes I needed an entire day of doing nothing. I didn't even watch TV in the evenings, which is something I used to enjoy doing. I just didn't want to have to concentrate on anything. Just like in the sauna. If lots of things were to happen one after the other, I'd feel under pressure because it could be that something might not work out, I'd come too late or I wouldn't be able to finish something that I needed to, like buy a bunch of flowers."

"Good. You've managed to realize 2 very important things,

1. Before your burnout you had practically no free time for yourself

2. Your body needs a lot of time to recover, as does your head, because too many things at once cause you to feel under pressure and stressed

That's not bad at all.

After a breakdown it can happen that the body reacts much earlier to external influences and sensations than it did before. This is some kind of safety precaution that the body uses to try and prevent a dangerous situation caused by stress from happening again. You have to be very patient. Your body and your mind just need more time to recover. And I mean REALLY recover not just change somehow. That means finding somewhere to "park" your mind, taking it out of gear, looking up to the sky and thinking of nothing. A fun evening with your friends doesn't help because you have to clear up afterwards. It's not the cleaning up which is the problem, but that it's not really relaxation; it's not a "reset" like you experience in the sauna.

Your task to prepare for the next session is to think about a new weekly schedule in which you include 3 x 20 minute breaks every day and one break of 60 minutes. This should be time for yourself with no external influences at all, so no calls or anything else. This should be a schedule for the time when you are back at work after the reintegration period. Don't take anything else into account - not your friends, family or work. The number 1 priority is that you have these breaks."

The result was a weakly schedule in which the focus was on periods of relaxation and breaks. I included time needed to work on projects, but there was no space for any overtime. There was time reserved for my family, but any activities for my voluntary work was excluded during the weekend. At the weekend, I had the option to spend time with my friends, but otherwise it remained free.

This plan seemed do-able, but it didn't answer the most important question I had:

Why did I lose it sometimes?

What could I do to stop it from happening?

What could I do if I couldn't stop it from happening?

My therapist made the following comment: "You are 50 years old and you aren't getting any younger. Always make sure that you can deal with the weekly schedule and your workload without running the risk of having a relapse. You shouldn't feel ashamed if at some point you need to reduce the number of hours you work. There are some people who have to change jobs or who even have to give up working completely. Be attentive and act according to your health. Don't ask yourself if you can afford it materialistically. You are going to have to if things go wrong.

I was recommended a very good book:

"Gelassen und sicher im Stress" by Professor Dr. Gert Kaluza. The author gives a lot of background information about the human psyche and how the body behaves as well as about the causes of stress and its possible consequences. It also gives good guidance and methods on how to recognize stress and overcome it. I think it is good to think about yourself and how you react, when and why and what you can do against these reactions or even how you can use it for good.

4.8) Working on the core problem at work:

In the middle of rehab (after the extension thanks to my infection and the danger of blood poisoning) we added an important point to the list:

"You told me in our first 2 sessions how the situation with being overworked gradually developed over several years. Your mother needed to be cared for and that was emotionally demanding, the voluntary work, renovating the house, the ever increasing pressure and stress at work. You dealt with all of this until your body reacted against it."

"Yes, that was over a period of about 6-9 months and during that time, the symptoms increased in intensity. I'd had sleepless nights before and especially during important projects. I think that's normal because everyone wants to do a good job. It was also normally only for a short period of time and then everything was fine again.

This time it just didn't stop and everything came together at the same time: terrible stomach problems, sleepless nights, brooding, not being able to switch off from work, the fear of not being able to succeed, waking up soaked in sweat, back pain, all the notes next to the bed etc. etc. "

"What did you do about it?"

"To start with I just thought about getting through it. It had always worked out well in the past and it should this time too. I thought that when the new colleague had been integrated into the team it would be better. But then he left and that happened twice in a row. The symptoms weren't getting any better by that point and so I went to the doctor. I then started to feel very unwell and unsure of myself. I hardly played any sport. If I had the time to, I often got very tired very quickly.

It was then that the symptoms began to be treated with medication. That helped for a short time, but because the actual cause wasn't treated or improved, it wasn't long before I couldn't cope without medication, but it didn't actually help. Very often I just couldn't sleep at all, and it would only happen if I was simply too exhausted to think about anything anymore. To try and help, it became more and more the case that I would have a beer in the evening. In the past I drank 1 or 2 bottles a week and that was because I enjoyed it or because it went with whatever we were having for dinner. Now I was using it more as an aid to help me sleep.

I realized this but I didn't want to take medication because I was concerned about becoming addicted. A bottle of beer on the other hand is nothing to be concerned about."

"So, you worked a lot on the symptoms and their consequences. That helped to start with, but it wasn't enough in the end to overcome the problem. You should have done something about the causes as well. What do you think could have been good things to do?"

"That's easy to say now! I couldn't just wimp out at work because the other colleagues were in exactly the same boat and the work had to be done somehow. The boss knew what the situation was and had tried to get some support for the department. He tried twice, but the applicants didn't want to stay even though we had all done our best to integrate them (See chapter 1). So what should we do? Just grit your teeth and get on with it just like we had done in the years before. There wasn't any other way!

The most likely thing for me to be able to reduce was the work I did in the parish, although the planning for the renovations of the church was about to begin. I couldn't just leave those guys in the lurch especially as I had been one of the people to bring about the project in the first place so that the continued existence of the parish could be ensured."

(I found out later that nothing would actually happen for a further 2 years, apart from the Council of Elders telling the parish that they needed to have some patience. That's the reason why I decided to step down from the Council and that way, managed to tick off something on the list of things to cut down on!)

"On the other hand, I don't earn any money from the voluntary work. It's not as if I need to in order to support the family. The election for the Council of Elders is in a year's time, and so I can stand down from my position then without any fuss. That's a ray of hope and then my head will be freer for the other things. Maybe by then things will be better. I think that would be a good first step."

"That sounds like a good idea." Her praise was enough to give me a bit more courage.

"What about your job? From what I have understood from what you have said, you like your work, you enjoy working with your colleagues, you are on good terms with your manager, but the amount of work is a lot to handle. You seem to have so many projects and tight deadlines that a lot of things remain uncompleted. You seem to have to run from one problem to the next even though, actually, you could be in the position to deal with these projects better if the working conditions allowed it."

"Yes", was my automatic response. My hands became clammy.

"You said in our first session that your current manager will retire in November, and his successor is already lined up, but you don't know who it is and neither do your colleagues."

"Yes, that's right."

"What do you think is going to happen?"

"That's what me and my colleagues have been worrying about the whole time."

"Why are you worrying about it?"

"Well, I definitely think it is difficult to find someone with the same professional experience as my current manager. Plus the new person will have to integrate into the team. That will definitely mean more work for us, but on top of that, there are certain things that our current manger worked on alone and we don't know anything about them.

I had a few scenarios in mind of what's going to happen:

1.) He will distinguish himself from us and we will just be the "foot soldiers". That won't work out anyway, in the long or the short term, and so we'll have to deal with a second change at some point.

2.) He'll know that we all rely on each other, and so we will work well together, but there will still be more work for us to do. We will have more friction and much more discussion during the initial stages.

It's not possible to judge in either situation if the new boss is going to agree with the department having to "carry me" if I can't give 120% anymore. I don't have any fears about what will happen with my colleagues. I'm pretty sure that the new guy will have his orders from above and he will be compared to his predecessor.

3.) He doesn't last very long and we have the same situation again. This scenario is similar to scenario 1, but it will happen much quicker and with less stress because I don't think he will create any stress.

In all of these scenarios, it definitely won't be easy at first." I could clearly feel the tension rising within me.

"What would be the worst case scenario for you?"

"Scenario 1, but also generally speaking, at the moment I don't know what I'm going to do if I can't deal with the pressure and demands of the job. I have a few ideas, but nothing set in stone. There are still some important questions left unanswered because I just don't know what's going to happen."

"What could you imagine could be a way out if the worst case actually happened?"

"That's not going to happen. Things always worked out in the past, so I'll find a way to get through it."

"But that's what you've always said, isn't it? That's nothing new, but what was the result?"

"Maybe I can reduce my hours. I took out a loan against my parents' house to tide us over if something went wrong over the next year. My eldest daughter will then probably have to live at home while she is training or studying and maybe even have to work a little to support herself."

I was avoiding the question and she noticed it. I was trying to find excuses. The anxiety was increasing and so was my pulse rate.

"You've already talked about this. This was the first part of your strategy. That was a substantial step. Most of your colleagues here either haven't made that step yet or haven't had the chance or the resources to do so.

And you haven't answered my question." She pulled me back into the ring for the next round. I wanted to run away, but she was in my way!

"What is the worst case scenario for you?"

I started to sweat.

"That……that I won't be able to cope with everything which is expected of me." My blood pressure was going in the same direction as my pulse: up.

"Is that going to have consequences?"

I lost my cool for the first time. I had to release the tension somehow: "Of course there'll be consequences!" I didn't want to talk anymore, so I stopped.

"What consequences?"

Silence

"Would you like to take a break or have something to drink?"

I was breathing hard and shouted: "I'll……I'll….I'll lose my job for goodness sake! Shit! I'll lose my job and will be out in the cold.

Of course I can look for another job, but everything works so well in the position I have right now. The work was always ideal and the area of responsibility and the colleagues are great. The boss is OK and the salary acceptable. I don't have to travel far to the office, so there isn't any stressful 2-3 hour commute everyday. Then everything got more complicated and stressful. If I get a new job, I'll have to perform well from the beginning and if things don't work out for me here, how am I going to cope with something new? Anyway, who is going to employ a burned out 50 year old? There's no chance, but even if there was, who is to say that I'd find something in the area? It might be that I only get to see my family at the weekends and I really don't want that!"

I was shaking. I took a deep breath in and breathed out slowly 3 times, and then did it again. I drank a glass of water and swallowed in a rhythm between the breaths. That relaxed me a little. After 5 minutes (or what felt like 15!) she asked me: "How are you feeling?"

"I'm scared that I won't ever be able to get over this. I'm so scared. It's that simple!"

"I can put myself in your position and I understand your thoughts and emotions."

"I need a way out. A realistic alternative. A Plan B. Something which I don't just talk about, but which I can be convinced will work if the worst case happens. But that's something I don't have yet. I also don't know how to get out of this cycle of panic if something happens, which causes me stress. How do I get out of this? Tell me, how do I get out?"

I stood up and started pacing up and down. She could feel my desperation.

Silence.

"I can't show you the way out, but I can help you to find it. I can tell you that you are closer to finding it than you think."

"Well, that's alright then," I said ironically. I become quite ironic when I feel tense, but it happens quite rarely.

Silence.

She hesitated a little, because she hadn't expected that reaction, but she dealt with it in a totally professional manner.

"I can count for you all the things that you have initiated and those you plan to do:

1. You decided to find a solution to your problem and fought for 7 months for a place in rehab because you knew that you couldn't do it alone. You were successful in your bid for a rehab place.
2. When I see you here and talk to my colleagues, who work with you in the other courses, I know that you push yourself to your limits. We've just seen that. You don't sit in the corner having lost all hope. I understand that your energy is waning after 8 months, but you've said yourself that you have been given a lot of new direction since being here and that you will structure your life differently than you did before. You will have different priorities in the future.
3. Before you came here you had already started thinking about a Plan B. You are ready to go without some things, which always used to be important to you. You've taken out a loan on your parents' house, giving yourself a lot of debt and you are also ready to sell if you have to. You are going to go without holidays. That means that you have already had a huge part of the burden to finance your family and the education of your children lifted from your shoulders. That means a lot.
4. On top of that, there are some alternatives, which we can help you with:

    1. We can talk with your employer and discuss all the options with them. For example part time work, no business trips, a reduced number of responsibilities, working in another department.

You have 20 years work experience in project management. You aren't a beginner. In most cases, companies don't let people like you go so easily. And if they do, then it'll be expensive for them! You have been there for 15 years. If I understand you correctly, the priority is to find a solution with your current employer and not anyone else, i.e. you want to try and stay in the same department, but if necessary, you could work in another.

You'll work on a reintegration plan for when you return to work with one of my colleagues. It won't be a rough and ready, sink or swim, all or nothing, all at once kind of approach. It'll be something that will happen step by step so that you can get used to the work and the office environment again. That also means that you can slowly get control of your fears as well because every day you'll have small successes. You'll be able to extend the different phases of the plan if you need to and, at the end, you can decide for yourself how able you are and then we can talk with your employer to try and find a solution. I'm very confident about that.

2. If we can't come to a mutual agreement then there is always the possibility to retrain. You'll be able to take advantage of support.

3. I don't think that you will not be able to work ever again. You want to find a solution and there is going to be one.

4. If nothing works out at all (which I don't think is going to happen), then there is still the possibility that you could claim a disability pension from the DRV. It isn't very much at all, but with your own contributions you would probably be fine.

Your courses aren't over yet. There will be other things that you will learn and experience about the connections between how your body and the human psyche work and react. A lot of things could still happen."

I looked at her, my therapist.

I breathed in and out slowly 3 times

"I will try."

"I think that's enough for today. Why don't you treat yourself to a time out.

Oh actually I have another question before you go," she said in true Columbo style as I reached for the door handle: "You talked about 3 scenarios and all of them had a negative outcome Why is that?"

"Because they are the things which I think are the most realistic and I can't think of any other possibilities at the moment."

"And what if the new guy is someone who has a lot of management experience, is very understanding of employees in special situations and knows to value your work experience and detailed knowledge of the job?"

"Then obviously that changes everything and I don't need to prepare myself for that. I want to prepare for the worst so that this fear and symptoms I have, which I can't control, disappear."

"OK, then have a good afternoon. Relax."

"I will. I'm doing Tai Chi anyway. Goodbye and sorry that I lost it."

"I've seen worse!"

"Thanks."

4.9) Next session: Helper syndrome, say NO:

"In the meantime you've met with the social therapist and discussed ways in which you can integrate back into work."

"Yes, that was really good. We talked about if I really want to go back to my previous job. I said that I definitely do. I don't want to not try and if it turns out that I can't do it for whatever reason then that's OK. At least I tried and didn't just give up and that is very important for me. If there were certain conditions which meant that it was highly unlikely to work out then that would be different. Then I wouldn't want to risk failing because it would be clear what the result would be. That isn't the case, though.

We discussed the following things:

1. I'm going to call my boss. Our relationship was always good and I know that he would appreciate it if everything weren't handled formally. I'll tell him the different stages of the reintegration we have discussed.
2. The social therapist will then talk to him and the HR Department to discuss once again how everything should work, what they need to take into consideration, including all the formalities they have to stick to.
3. Then it's all about the paperwork: a description of the reintegration, collecting the written confirmation from the employer that they are happy with everything etc. As soon as my employer has signed the documentation and sent it back, then everything is ready.

I'm going to start by working 2 hours everyday in the first week. It's not much, but it'll help me get used to the office again and I'll be able to say "hello" to everyone. It's important for me and I don't want to risk anything. I'd prefer to do it for a few weeks longer than have to completely stop. That's not going to help, but will make everything even harder. I just need to take small, slow, patient steps, which bring some kind of success. It's planned that I'll work 1-2 hours more every week and that the whole period should last 10 weeks until I'm working 7.5 hours a day again. There are no business trips planned during this time."

"That sounds really good. When are you going to talk to your manager?"

"This week. I don't want to put it off and I don't have all the time in the world anyway!"

"Are you going to do it by yourself?"

"Yes."

"And how do you feel when you think about it?"

"A little nervous, but it's the first step. I'm going to have to take these steps by myself anyway, so I'd better start! If I have any problems, I'll let you know in the morning meeting."

"Good. So when you are back at work and the first part of the reintegration phase is behind you, you will probably be trusted with an increasing amount of responsibilities. How do you feel when you think about that?"

"I'm actually looking forward to it. I want to be able to do the things I always used to be able to do. I'm a little unsure and am afraid because I don't know how my body is going to react when the pressure starts to build and if I'll have the same symptoms as before. I'll try and use all the different relaxation methods I've learned about here. That'll be possible in my office during the reintegration phase. It'll be more problematic when I start going on business trips. I can't really ask for a 30 minute tai chi break!"

"Why not?" she interrupted.

"I can't really stop a meeting and then come back 20-30 minutes later after making all the others wait. How do you think that's going to work?" I responded directly.

"You can control a lot of things, Mr. Dietrich. As you have already noticed and reported, you are very good at recognizing your physical symptoms early. That is very helpful. You are learning relaxation techniques through breathing exercises and that can help you too because you can give yourself time to react appropriately. It's quite normal to ask for a break during a meeting and a good meeting agenda includes breaks at certain points. It's also very useful that you don't have to take part in these meetings alone at the beginning and that means not everything is relying on you. You can hand over to someone else and that takes the pressure off you and you can slowly collect the successes we have talked about before until you feel ready to do more. You will still be with another person, but you can try as long as you like to lead the meeting until it works. With planning and discussions you can also control a lot of things when it comes to your colleagues. It doesn't have to be a jump into the deep end. It shouldn't be anyway because that would

106

be irresponsible. You should approach it as if you are new to the job, but with the huge advantage that you have all your years of work experience."

"It doesn't sound unrealistic at all." She smirked slightly before she started her next "attack".

"When the management change takes place and one of your 3 scenarios becomes reality, what are you going to do?"

"If the reintegration has gone well then I'm just going to have to grit my teeth and try to get on with my work."

"What does that mean "try to get on with my work?""

"That I work to the best of my ability when I am asked to do so. What other option do I have?"

"I don't want to rule out that you will be able to do the vast majority of the work you previously did. In all probability you will be so stable again that you will be able to take on the responsibilities associated with it. It is, however, also probable that this entire development process will last longer than the "official" reintegration phases. That means that your new manager could end up demanding things from you that you are unable or unwilling to do at that time."

She had got straight to the heart of the matter. I wanted to run out of the nearest door, but it was as if she was standing in my way with the key in her hand.

"What should I do then? I've got to get through if that's what is expected of me. What alternative do I have?"

"I don't understand you Mr. Dietrich", she said for the first time. "Isn't that exactly the same situation which led to what happened on 23.11.2011 at 8am?"

My blood pressure was shooting up like a paraglider riding a thermal current.

"Do you really want to put yourself in a situation which you already know the outcome of?" I felt like she was pushing me into the corner of the ring again. "Have you forgotten what the doctor in the Emergency Department said to you just as he briefly stopped your heart to get it back into rhythm.....as he briefly stopped your heart to get it back into rhythm..... as he briefly stopped your heart to get it back into rhythm." Those words kept coming back to me like an echo. "I don't understand that you rightly have the strategy to sell the house and take the loan, but that you don't want to use it. Why do you want to take such a risk? What's more important, your job or your health? Without you, there isn't any job. Without you, your family has to deal with the consequences of your mistakes. So, what is more important?"

"But what should I do if I end up risking my job?"

"What about if you win back your life in doing so? Of course it'll be another kind of life. We've already talked about it. It'll be a life without the risk of what the doctor in the Emergency Department told you could happen."

She was right. She was right even though it hurt to accept that. She was right. If the worst-case scenario became reality, then I had to accept that I couldn't handle it. I would have to admit that I wasn't the person I used to be. I would have to concede that I couldn't rise to the challenge anymore. If I were given a task to do, which I was unable to do at the time of asking, I would have to say: "I can't do that yet. I need some more time. I don't know for sure right now if I'll be able to do it later. For my own protection, I have to say NO." And then I would have to see how the new boss reacted. I was going to have to get used to that idea. I will get used to it. I will get used to it for my children, Marliese and me! What's more I had to accept that situations aren't only black and white. Most of the time, a solution is reached because both sides make compromises. You set the benchmark as high as possible to start with in order to achieve the best you can, but at the end, you are satisfied with whatever was achievable. "Things are never as bad as they seem."

"I would say NO," I answered. She smiled.

4.10) The "Fear" Group:

I have limited myself to the points that I can remember and that were important for me. I won't describe the entire course content because that would go too far. Apologies for the amateurish account, but I think the result is the same!

The "Fear" group took place twice a week and went on for 4 weeks. Participation had to be confirmed with a signature on my timetable, just like with all the other courses.

Today was the third meeting. We focused on various topics related to fear in each session. As preparation, we all had to think in which situation and under what circumstances we felt fear, stress, pressure etc. These situations were then discussed.

Each participant talked about their own situations and then the therapist put together all of our experiences and showed us some research basics. I thought this was a good method because you automatically have a connection between your own situation and the medical findings. This led to an "aha" moment more often than you would expect!

On this particular day the topic was the interaction of stress and fear in everyday life.

In the following picture, I have tried to illustrate the connections using my notes and sketches from the course at the clinic.

1.) The Fear Threshold (FS) is different depending on the situation. It can be changed through training. If there is a particularly negative experience, it can be reduced. Training in confrontation techniques can raise it.

2.) Going over the Fear Threshold can lead to panic (striking out, anger) or uncontrollable physical reactions (hyperventilation).

3.) Calm people, who generally have a low base tension level and a high Fear Threshold very rarely panic because the tension levels seldom go over the Fear Threshold, even in dangerous situations. People with high base tension levels (choleric) lose their tempers very quickly because they go over the Fear Threshold more easily.

4.) People who generally have a low Fear Threshold have the same problem. (Low self confidence).

5.) Things become critical when the Threshold drops very low because of external factors (Overwork, stress, traumatic event etc.) This is the body's way of protecting itself, but it means that everyday activities are seen by the body as dangerous or simply too much. The result is a lower ability to deal with stress. The Fear Threshold is connected to an unconscious estimation of the situation. As mentioned above, this can be trained.

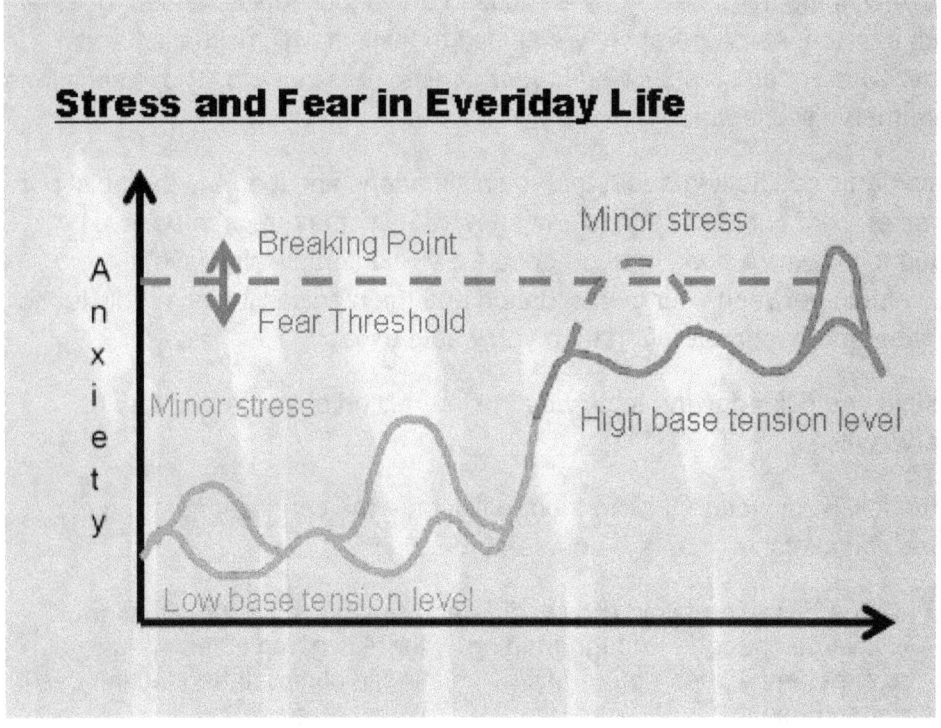

Qualitative connection between the breaking point/Fear Threshold, base tension levels and stress.

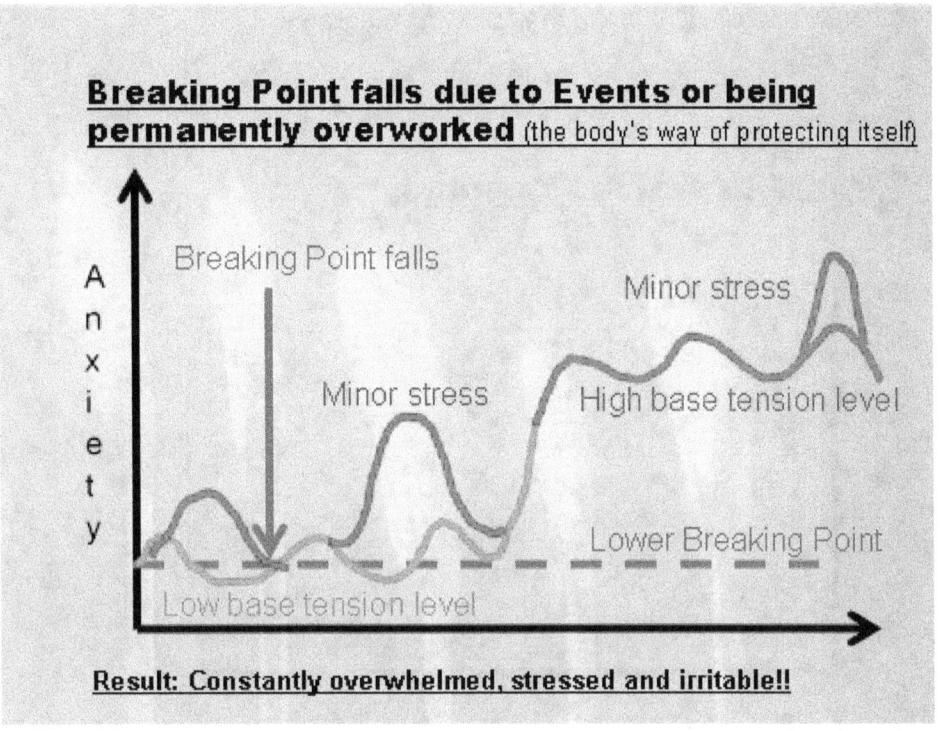

Breaking Point falls due to Events or being permanently overworked (the body's way of protecting itself)

Anxiety

Breaking Point falls

Minor stress

Minor stress

High base tension level

Lower Breaking Point

Low base tension level

Result: Constantly overwhelmed, stressed and irritable!!

Illustration of the situation in Point 5. The result can be permanent overload.

In the illustration, it is easy to see what possibilities there are to positively influence the situation:

1. Trained in small steps and with patience. (Confrontation training, see the section "Fear" Group, Amygdala)

2. I had to work on my "stress profile". In a critical situation it's important to remain calm, not to flare up internally or see everything in a pessimistic light. It's important to differentiate between important and less important things. Relaxation training is very important for that and has become very important for me.

3. Reduce the frequency and number of events, which lead to tension. Quite simply that means: slim down. This is easiest when it comes to non-existential activities: hobbies and voluntary work. Organizationally, things can also be simplified at work without having to take any radical steps straight away. It's like driving a car. If you put your foot down, you go quickly, but you only go a long way if you ration the fuel. These are individual decisions that everyone has to make by him or herself.

Qualitative illustration in the following diagrams.

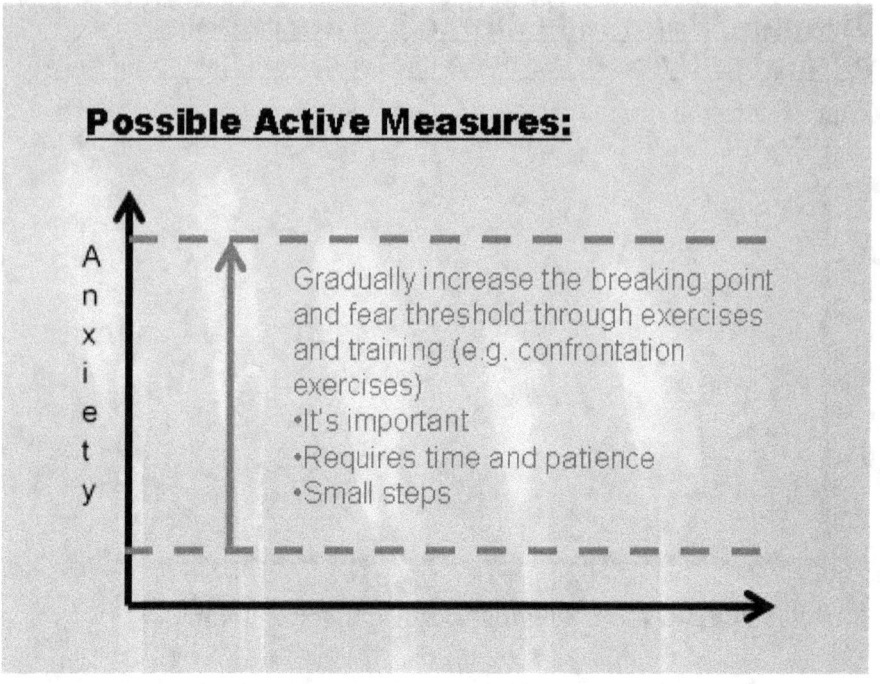

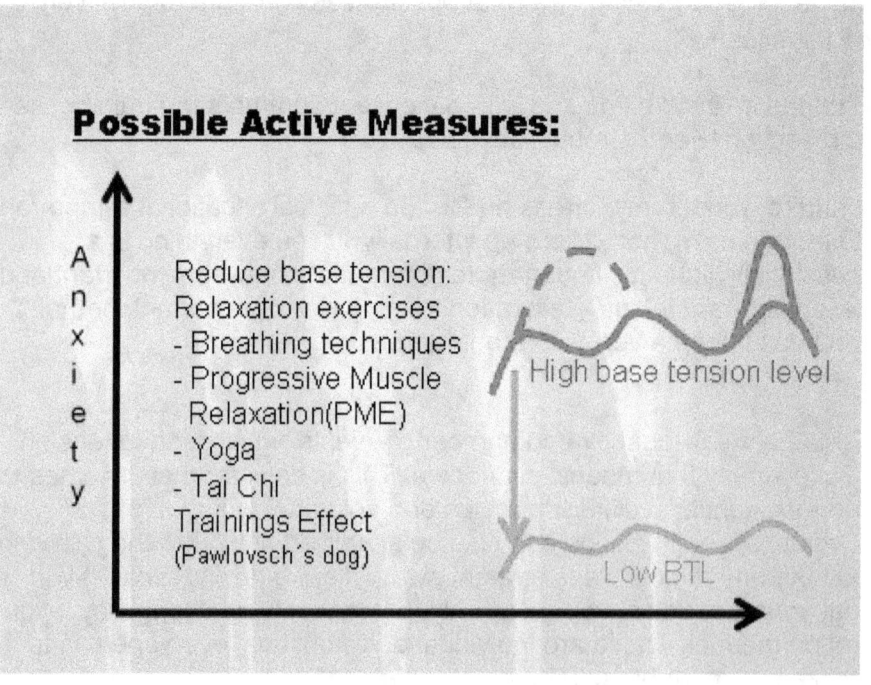

If I have built up some kind of protection because of a traumatic event, it can happen that permanently avoiding a situation can lead to being increasingly unable to deal with it and, in the end, would mean always wanting to avoid it.

Possible Consequences of Cycle of Fear:

➤ **Anxiety disorder**

➤ **Maintaining the anxiety disorder**
(Avoiding the situation)
(Negative thinking: driving is dangerous anyway)

Breaking out of the Cycle of Fear:

➤ **Try things anyway (Confrontation)**
➤ **With external help and guidance**
➤ **Take small steps**
„I can do it" (Successes)
➤ **Draw from succeses**
➤ **Reward yourself for successes**

If I want to overcome my Fear Threshold, then I would have to negotiate the situation and gain experience so that it doesn't become dangerous and I can control and contain it. Small steps are important here because you can slowly build up self-confidence and, if the situation is divided into smaller portions, it is easier to deal with.

For example: driving again after having an accident:

- On the first day, just sit in the car again to get acquainted with being in those surroundings again
- On the second day, try out all the controls while the car is stationary.
- After this, start the engine.
- Be in the car as a passenger.
- Drive yourself around a car park.
- Take a few driving classes.
- Drive yourself along an isolated route.
- Drive in the city outside of rush hour.
- Etc.

Let's continue with the course in the clinic…

A week later in the following session, we discussed the topic: perception and the body's reaction.
Perceptions, stimuli, senses. Everybody knows those: sight, touch, smell, taste, and sound.

The brain is stimulated and we react according to what situation we find ourselves in, i.e. where we are and how we are feeling. This is also nothing new.

The therapist drew a human brain on the board with an eye, ear, finger, mouth and nose from which arrows pointed towards the brain. So far, so good.

Then came something new, at least for me as I've never really had anything to do with this topic and so was a total amateur.

The therapist drew a black point underneath the brain. She doubled all the arrows from the pictures of the organs down to this point before writing the description of the point next to it on the board.

"Has anyone heard of AMYGDALA in the human brain?"

No idea. No one answered.

"Then I'll tell you a little bit about this part of our brains."

"The Amygdala goes back to the origins of man. Among other things, it controls our spontaneous behavior in dangerous situations. It reacts to the same stimuli that we are conscious of, but many times faster than our cognitive brain. It controls adrenalin production using the sympathetic nervous system, which instantly helps us to fight or flee in times of danger. The Amygdala decides what our first reaction will be in these situations: can I overcome this = fight, or not, and so we experience fear = flight.

Why doesn't this first reaction work in parallel with our normal brain and perception processes? It's quite simple and I can give you an example from the time of our ancestors:

You are hunting in the forest when, behind you, you hear a branch snap. Does that mean there is danger? By the time you turn round and have decided what you want to do, the bear will be on you. What's more, in order to have lightning quick reactions to turn your head round, you need some kind of signal to do so before you think too long about it. And that's what Amygdala is responsible for.

"So, in simple terms, does that mean that we "unconsciously" react before we have properly realized what is going on?"

"Exactly. Amygdala puts you in the position to be able to defend yourself as soon as the situation has been properly recognized. Argh, a bear! Normally you'd react by running away."

That was nothing new for me. Of course we had all heard of subconsciousness and reflexes. You always need good reflexes if you play sport. What was new was to what extent everything was connected.

"It is possible to train the Amygdala to a certain extent. You can improve your reflexes and reactions and reduce fear through training. For example, if you have a fear of spiders, you can train by putting yourself through a situation with them so that you can experience that nothing will happen. This is Confrontation Training." (This is also layman's terms, but hopefully I have explained it as clearly as possible).

"Can it work the other way around as well? I mean that I suddenly fear something and the Amygdala springs into action, but I never used to have any fear of this situation?"

"Yes."

The others continued to discuss this, but I lost track as I was lost in thought. I stared at the diagram on the board and thought about it. I focused on the black point and at the arrows from the eye, nose and ear pointing at it. This controls the adrenalin in my body. It can instantly make me ready to fight. The therapist had said it is faster than my cognitive brain and faster than I can think. It is faster than me. It is faster than me.....

I interrupted the discussion at the next possible point with a question: "What happens to the adrenalin if the Amygdala has got it wrong and there isn't any danger?"

"Then you probably won't react in any physical way (fight or flight) and the adrenalin is surplus to requirements in your system."

"What could that lead to?"

"If it is a small amount, you can normally calm yourself down quite quickly. Also, when the mind realizes that there is no danger, the parasympathetic nervous system normally balances the levels after a short period of time."

OK. My GP had said that something in my system wasn't working as it should, so I continued my questioning. That's why she was there.

"What happens if this balancing doesn't work for some reason?"

"If you have an excess of adrenalin, which you cannot control, then you will experience anxiety, nervousness, shaking, it can lead to hyperventilation and other physical problems, but also to panic attacks."

I had her and now I wasn't going to back down! I was on the right track to being able to explain everything. I was so near! I carried on with my questions:

"Could it be, for example, that I develop some kind of fear because something at work had gone wrong and I worry that it could happen again, and that Amygdala reacts in a way like you explained with our ancestors, and produces adrenalin, which means I find myself reacting in such a way as to protect myself, even though there isn't any danger?"

"It's possible, but you have to consider that every person reacts differently."

116

"So when I am agitated and I can't calm myself down because I still fear that the same situation will be repeated or that it will be even worse, could it be that the situation then escalates?"

"Yes, as I said, normally you figure out that there is no danger present and you can calm yourself down with help of the parasympathetic nervous system. If the fear remains, the situation could worsen and end in panic."

"If I know that I am in this cycle of fear, how can I break out of it?"

"You can try calming down using relaxation techniques and that's why you learn various methods while you are here."

"What if that doesn't help because the adrenalin levels are just too high or I just can't do it?"

"Then it's good to reduce them by using the adrenalin for what it is actually for: movement, sport, some kind of physical activity."

I looked at the therapist. "That should work? When I'm already agitated and hectic and I don't have a clue why, I should exert myself more by doing sport?"

"Everyone reacts differently and has different limitations. If the cause is an uncontrollable adrenalin production and you can't find any other way to calm yourself down, then you should try it. You are here in this clinic for exactly that reason - to learn things."

"OK," I answered. "I'll try it out."

Wow. If that actually worked! This was exactly the point that I had never understood. I never would have had the idea to do sport, especially as I didn't really seem to have any control of myself.

That would be fantastic if it worked!!!

This was essentially confrontation training: create a certain situation which creates fear and then try and control the body's reaction by remaining in that situation until the fear and the symptoms have started to disappear. If everything is working normally, the parasympathetic nervous system can reduce the levels of tension after a while.

Fear has a lot to do with learning processes. It's as easy to forget it as it is to learn to have it. This needs time and patience because the body needs to experience that the situation we are in isn't actually dangerous for us. It's important to repeat these experiences through confrontation.

As a result, the body learns that the situation isn't dangerous, and so the next time we find ourselves in it, the symptoms will appear in a limited form or not at all. It's important to only do this with the support and guidance of a medical profession if you have psychological problems.

In the following diagram, I have tried to illustrate the connection between our conscious perceptions (sight, sound, smell etc.) and our reflex evaluation of a situation through Amygdala. It is based on the drawings I made during the seminars.

Our perceptions are transmitted simultaneously to our "conscious brain" and Amygdala (Amy) instantly evaluates the reaction and produces adrenalin as a precautionary protective measure in case of danger. The body can then react appropriately depending on what the conscious brain then reports back.

When the adrenalin and oxygen have been used up (the sympathetic nervous system doesn't produce anymore because the danger has passed), the parasympathetic nervous system balances everything. The result of this is often feelings of exhaustion (It's very simplified so that I can also understand it!)

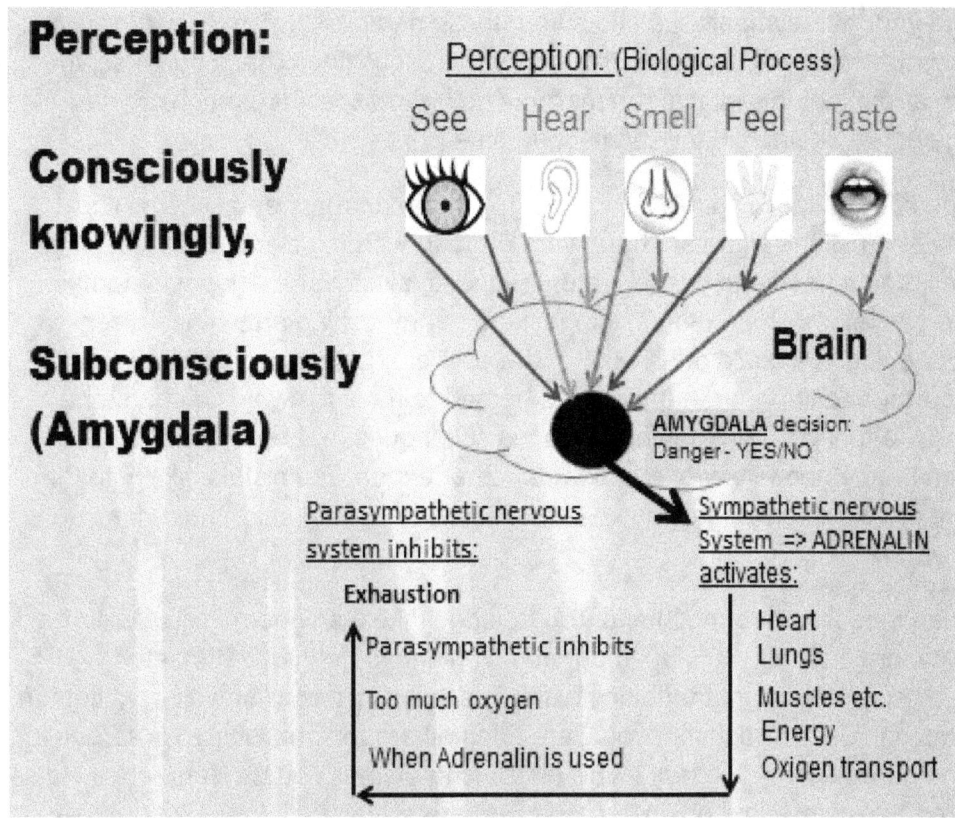

Perception:

Consciously knowingly,

Subconsciously (Amygdala)

Perception: (Biological Process)

See   Hear   Smell   Feel   Taste

Brain

AMYGDALA decision: Danger - YES/NO

Parasympathetic nervous system inhibits:

Exhaustion

Parasympathetic inhibits

Too much oxygen

When Adrenalin is used

Sympathetic nervous System => ADRENALIN activates:

Heart
Lungs

Muscles etc.
Energy
Oxigen transport

4.11) My friend Amygdala:

I stood in my room C103 and looked in the mirror in the hall. I looked her in the eyes. We stared at each other for a while in that mirror.

Then I spoke to her.

"Hello Amygdala. What are we going to do with each other? I didn't know until today that you existed, but we live in the same house as each other. We both live in the same guy here in this mirror. We rely on each other – You can't survive without me and I can't without you. That means we have to get along with each other.

I found out today that you exist in the head of the guy in this mirror. I also found out that you want to take care of me. That's great, but you've become a bit confused because I expected too much of you and now you shut down when something happens you are afraid of. Every time when you think that there is a situation, which is going to create stress, you put on the breaks

119

and your parasympathetic and sympathetic nervous system and adrenalin go crazy. Just like that even though everything is fine. That's because you are afraid that this idiot in the mirror is going to expect too much of you again, just like he did for such a long time.

You know what? You are right. The guy in the mirror is an asshole. You gave him all the signals. There were enough warning signs – not sleeping well, being unable to concentrate, tiredness, sweating, back pain, stomach cramps, stomach problems, indigestion, nearly getting a stomach ulcer – everything you could offer, but no, the asshole had to carry on. He was smarter and stronger than you and he had to have his way. Of course he had the fear of failing, letting down his colleagues, not being able to cope with the demands of work, making another expensive mistake like with that one project. If only he could've opened his mouth and said: "no. I can't do it anymore.

Then it became too much and **you** couldn't take it anymore. You were afraid. Very afraid. Then you flipped out and went into safety mode to defend against an opponent that didn't exist. There was no bear or wolf or knifeman who wanted to attack, but you were firing all around you with your adrenalin. And here we are. The guy in the mirror is to blame. You didn't do anything wrong. You just shut down because you are still afraid if there is some stress or you remember situations where the pressure was too high. I've understood that now.

So, I understand you now. I know that you are in me right there in my head. I also know what makes you tick and why.

What are we going to do with each other?"

I looked at her in the eye and I knew that she could see me and I could sense her.

"Listen to me. I'm sure you don't want go stale in there and I don't want that either. You don't want to panic just standing in front of the dishwasher or at work or when the phone rings. We both have the same goal. We both want to get out of this damn hole, get back on our feet, laugh, be happy and not hide ourselves away. We want to be able to do a job, it doesn't matter which one, as long as we can lead a normal life.

OK. At least we are both going in the same direction. That's a good start. Pay attention then. This is the plan: after all the examinations, I know that physically, I'm in good shape and I don't have any limitations when it comes to sport. As the GP said, mechanically, everything is fine, so on that side, and nothing can go wrong. This is what I'm going to do:

1.) Get myself into shape physically to make sure that I don't have so much to worry about in that respect should I push you to your limits again. But I also will take care not to overdo things again, no more marathon, that's a promise!

2.) I will do anything, and I mean anything in terms of relaxation techniques. I'll go to all the courses here and take what I can from them so that I can use some of what I learn regardless of what I situation I find myself in if you give me a sign in the future that I'm doing too much or that I'm expecting too much of you.

3.) This way I'll always try and stop in time so that you don't flip out again.

4.) If it gets too much for you again, I know now how to use up all your adrenalin: sport, movement, vent, full throttle. Nothing will happen. My body can take it.

5.) That way we have each other under control. You watch out for me and I'll take more care. You'll be able to get back to working under normal conditions. I'll expect a little bit more of you every so often and we'll see how you react. If it's too much, then I'll react to that. We'll take it step by step.

6.) We have all the doctors we need here. This is the best place for us to test our new training. We know what we have to do and if something goes wrong, we are in safe hands.

Don't you think that's a good deal for both of us? We'll both be able to get ourselves out of this hole. It doesn't matter how long it takes, we are going to see it through. You and me. I do projects that go on for years, so it's no problem to have a personal one, especially when it's about my life. It doesn't matter if it takes 1 or 2 years if it wins me 20.

If we have or problem or there's something we can't deal with, then we'll change it. It's about the rest of our lives and nothing is more important than my health, my family and me. It took me quite a long time to get that, I know.

So let's go RIGHT NOW!

Hey, I've got another little trick up my sleeve, which I've just thought of. I've just learned that you are really fast, faster than I can think. When I'm feeling good, you feel that. You see and hear everything that I perceive. Every time I feel good, I'll make sure I look into something that reflects then you will see and feel how well we are doing. It'll be fun to see that guy every morning in the mirror when he cuts himself shaving and shouts "oh, shit!", right?"

I looked us both in the eye in the mirror and started to smirk. "Come on Amy. This is our dance, so let's dance."

I know that she heard me! There was a benefit for me. I didn't have to watch out for Amy's feet like I do with my wife! Her feet were mine and I am a miserable dancer.

Was I crazy for doing that? Talking to myself in the mirror? NO, I wasn't. Every sportsman and team does something like that before an important competition and this competition was about me and the rest of my life. Everything that I learned about myself I would try and use somehow. Everything else would be really stupid!

There is the expression: "if you can't beat your opponent, make him your friend." I'm going to add something to that…..then you will both be stronger.

Breaking out of the Cycle of Fear:

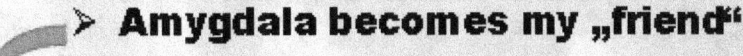

- ➢ Amygdala becomes my „friend"
- ➢ No internal fear or pressure
- ➢ No „fighting against your weaker self"
- ➢ Adress issues together with Amie
- ➢ „If you want to go fast, go alone, if you want to go far, go together" (African proverb)

This was going to be quite a long road, but you don't need any tools from the DIY store to go down it. They won't get you very far. You need other tools. You just need to get to know what they are. You have to learn to handle them and someone has to show you how.

You need patience because it won't happen quickly.

You need courage because you will always have to deal with difficult situations, but you don't know how it is going to work out.

You need hope so that you don't give up even after a set back.

You need to have the ability to be happy about the small things - the small steps that give you courage.

You need the willpower to work on and change yourself, to set new priorities and set aside unnecessary, stressful things.

You can set your own targets. The means, tools and the way you get there can be learned from the therapists, courses and other patients.

You can set your targets, but there is no schedule, no project timetable, no milestones, no time when the project has to be completed. It will probably be a life long project so take your time. "The journey is the reward."

Today is 26.07.13. It's so great that I can just write this down. It's even kind of fun. It was such a strange feeling back then to finally have a solution, a way out, a method to get out of this situation and it has worked since then. In small, very small steps, I trained myself and 1 year later, I am still training myself. It's like running a marathon. I control my breathing and do 10 minutes of tai chi in the quiet room at work. Most of the time, the colleagues don't even realize what I am doing. But that isn't important. I'm back and that is all that matters! Amy is also important and she has become my best friend. It's no wonder now that she knows that I'm taking better care of her. As I said before, we both have the same goal after all.

A second comparison has just come to mind:

At our kindergarten, we have the normal groups, but also a group for disabled children. Everyday, the groups do things together so that they can be integrated more easily and the healthy children can learn how to deal with certain disabilities. They sometimes have little sports competitions (e.g. running, jumping etc.), whereby teams are created with one healthy and one disabled child. The aim is to complete a task together and, depending on the task, the time as a team also plays a role.

There are often different strategies during these games:

1.) The healthy child runs as quickly as he can to be first and to gain as much time as possible from the other teams. He then stands at the finishing line to cheer on his teammate, who works really hard, but sometimes won't make it to the end. The worst case is hat the healthy child becomes very frustrated or angry (some kids are like that), because he gave everything he could, but the team lost because the disabled child hadn't managed the task. Both are disappointed and the disabled child won't want to take part at all next time because he will be even more aware of his limitations.

2.) Strategy number 2 involves giving each other a high five at the start and then doing the task together. The healthy child supports, pushes or helps his teammate in any way he can. In that way, both make it to the finishing line and it's often the case that the time needed isn't important. The children had so much fun and are happy that they managed to do the task together. The team then stay together fort he next task.

So Amy, I am happy to go at your speed so that at some point, together we can throw your crutches in the bin, which I was responsible for in the first place. I promise I won't open that bin again as well!

4.12) A lecture by my therapist:

As is sometimes the case, a few days later I had the opportunity to put my new findings to the test.

I was given another questionnaire with over 200 questions half way through my stay, after which my therapist gave a lecture. I thought I would work through as many questions as possible and then go. Somehow or other, I got engrossed in the questions because some of them had been written in quite a complicated way (maybe that was done on purpose). I was totally stressed when I looked at the clock. Oh damn. I only had 5 minutes and I had wanted to rest beforehand, but I had got so caught up with the stupid questions and I couldn't concentrate on anything. It didn't matter. I had to go.

I found a free seat in the middle row and sat myself in the aisle seat. The lecture began, but I can't remember right now what the topic was. I wasn't taking anything in after 15 minutes anyway. I couldn't concentrate. The questions, the noise levels (which weren't actually so high), the constant to-ing and fro-ing had taken its toll.

O.K. so what have we learned?

First of all relaxed breathing. Eyes closed, breathe in slowly, count to 3 and picture something relaxing.

The discussion continued around me. I breathed in and out 3 times. My mind continued to race. Shit. I wasn't going to be able to do it. I couldn't switch off. I tried again, but it didn't work.

Second: change where you are. Get out of the environment that's causing the stress. I went up to my therapist and explained to her in as few words as possible how I was feeling and what I was going to do: "I have to leave now!" She answered "It's OK. I've been watching you the whole time. If you don't feel any better, let us know straight away."

"OK."

I opened the door and went out. I felt relief as soon as I left the room. I went into the corridor and breathed in and out slowly. My head felt a little better because the noise levels had dropped, but I still felt tense. OK.

Third: use up that excess adrenalin. The stairwell was in front of me, but there was only one floor unfortunately. I ran up and down taking 2 steps at a time, 5 times, 10 times. Hey it was getting better! I was panting.

Now I wanted to know: Fitness room, punch bag. I told the therapist where she would be able to find me and off I went. I was already wearing loose clothing so I didn't need to change. I hung up the punch bag (about 25kg) and just started hitting it. Right, left, right, left. The bag was swinging. I took a step forward and my punches kept it at an angle. Right, left, again and again. I began sweating and to breath more quickly just like I did when running. I switched between slow and fast intervals and back to get my breath. 10 minutes. Come on keep going! 15 minutes. The sweat was dripping onto the floor. I screamed out my anger, the anger I had about myself, which I didn't have under control. The anger that I had caused so many problems. The anger at everything I could think of. My knuckles were starting to ache: what's all this fighting?! It hurts!

20 minutes and the floor was wet, my hands were hurting, I was exhausted, I was puffing like a locomotive climbing a mountain. It had been a while since I'd done anything like this and I wasn't really in top condition anymore.

I sat down on the bench. The door opened and the guy I had arrived with looked in: "is everything OK?" he saw me puffing away and I gave him the thumbs up. "Everything's fine." He left.

I was alone again and I jogged slowly around the room. My breathing slowed, I calmed down and I felt good. The tension was gone. It's gone. Totally gone. I felt tired and I was soaked in sweat, but I felt great. I started to grin slightly and then I stuck my hand in the air and shouted: Yeeeaaahhhh!!!

Afterwards, I said quietly: Thank God.

It seemed like, after 7 months of trying, I had found a plausible way for me to cope.....and it worked! I had finally understood why I hadn't got anywhere before. This was a way out of this cycle of fear. The fear that I'd be stuck in this rut, that I wouldn't be able to find a way out or that maybe there wasn't a way out. I had found a solution for me. It was like breathing in fresh air, like a sunrise. It was damn good!

I decided to take in as much as I could from the courses: relaxation, sport, jogging, creative group, "fear" group, social competence and and and..... I didn't want to leave any stone unturned when it came to learning about methods or tools. That's the reason I had come to rehab in the first place after all.

I remembered in the "fear" group when we had talked about dog training (where saliva could be made to be produced for food even when there was none. It was done using only an alarm clock after the dog had gotten used to the fact that there was always food when the alarm rang. See appendix) and how you can train yourself to overcome your fears using confrontation training. Or, how you can take control of Amy. I thought that I would start setting the alarm clock for us both and then we could dance.

4.13) "The Thinking Trap":

The topic of being able to switch off was important for me.

Switching off from the problems at work when I was at home and things were too much.

Being able to switch off when I went to bed.

Switching off and going back to sleep when I wake up in the middle of the night.

Thinking about what I am doing at the moment instead of constantly having the same thoughts and problems going around in my head about unfinished work and upcoming appointments.

When you have trained this it's really easy and it happens on demand.

The first time I recognized this was when I was doing the breathing exercises. A therapist had read a relaxing story with the same rhythm as slow breathing. After a little while, we automatically got used to this rhythmic breathing. We also had to think of a peaceful picture, i.e. a favorite situation, which would help us relax, e.g. walking by the sea. Doing that meant "being" in another place. We trained our bodies to relax with these thoughts and the breathing techniques and this was something that could be done anywhere. In the end it was the case that we felt relaxed after only a few minutes and our minds were free from all thoughts.

Here are a few tips on how to get out of the "Thinking Trap" (the more you train, the better it works):

Take a break, change your location and get some fresh air, distract yourself with activities and sport, self control, meditation techniques, relaxation training, talk about your problems and your thoughts with other people, write down your thoughts because you don't forget what you write down and it is sometimes important to remember things.

4.14) Social Competence:

At first this sounded quite complicated, but it really only means how friendly, polite and appreciative you are when you have contact with other people. This also affects situations of conflict (Problem solving group). In these situations it is more difficult to forget your emotions so that you can deal with the problem/conflict in a targeted way.

Coincidentally, the therapist was the same person who had led a part of the creative group and had given me the tip about canvas frames. I found her to be very sharp and showed us, with the help of small role-plays, how to avoid or fend off daily tension, misunderstandings or insecurities. At first I didn't think that this would help, but I was very wrong.

The most important questions that were dealt with were:

What is the goal? How can we achieve it? What are the conditions? What could happen? What tools do we have at our disposal? Is it realistic? Etc.

It's not easy to approach difficult discussions or conflict resolutions when all you have are arguments. Everyone should be able to save face and never go home feeling like the "loser". If that happens, then that person might not be completely motivated the next time round. Sometimes it's all about the everyday things like telling the other person that you are in a bad mood and taking every little thing with a pinch of salt. You should be able to concede a point now and again and not always have to have the last word. You should be able to admit your mistakes and apologize for them. You should also be able to accept apologies and not continually talk about what had happened (I knew it, but nobody ever listens to me) etc.

In the social competency seminar, we did so many role-plays of different situations to practice how to deal with each other in various situations or simply how to be friendlier in daily life, to be thankful, to smile more often or to say sorry.

Is this just something for wimps? No, absolutely not. I once tried to greet strangers on the street. 70% responded to it. That shows that all you have to do is try. Of course I don't walk through the streets every day greeting the whole world, but it was an interesting experiment.

And who normally refuses to accept an apology when someone has messed up? It can happen to everyone after all.

A good mood and friendly gestures can motivate those around you and you will also get positive feedback in return.

Why is it that some relationships work and others don't? The first impression is often something like looks, outfit, money etc. It's normal to do this and for some reason there is a spark at this point. Whether this will lead to a fire or not will be decided by how both sides work with each other on the points I discussed above. If there is no appreciation etc., then the bank account can be as full and the figure as curvy as you like, but the relationship won't last.

The same theory can be used when discussing bringing up children. At least that's what we discovered.

Humor is also very important. Using humor is a good way to get a lot across to the other side without making them feel like they have been pushed into a corner. You shouldn't take everything deadly seriously. Brush some things aside if it isn't too important. Everybody has a bad day now and again.

I've been doing my job for almost 25 years and have worked on around 200 projects. That includes warehouses and conveyance systems (new builds as well of rebuilds of systems already in operation). In the 5 previous companies, the focus was on the technical system planning, creating offers and executing them for the customer. These days, I still do the planning, but I also play the role of a customer in my department. In my experience, 30-40% of a successfully functioning and on time system is dependent on constructive cooperation and open communication with our partners during the entire project. They of course, have to be able to communicate well with us! How you treat each other when a problem arises or there are difficulties is decisive. In this respect, social competence plays a very important role.

I have seen various warehouses in different industries and have also planned production process systems. This involves taking measurements, having meetings and doing inspections on site in order to note down the customer's demands and any special local conditions.

When I did warehouse inspections for a previous company, it was relatively easy for me to see or sense the lie of the land because of how the employees behaved. Discussions would often become very tough if a department or warehouse manager marched through the warehouse. Some of the employees would become very hectic and nervous while others would be relieved that they were out of the line of fire. It would also be difficult to get some information because it would often have to be clarified who was responsible for what and if that was still the current situation. This also meant that cooperation was pretty difficult once the building work had started.

I had a very positive experience working on a particular project because every department, from the manager to the caretaker, (even when the project was delayed) was excellent. From the moment we first walked through the warehouse, there was a very relaxed atmosphere and the manager greeted his employees.

"There is a very strong feeling of being part of a family in our company. A lot of our employees have been here for 20 years or more and we are proud of that" I was told.

"I've sometimes heard the argument from other people I do projects with that older employees are not as flexible, are slower and more expensive," I responded.

The response surprised me: "Most people want to work. They spend about 50-60% of their time doing it every day. That means that they want to do something meaningful, something enjoyable, something that makes them complete, something productive, but where you can also have fun. That's the task of someone in a management position – to recognize the skills of the employees and then to put them in a position, which will bring the most benefits for the company in the long-term. This includes being friendly, cooperative and constructive with each other. Recognition and appreciation play a big role. If everything comes together and the employee feels good, then there isn't really any need for any more motivation. This comes automatically. Of course the salary always plays a part in increasing motivation, but if none of the other factors are right, then the salary won't make up for it. I save a lot of money because the employees don't put such a high value on the salary they earn. It's very difficult to measure the experience of an employee who has been here for many years. It depends a lot on what exactly the employee is doing and what qualifications he or she has. The more complex and broad the area of responsibility, the more important experience becomes. An employee who needs twice the amount of time to complete a project, but can do so without making any mistakes is more productive than one who needs half the time, but has to do 3 times as much rework because he didn't have the experience, and so made mistakes in the development stage. These mistakes could result in follow-up costs."

Despite the complexities and all of the building work that had to be done while the system was still in operation, the project ran very well. Every problem, question or piece of information was dealt with promptly. Everyone knew who was responsible for what, there were short decision making processes and every employee had sole responsibility for his or her own tasks.

It's important to understand that pastoral care should also be considered – being able to listen when there are problems, taking someone seriously, comforting people in times of mourning (at my age, this is happening more and more often. The hits just keep on coming. That's life I suppose.) etc. Social competence extends to all areas of life.

<u>4.15) General health care behavior:</u>

I'll sum this up for my personal situation:

I am no top athlete, but if I hadn't had a basic level of fitness, had consumed too much alcohol, coke, coffee or nicotine, I might not have survived the 23.11.2011 without some physical damage if I had survived at all.

In my view, the advantage I had in terms of my health at the time of my burnout was that I was able to recognize the signals of tiredness, exhaustion etc. my body was giving me. As a result, and also because I hadn't tried to give myself a boost by drinking too much coffee, Coke or Red Bull, I didn't spend too much time in the danger zone. This meant I could physically regenerate in a relatively short period of time. My GP told me "physically, no damage had been done."

Everybody knows about coffee and beer and the question "How much can you handle?" I've tried to illustrate the habituation effect and the resulting vicious circle in the following 2 diagrams. I'm sure there are better scientific explanations and maybe the terms I've used are too simple, but I think it's enough for this situation.

The strain/performance the body has to undergo/achieve during the day can be balanced out again at night or during breaks. This is what happens to the body when playing sport. The body can regenerate quickly or slowly, depending on the person. Everybody has his/her individual "balance", which can also be trained. We all know that poor bakers always have to get up very early in the morning so that we have freshly baked bread. They need to train themselves to do this over time.

The following picture shows a normal situation when everything is OK. The relaxation phase at night balances out the stresses of the day:

Regeneration by Pauses or Sleep (qualitative)

Normally the space inside the curves is equal. The regeneration phase compensates the stress and tautness during the day. The duration may be different, when sleeping phase may be more intensive. (good deep sleep).

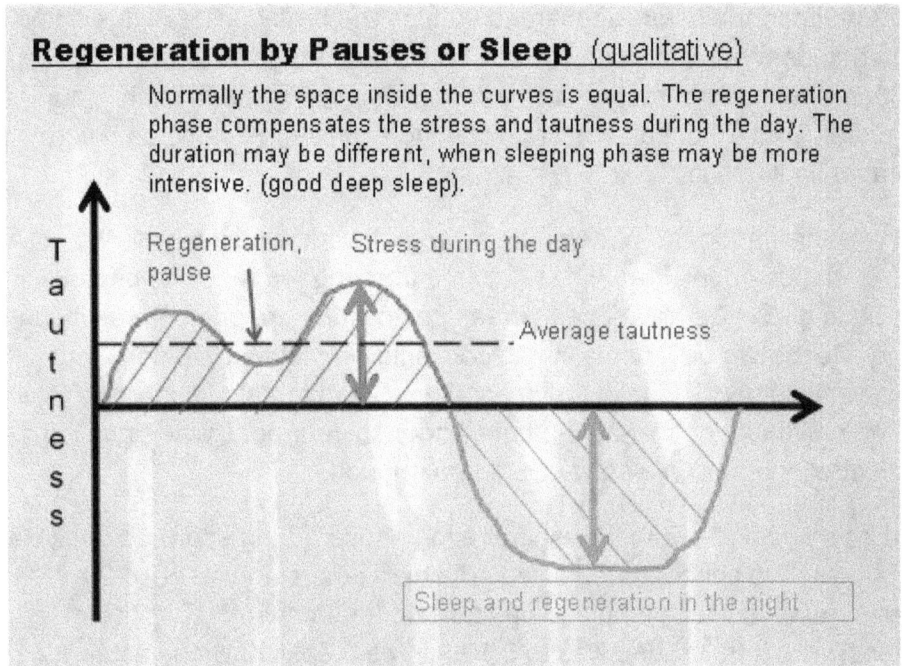

The following shows how the body is pushed to perform with caffeine or nicotine even though it is signalling the need for a break through tiredness:

Impact of Caffeine on Regeneration (qualitative)

Shifting of regeneration level by caffeine / nicotine etc.
Body tries to balance that out=> Habituation => more caffeine needed for same performance

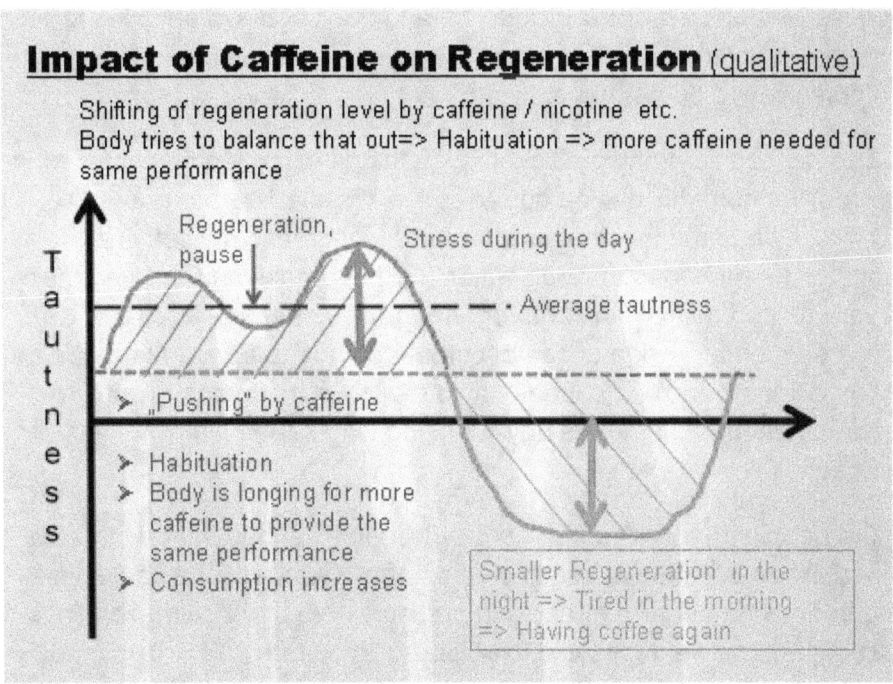

There is no opportunity for regeneration during the break. Instead, the body is pushed to perform at the same levels as before. It tries to balance out the stress because it has to recover somehow. The result is habituation. You need a "starter dose" of caffeine or nicotine to achieve the same as before => spiral of habituation.

And why is this important? When we get tired at work, we simply drink a coffee. Everybody does that. It has to come from a good machine because it should taste good. We have one at breakfast to wake up, one before lunch and one after eating because all the blood is flowing to your stomach and you feel very sleepy. Then you have another at 4pm to help you through the afternoon and then you've had 4-5 cups although your body was signaling that it needed a break. We don't give it one, though.

It could be so easy: As with the regeneration phase during sport, it's possible to train yourself to concentrate at work. Maybe at the start you need 20 minutes to relax, but with training you could get that down to 10 minutes. Why don't we just treat ourselves to 3 10-minute breaks now and again? That could be a short walk in the fresh air to completely refresh ourselves so that we don't go home in the evening absolutely exhausted, but wake up the next morning feeling like new. We all know about this. Every doctor tells us about it and it's also written about in all magazines, so why don't we do it? It's because we think we aren't productive and don't achieve anything in these breaks. It could be that we actually achieve more because we tare training ourselves to be permanently fit.

I have also noticed something else. I think 2 things can often be confused. If we are tired, we normally drink a cup of coffee because it's a pick me up, and it works. Due to the fact that I can't afford to increase my caffeine consumption, I switched to drinking water. Taking breaks and drinking the water really helped me to relax and regenerate. It's often the case that we don't drink enough at work and can become tired due to dehydration. We try and improve this by drinking coffee only to realize in the evening that we haven't drunk enough during the day. Drinking water seems to work very well for me.

I know 3-4 people in my circle of friends whose lives ended after a stroke or bypass operation because of constricted coronary arteries. The cause was smoking or drinking but also stress and pressure. We all know these things, but most of the time we don't want to believe it to be true. We will have to pay the penalty that's for sure. My father was a chain-smoker. My aunt smoked and I know people, who can't get through a day without drinking. The risks become greater when you are 50 or over, but the quality of life we enjoy rapidly decreases as well. My neighbor ran a marathon at the age of 60. Today he is 72. It's amazing what he can still do while others of the same age are already using a walker. That's at least 15 years of a more active and healthy life.

I drink 1-2 beers now and again, but I don't drink to try and sleep anymore.

So, what is the definition of "health"? (WHO):

"Health is a state of complete physical, mental and social well-being and not merely the absence of disease or infirmity."

That means that mental health is also important.

Briefly summarized and according to my understanding.

The basis for good health is a balanced diet, regular endurance sport (3 times a week for at least 30 minutes so that you are sweating and out of breath. Continuous exercise is better than one off training), strengthening your heart, improving circulation and increasing heart and lung capacities. Improving stamina and resilience, strengthening the immune system and metabolism leads to an increased production of positive hormones and then to an improvement in your psychological well-being.

It's important to consider your "conscious behavior or experience of situations or actions". If I can concentrate on something or do something consciously, then it will be much more successful than if I'm distracted or I'm jumping between different tasks. If you are doing something important, everything else should be set to one side so that you aren't disturbed. It's the same situation as when in a meeting. You should turn your mobile phone off there, just as you would in the cinema.....

Why think about it any longer? There isn't a better alternative. Maybe I'll be able to do another half marathon. At the very least I'll cycle the 10km to work everyday instead of taking the car. It'll be a good start, it'll do me good and I will be able to save some fuel for my daughter....

4.16) The creative area. Painting my Triptych at home, pottery etc.

I had been at CB for about 5 weeks. Rehab had been extended thanks to that great knee infection because I hadn't been able to take part in any of the relaxation training such as tai chi or yoga. This was to stop me from moving my knee, which might have led to the infection spreading.

Everything seemed to be better by this point though and the physical therapy for my knee was progressing well, but I've already written about that.

I could also take part in the creative group again. While I had been holed up in my room, unable to move very far, I had painted like there was no tomorrow. Mickey Mouse, Donald Duck, Daisy Duck etc. etc. This is something that is normally forbidden, but because I couldn't really do anything else, the ladies turned a blind eye. By the end of this period I had about 20 Disney portraits – some for my own family, but most were for when other patients, who I had gotten to know, left. It took around 3.5 hours to finish a 30 x 40 cm picture of Daisy.

What was interesting was despite concentrating on the painting, my mind was able to be free of any stress. That was new for me. In the past, concentrating on something had always meant feeling very tense. I continued to train that and provided CB with the pictures, if they wanted them or not.

I had an idea 2 weeks before the end of my stay: 15 years ago I had painted a motive of 22 Disney characters on the side of the garage for the children (Ok, I admit it. I had enjoyed doing it!) I had suggested to my therapist that we could use this as some kind of group work. (Originally, the painting had been put together from 8 covers of a weekly magazine). "Do you think you can do it?"

"I'll give it a go. It can't go so wrong."

"How do you want to organize this?"

I explained the story above.

I had begun to notice that I was getting better at being able to "switch off". I just had to think about something else, but not about going to back to work, home or the problems with the church renovation. I just had to draw a line under it all, listen to a relaxing CD and nothing else. It did me a lot of good and I knew that I would carry on doing the same when I got home. (And I did! I painted another 4 pictures for a birthday, move, wedding and a good friend.)

I always put the frames out in the corridor in front of the door to my room so that they would dry. Those people who were on the same corridor as me always took a look at them on their way to the canteen and gave their opinions.

In the end, I finished the picture by myself. That was OK by me though. The most important thing was that I tried to see this "project" through. It didn't matter if it was completely finished in time or if there were 1, 2 or 3 pictures in the end. It was only important that there was something I could work on, that I believed in myself and that Amy cooperated.

Amy DID cooperate and it was as if she was pleased with how the picture slowly came together. The picture was finished on the second last day in rehab. All 3 of them were finished. It was definitely a great feeling of success. Something totally different – no conveyor system, no technical commissioning, no renovation or rebuild. I was really pleased. My therapist thought I should take it to the farewell meeting the following morning. I wasn't sure about that, but most people had already seen it in the corridor anyway.

"I have another question. What are you going to do with the pictures? How are you going to get them home?"

"Hmm. Yes, that's a good question. I hadn't really thought about what I was going to do with them. Could you use them to decorate the rooms in the clinic?"

"No, sorry. The room decoration is strictly controlled."

Fortunately, I found a solution in the morning meeting the next day.

Most people thought the pictures were fun and thought it was nice that I had managed to finish them at the last minute (there were some parallels to my projects at work here!) One woman said: "They are great for kids. What about giving them to a kindergarten or the children's cancer hospital in Chemnitz?" That was exactly it. Bulls eye! The children's hospital! It couldn't have been more perfect. I thanked her 100 times for her suggestion. My therapist said that she was prepared to get in touch with the director of the hospital to ask if they were interested and, if they were, to hand over the pictures. She said she would keep me updated by mail.

Everything worked out well in the end. The director of the hospital thanked me for the pictures and now, there is a piece of me hanging in the children's hospital. At some point I'm sure they will be taken down when the room is renovated, but I don't care about that. It was my first project and it had worked and that was all that mattered!

A project leader had painted some Disney pictures because he couldn't do anything else and then they had ended up in a children's hospital. It's quite soppy really, isn't it? Like I said, I really couldn't care less. It helped me to switch off and hopefully the children are enjoying looking at them. Nothing else matters.

I also managed to build quite a nice Smurf house for my youngest daughter in the creative group. It became quite hard. Things like that are always hard because I can't really do delicate, but she was really happy to get something from her Dad in rehab.

4.17) Bio Feedback:

I registered for the "Bio Feedback" course. As before I went to my counselor to arrange an appointment after speaking to and getting the suggestion from my therapist. My counselor told me that she was running that course as well and we could start the next morning as I had some free time in my timetable. I asked what exactly the course was about. She told me I would see the next morning.

Around 10:30am the next day, I went to Bio Feedback:

"In Bio Feedback we can measure and determine how sensitive you are to external influences and perceptions and, in your case, how you react to mental pressures. Afterwards you will be able to test how well you can use the relaxation exercises and methods you have learned here." The counselor put some kind of cover over my middle finger on my left hand. In this cover were 3 sensors to measure blood pressure, pulse and skin resistance. We know the first 2 already, but what is skin resistance? This is how I understood the explanation: "The reading changes as soon as you feel some kind of stress and it is an indicator of the degree of the tension you are feeling. That's how we can measure your stress levels," she explained.

I sat comfortably in the Ikea seat and she turned on the monitor. All 3 readings were normal. Everything was fine. The scale, which showed tension levels, ranged from 0-10. 4 was the number where stress was being felt. I was registering at 0.5. "Mr. Dietrich you seem to be relaxed. Let's see what you are like under stress. "Frau Meier, why have the values jumped up like that? I can't feel anything and I'm just sitting here in my chair. Are you sure the sensors are correctly connected? Maybe there is a loose connection?" The values had jumped from 0.5-1.5 in about a second. How was that possible?

"No Mr. Dietrich. Everything is fine. Do you remember when that happened? I told you that I was going to put you under stress. This happens with most patients, who have been overworked. Just saying what is going to happen is enough to see some kind of reaction."

"Yes, but I can't feel anything."

"You can't consciously feel anything, but a release of adrenalin has already been triggered because your body is preparing to fight."

I understood. Amygdala had stepped in. She had control of me even though I hadn't noticed anything. I was ready to defend myself against an attacker or to run away. My reflexes were ready. The problem was I didn't need any of this. I was just sitting comfortably in my Ikea chair.

"Mr. Dietrich, looking at how the values changed, I would say that you normally have good reactions and reflexes."

"Yes, normally."

"You see, in the Fear Group, you discussed the part of the brain called Amygdala. In the wild you would be able to survive quite well because your warning system works very well. At the moment you are like a nervous Porsche driver - you are nervous about putting your foot on the gas too hard."

That was a technical description of the situation, but I understood what she meant. A Porsche? Wow. It means I never have to buy one if I am one myself. Even if I am one which goes too fast! That means being uncontrollable and hitting 200 km/h too fast. My GP had already said that some part of my "control system" wasn't working as it should. This seemed to be a clear technical description of a psychological diagnosis.

"So now that you know, let's start the test."

Some geometric shapes of various colors appeared on the screen, which seemed to fly at me. On the right side of the screen, the same shapes were organized together. On the left side were the colors. I was supposed to use the mouse to match the shapes to the colors. The shapes on the screen started to fly around more quickly depending on how fast I could work. My stress value climbed to 4, but it was only a question of concentration. There was absolutely nothing to fear here. I realized that I wouldn't be able to beat the computer, and so I thought up a strategy and let every second or third shape go by. As soon as I did that, I became more relaxed and by the end of the test, I had achieved an average score.

"You can see from the results that tension levels rose very quickly at the beginning, but after you had gotten used to what you were doing, they continued to drop. How did you do that? What normally happens is that the tension levels continue to rise until the patient can't take it anymore."

"I realized that I wouldn't be able to beat the computer, and so I relaxed."

"That's exactly what the results show. That means that at some point during the test, you tried to control the levels of stress you were experiencing. That's good. Let's carry on, shall we? I'm going to leave the room. I'll turn on some relaxing music and you should try to relax."

"OK." She turned on the music and left.

Right, so time to relax!

I tried the breathing techniques, breathing in deeply for 3 seconds and then back out, then in for 3 seconds. I had my relaxing picture in my mind, just like I had had before. I became calmer and my breathing became slower and steadier. I felt like a bird high up in a tree in the jungle, looking down on the animals below me. It was a wonderful feeling.

The door opened and I "woke up". "Mr. Dietrich, you are back down to 1. That's good."

It was then that I knew that I could do it.

That was one of the most important moments of the entire time in rehab. It was proof of how and why I react to stressful situations!

Most of the time, as in school, we had written up the contents of the course on the board and had then received some kind of handouts as a summary of what we had done. That was great because we didn't just get theoretical information, but we listened to the experiences of others in each of the courses. We saw that the results were real. We didn't have to search for the people to find out how they were because they were sitting right next to us. It was then also possible to talk to that person after the course had finished.

"Downhill" run:

After I had gotten over all the problems with the infection in my knee and had been given the all clear to do sports again, I needed to work on getting my knee back to full flexibility again. I couldn't bend it to 90° to start with, and so I did 20 knee bends and stretching exercises 3 times a day in my room until it became too painful. The doctor had said it would be OK because the infection had gone. I needed another week or so before my knee was almost completely better and I could play volleyball and jog again. It was after this that I got the important results from the Bio Feedback session. Suddenly I had hope again, just like it was when I had spoken with Amy. It didn't matter how long it would take. I was going to try again and again and again, but slowly so that Amy could keep up. I was a marathon runner. I knew how you had to prepare yourself in stages to reach your goal. (Even though I had collapsed during the second marathon, I had carried on). It might take 1 or 2 years or maybe longer, but it didn't matter. A friend had needed 4 years. It was only important that I got back to having some kind of normal life again.

We had a really beautiful warm day and I decided that I would pull on my running shoes and do a lap in the forest.

Everything was perfect. It wasn't too warm and there was a light breeze. I changed into my jogging clothes and went to fill in the Absence Book. Reason: Jogging. Where: In the forest. And off I went.

The area around the clinic was a little hilly and in some sections, you could really push yourself to your limits. One week before, another patient at the clinic had shown me a great route with wonderful views. The highest point was a tower with 180 steps and a 360° view. This was the perfect place to go in that weather. This was one of the most beautiful runs I had ever been on. This wasn't a competition; there were no other people, no one to chat with. I wasn't really in the best condition as I had been banned from doing any sport thanks to the infection, but I had found my self-confidence again a few days previously and this was a great feeling. I had a goal and now I had found a possible way to achieve it. It was great. Simply great. I felt good at that moment. I ran slowly up the hill. There was no rush, no time limit, and no pressure. I enjoyed every step up that hill. I could feel every tree root and stone under my shoes. I could taste all the drops of sweat that had fallen from my face onto my lips. I inhaled as much of the warm air into my lungs as possible. I had a break at the first viewpoint and took in the view with the rolling hills. I took a sip out of my water bottle, checked my pulse, but felt ready for the second climb up to the tower. My thighs were starting to burn slightly after 30 minutes of running uphill. As I said, I hadn't prepared at all. I was out of breath by the time I reached the tower. I had a breather and then tackled the 180 steps up the tower until the wonderful view reappeared. I probably spent about half an hour up there despite being soaked with sweat. I tried to save every element of the view in my mind – the forest, the wind turbines in the distance, the fields and the view of the clouds and the sky.

I started to make my way down and ran back to CB. Of course, the way back was downhill. Thank God it was downhill! I let myself go in the forest. My strides were getting longer. My lungs were working like a compressor and my legs were going full throttle. It was working again and it was great. I ran as fast as I could, as if someone was behind me, but nobody was there. I held out my arms and screamed in elation in the forest as loudly as I could. YESSSSSSSSS!!!!!!!! Once, twice, 5 times. I let it all out.

Before I fell over, I had to stop due to purely biological reasons. I had to slow down. 2 walkers looked at me a bit perplexed. They were probably wondering if I was the idiot, who had just been screaming in the forest as I was the next person to come past them. Things like that happen now and again near psychiatric clinics.

I was exhausted and happy. I showered and looked forward to dinner.

4.18) Relaxation Therapy:

Everything that we learned and practiced with regard to relaxation therapy in rehab was and still is the most important tool for me to control myself and keep myself emotionally stabile in stressful situations. Doing this meant that my breaking point rose just as it would during training for a run. I also noticed that I sometimes seemed to be able to react differently in certain situations than I had been before. Apparently you can also train that. Of course it depends if you can get your body and soul used to certain ways of behaving so that you can relax. Once the body has gotten used to connecting this kind of behavior to relaxation, then it becomes easier to behave in this particular way in everyday situations and then also relax. It shouldn't matter if you're standing on a train or at the station where there is a lot of hustle and bustle around.

If I'm in a "Thinking Trap" or I'm considering a problem, but I'm not making any progress and I suddenly realize that Amy is making herself known, 90% of the time I am able to switch off: slowing down my breathing and thinking of a relaxing image (e.g. beach or sunset) and then the thoughts stop. Immediately. It also works when I wake up in the middle of the night and I can't get back to sleep straight away. Slow down the breathing so that it's very slow but deep, breathing out, repeating the process until I fall asleep. It really works for me. I couldn't do it in the past. I was stuck in my thoughts about what I had to do the next day then I would check the alarm clock every 10 minutes hoping to see that the night was almost over.

I had always thought that it was rubbish. I was either tired and could sleep or I couldn't. Today I am happy that rehab taught me something different.

Standing up? How could you possibly do these relaxation exercises standing up? With tai chi! You have to slow down all your movements as well as your breathing, taking deep breaths in and out. During the reintegration phase, I managed to calm myself down just before a panic attack or hyperventilating around 5 times by doing tai chi in the relaxation room at work (Amy wasn't as good then as she is now). It doesn't matter if you can do the exercises perfectly or not. It's only important that the body gets used to this relaxing behavior. We learned this in rehab: it's like the dog you always feed when the alarm rings. In the end, the dog shows the same behavior when the alarm rings but there isn't any food. This will change again if you stop training, so it's important to keep at it!

This is also something you can learn by yourself.

We had a therapist who helped us with breathing exercises, who always read a text very slowly and quietly. She had such a calming voice that 50% of the group had fallen asleep half way through regardless of what we had been doing before.

You should try everything to see what suits you best: breathing exercises while lying down listening to relaxing music, tai chi, progressive muscle relaxation while lying or sitting (this is good practice if you have stress at work), yoga. The breathing exercises help me cope in most everyday situations and most people around me don't even realize I'm doing them. My basic tension levels are much lower than they were before, but I always have to train that because the maximum limit of stress I can deal with is also lower than it used to be.

Types of mental stress
(from my own experience and therefore not an exhaustive list):

Over the course of time, I have tried to find out what causes me mental stress, why this is the case and what I can do to prevent it from happening, or even what I can do if I am acutely affected.

As an engineer, it is easier for me to understand a process with the help of a model:

Thoughts are an energy-consuming process in which "new materials" have to be added and "used materials" are removed. The higher the "energy consumption", the more stressful the process. This is true of sports as well and, as with sports, it is possible to do some training (reduce "energy consumption", improve regeneration). It is not only the process that can be improved through careful training so as to not overload yourself, but also the regeneration phase as well. This all seems to be completely routine because we are used to it, but in this situation, the brain is working normally. What happens though, when the dishwasher becomes too much to deal with?

I was able to roughly differentiate between the various stressful situations during my burnout as follows:

1. Normal thinking: "What could possible be stressful about normal thinking? I do it every day. I am sometimes tired, but so what? After a short break and a cup of coffee, I can carry on."

Everybody has this attitude, but what I didn't know was that there could be situations when a normal conversation could be so exhausting that I had to have a lie down afterwards. This didn't help, though because I would have other thoughts running through my mind making it impossible to switch off meaning there was no chance of relaxation or recovery. I was getting up in the morning feeling as tired as when I'd gone to bed. It was also the case that I'd start thinking about things while gardening (which had always been a form of relaxation) and would become so mentally exhausted that I would have to go in and lie down.

This is Stress Level 0 in the acute burnout phase. How do I get myself out of this? Don't think about anything! How do I think about nothing?

How can I control my thoughts, empty my head, stop all the things racing through my mind like a policeman does with the traffic? This is something I learned during rehabilitation – to put the brakes on my thoughts. It's possible to influence certain processes within the body by learning how to control others.

Breathing and moving are examples of processes, which are very easy to consciously control. Slow and deep breathing as well as slow movements mean calm and relaxation. As already described, I simply breathe very deeply and as slowly as possible to stop the racing thoughts in my head meaning that the regeneration process can begin. This could be a short-term solution, but could still be enough to lead to a recovery phase if repeated. Doing this when I wake up early in the morning can mean I fall back to sleep or I can regenerate despite being awake.

The same is true of eating. Eat slowly. Chew slowly. Breathe slowly. Bring the spoon up to your mouth slowly....... We are normally so rushed when eating and we often talk a lot at the same time and that's fine if you have a normal level of resilience, but at Level 0, every period of relaxation is good for you.

2. Normal activities requiring concentration: This is my second category. Routine work that we often do, but normally to make sure that nothing goes wrong. This also includes part of our jobs. This is influenced by how well it is possible to concentrate or if there are constant interruptions thanks to the phone ringing or people asking questions etc. If necessary, I will simply take a short break, eat or drink something (not coffee!), get some fresh air at the window or take a short walk at lunchtime. This is also something that can be trained – fresh air => relaxation. Sport,

movement and taking the stairs instead of the lift leads to a better metabolism, which can help to "remove" any "wasteful thoughts" in your head. What's more, sport can help a person switch off.

3. New activities requiring concentration (In addition: Learning effect): This works in the same way as the second category, but there are times at work when I have all phone calls redirected to the secretaries. As a person gets older, they don't learn things as quickly as the used to. It's often necessary to repeat things until they become a part of our long-term memories. What normally happens is we try to do something using the "old method" because we have experience in this way and it is also quicker. The new method can be more difficult in the beginning. When I was at home with a lot of time on my hands before going to the Rehabilitation Clinic, I considered learning to play the piano. You know, only children's songs. My daughter, Sara, was immediately on board as she had had lessons herself. The difference between category 2 and 3 became quite clear at this point. Holding meetings in English is not as stressful as trying to play the piano for 20 minutes! Having to coordinate 2 hands, several fingers and one foot whilst trying to keep time and make it sound like it should required high levels of concentration leading to exhaustion. (I definitely won't be the next Lang Lang!) It was a disaster! When you type, you are also fast, but at least the letters are typed one after the other. When playing the piano, you have to be able to do 3 things all at once.

4. Making right or wrong decisions, consequences: The next level for me was decision making. A person has to be able to weigh up the arguments, decide what is good or bad, right or wrong, and consider the consequences of each course of action. When it comes to making a decision, there is a big difference compared to the stresses in categories 1-3: the stress here is caused by having to take responsibility if something goes wrong. It's at this point that fear becomes a factor in our subconscious. "What happens if.....? Hopefully it will turn out well." It depends what the decision is that has to be made. The longer you drag it out, the more unsure you become and the higher the stress levels become. So, plan your course of action, collect arguments, weigh them up, make a decision and document it for the future. This can be practiced: make a list of the pros and cons with a weighting for each point if you need to. Evaluate the consequences. This means you can make a decision to the best of your knowledge. If it is an important decision, you can also ask others for advice. If needs must, you have to be able to react accordingly. At the time the decision was made, it was the right thing to do. Of course hindsight is a beautiful thing.

5. Conflict situations (with rational solutions), group decisions: The next level for me is making decisions in a group. This is similar to number 4, but there are more parties with their own views and arguments and that makes everything more complex. The situation can be controlled if everything is presented rationally and there are good reasons for the arguments and everyone involved accepts other people's points-of-view and are happy to work together towards the common goal. It's possible to train for this situation in a similar way to number 4 by writing up a list of pros and cons etc. It is important to keep things professional and make sure that there is consensus among the group. If this works well (I recently had a very positive experience at work involving a very important and expensive decision) and the decision making process is well documented, it can be a relief later on because the stress isn't just on your own shoulders, but on everyone's in the group, who should also be working on the task with you anyway.

6. Emotional conflict situations (without rational solutions): This is the most difficult kind of stress for me to deal with. You just don't know how things are going to turn out. Who is going to give up on it all? Does everyone have the goal to reach a solution, which is good for the project or the task? Are the people only taking their own interests into account? (These questions can be put to most politicians as well). In this situation, fears about whether or not a project can be completed quickly grow. Frustration and fear come before a failure. I currently only have one method of dealing with this: create some kind of distance if it's possible. You should also try and document everything so that it is possible to see later on why no decision was made. The most important thing is not to let things affect you emotionally. I know that in most situations this is much easier said than done.

7. The frequency of the stress and time pressure play an important role in all situations. What do I do if I can't finish my tasks within the allotted time? Was the schedule realistic? Would I have been able to work/decide better if I had had the required time? Also in this situation it is important to document and communicate: at this time, I was able to clarify these points. Others are still ongoing. Disclose all arguments.

In the meantime I have managed to get to grips with all of these types of mental stress (apart from the last one. Sometimes I think I could still do......Never mind!). This means that I feel more secure and it reduces the stress levels and the feelings of insecurity felt before the next comparable situations. This is experience, but of course it depends on the situation. I understand that these things won't necessarily work for everybody. They are simply examples, which show how I tried to understand my situation and symptoms in order to come up with suitable strategies for dealing with them. I am sure you have your own experiences.

4.19) Social therapist: Reintegration:

I was positively surprised by the conversation I had with my social therapist. We had discussed the entire situation at work with my boss and my colleagues. I didn't have any problems in terms of contact and support. I was amazed by the frankness from the very beginning – could I imagine returning to my old job? If not, why not? And what about the next steps looking for an alternative? I had thought that our first try would be more like: How am I going to cope being back at the office? The way the first questions were put meant that we didn't feel under any pressure at all.

I had decided that the right way for me was to try and get back to my old job because the problem hadn't been there.

After I had made that decision, we discussed together how to proceed.

Together we created a plan for how the reintegration should work. After this had been done, I telephoned my boss because I wanted to discuss things with him first. The social therapist then formalized the rest of the details with him and the HR Department. She also advised on what we needed to be careful of during this time. This was especially important because there had to be intensive communication between the boss, HR and myself about the state of my health, the level of stress I could deal with and potential problems that could crop up. This should mean that we would be able to react immediately if something came up. After about 4 weeks, I suffered a black out and we were able to talk about it together and find a solution that was acceptable for both sides (See the chapter: Reintegration).

Half a year later in the same situation, I didn't experience any stress anymore. It had been better for me to take my time instead of forcing myself too early into something I wasn't ready for. I later worked on the project, which had caused the problems, but managed to do the complete layout planning and budgeting (with the help of a younger colleague due to time pressure) as well as I had been able to do before my burnout. That was a damn good feeling: I could do it! There hadn't been a huge amount of time pressure, but I had managed to overcome another hurdle.

The therapist advised me to have my potential degree of disability formally checked out after giving me my previous files and final report from the clinic.

<u>4.20) Group therapy:</u>

Why was group therapy so important for me compared to the one-on-one conversations or those with my therapist at home?

- You aren't on your own with your problems in group therapy. There are other people with similar situations. You aren't isolated.

- You open up to the people. You don't let things eat you up.

- All participants sign a confidentiality agreement, so there is no risk that anything will leak out. The group is like a sealed room.

- Everything you hear isn't from a third person. It's authentic, including all the emotions that come up. Everything is "real".

- It is emotional. You can get everything out and it is deep. Very deep. This way, you can get to the root of the problem.

- You realize that other people feel the same way as you and maybe they are even worse.

- You build relationships with others and you can help each other.

- You aren't afraid about being isolated when you go back home.

- You can deal with the situation and your problems much better.

- You can get ideas about different approaches from other people and the therapists on how to get out of the hole.

- The whole situation can hurt a lot, but not only those who are directly affected. It happened more than once that a large part of the group were unable to know what to do next. Me too. Tears flowed freely and some of them were mine. All pieces of advice we were given had some kind of a positive effect or led to a light-bulb moment.

There were usually 6-10 patients in group therapy who had different clinical symptoms. Normally, 2 or 3 of them were similar. A therapist led the group and also acted as the compere. Everything that was said in the group was strictly confidential. Nobody said anything about what was said when outside the door. The group only changed if new patients were admitted or others were discharged from the clinic. We always decided on what the topic of the session would be ourselves. The condition of one of the members of the group would always be talked about. The person being talked about would talk about their situation, background, and feelings and describe their problem. It's hard. Really hard. You out yourself as much as you can. This sometimes ends in tears and emotional outbursts.

The group discusses the problem and you discuss it with them. You are suddenly in the middle of your own world of problems, which you often try and push to the back of your mind and that is difficult. You are confronted with questions, which basically turn your life upside down. You have to set new priorities and give up on some things, which had always been important to you. You have to learn to limit yourself to the essentials because everything else has become too much. As I said before, it's very hard.

Example of father's suicide threat:

I have an example I can't get out of my head anymore. Strangely this has nothing to do with burnout, but the consequence of trying to distance yourself from responsibility you can't handle anymore. It's also about the consequences of saying NO when you can't cope anymore before you start suffering.

One of the patients, who had his own family, had been supporting his father financially for many years. The father then passed the money on to his wife because he felt guilty for having an affair. The mother had no idea where the money was really coming from. She had assumed it was from her husband, and so she spent the money on pointless things to try and make up for his cheating. The patient couldn't really afford these payments and his father threatened suicide. He had already tried to take his own life 9 times. That pushed the patient over the edge. He didn't know what he should do. His family was suffering, but he didn't want to let his father down and be responsible for his suicide. After explaining his situation, he broke down in tears.

Some of the rest of us in the group were also in tears. I was speechless. This wasn't a film. Nothing was being acted out. It was real life. This sucked! We were all at a loss as to what to say. What do you say to someone in that situation? Simple kindness just wasn't going to cut it.

We tried to give some advice and also analyzed the relationship between father, mother and son and suggested that all 3 sit down together and talk about it as the mother still didn't know what was going on. We also discussed numerous ways of how the conversation should unfold so that the topic could be broached cautiously. It was all helpful, but somehow it didn't really get to the heart of the problem. We were just beating around the bush. Nobody could think of a really good solution.

Suddenly the therapist thought she would add to the conversation:

"You could hand the responsibility for your father's life back to him. It's important for your health and for your family's future. Your father is an adult and he has to take responsibility for himself. He is healthy and of sound mind. It's not your responsibility or your fault. Hand back the responsibility regardless of what he threatens to do. If he really wants to take his own life then he will find a way to do it and you won't be able to stop it."

There was deadly silence. A fly buzzed around the room without any knowledge of what was being discussed. We were speechless again, but this time because we were in shock.

What had the therapist just said? Basically he had told him to let his father do what he wanted. If he wanted to kill himself, then that would be his own problem.

The problem is, this was his father and he was going to feel guilty if something happened, and the therapist just said, hey let your Dad do what he wants. He's a grown up so why should you worry about it.

Had the therapist gone completely mad?

He had coolly analyzed what was happening and set priorities with one goal in mind: he wanted to help the patient out of his desperate situation while we had become entangled in our own emotions.

The heart of the problem was this:

The father needed help. The patient had given him what he could and since then the father had used him and put him under pressure. He had threatened suicide. He wanted to pass the buck for his bad behavior and its consequences onto his son.

Now the son couldn't afford to help anymore without there being consequences for him. A limit had been reached. You can only give as long as you have something to give. What's more, the father wasn't actually acting like a father to his son.

In this situation, you need to be strict and say: "I can't do it anymore. You have to take responsibility for yourself. I've helped as much as I can and now it's up to you."

If you take away all the emotions and the family relationships, it's actually quite easy, but you need to be in that frame of mind first to be able to see it in that way. I can't imagine being strong enough to be able to do that if the 10th attempted suicide was successful.

But what has all this got to do with me?

It's quite easy: if you have reached your limit taking care of someone else, then you should make them take care of themselves again. It is their own responsibility after all! So why can't the same thing be possible for me at work? You know, postpone a project now and again, cancel an appointment or not take on a project at all because I feel I won't be able to cope with it. It has nothing to do with making excuses or not having any motivation to do it. I want to do my job well, but there are also limits and the best person to know what they are is you. It's OK to tell people what those limits are as well. If you know your limits then you can act more responsibly than if you tell yourself you can do something and then you mess up the project. If you say no, then it is the responsibility of the manager to find a solution. Maybe the project can be shared between 2 people or it really does have to be postponed. If your own health is suffering as a result of the pressure and you fail in your job, the results can be much worse and also more expensive. This has nothing to do with any kind of weakness. On the contrary, it's all about acting responsibly. It could be that an employee exploits the situation so that he or she only has to work at 50%, but the manger should notice that. He should also know which of his employees he can trust. Trust goes both ways and the results should be the best for the long-term.

I was starting to realize that there are people, who were in more trouble than I was. This was also a good insight.

We asked the therapist:

"How can you stay so clear headed and analytical in these emotionally difficult cases?"

"I listen very closely to the patients. I try to put myself in their situation and to empathize with them, but I have to try and keep some kind of distance so that I don't suffer emotionally in the same way as the patient does. If I did that, I wouldn't be able to evaluate, judge or advise on the situation professionally."

This and the sentence that you can hand responsibility back for things you can no longer cope with (or simply, say "no"!) were two of the most important things I took with me when I left the clinic.

Sudden cardiac arrest. ATS-example:

Another member of the group therapy told us this story:

"I had taken a day off because I'd had so much to do and I needed to take a break. I was at home and my wife went to work in the morning. I had planned to have a quiet day doing some work in the garden etc. My 2 daughters, who are 16 and 19, were at home that day because one of them had had classes cancelled and the other had had her boyfriend stay the night at ours the day before. On any other morning I would've been alone at home.

After breakfast I went out onto the terrace. All I remember is that I wanted to open the door, but I suddenly felt this stabbing pain near my heart. I lost consciousness and fell backwards. By chance, my youngest daughter heard the fall on her way back to her room from the bathroom. She came downstairs and saw me lying on the floor and screamed to her sister and the boyfriend. She could see that I wasn't breathing and she registered that I didn't have a pulse. I owe my life to the professional, logical and clear actions of my children. My eldest daughter and her boyfriend immediately started heart massage and mouth-to-mouth resuscitation. They had learned it not long before for their driver's license. My youngest called the ambulance and calmly explained the situation. Thankfully, there was an ambulance in the area and it was there within 10 minutes. The paramedics saw exactly the extent of the problem and used the defibrillator to shock me back to life. My heart began to beat again, but irregularly and with fibrillation. I remained unconscious and, once I got to the hospital, they decided to keep me sedated to let my body cool to 32°C so that my brain would be able to recover better. At that point it wasn't clear how long it had been starved of oxygen. I woke up one week later in a state of confusion, but it wasn't long before I could remember things again.

Diagnosis: ATS-Syndrome, sudden cardiac arrest. Cause: Unknown. Treatment: Automatic defibrillator implant, which I'll need for the rest of my life. It will fire up my heart every time it needs to.

I now have the defibrillator inside me just under my arm. It took some getting used to and it reminds me every day about what happened.

I can't stop worrying that something like that is going to happen again. The thought that I was actually dead has changed me. I just can't get over it"

Everyone was speechless. That must be a really strange feeling to know you were clinically dead. What would Amygdala think about being in a coma for a week?

Of course the guy was pleased that he was alive and he is incredibly grateful to his children and doctors, but the fear remained.

I seemed to be in relatively good shape compared to him. He definitely was much worse off.

4.21) Burnout Situation, - Social Network + Diagram:

During our group work, we had discussed the topic of burnout and had a look at the daily demands an average person has to deal with. Nowadays, if you think that the person lives in a normal family with 1 or 2 children, that means that the parents have a lot of tasks, expectations and social events to have to cope with.

You and I are in the middle of everything. Then there is the partner to consider. Of course, both people then have a profession. Most of the time, both people have to/want to work. This means 8 hours of the day is taken up in the office and you have responsibilities. Even at home and when you are out and about, you can now be contacted via per email, telephone and also pricvtely via Facebook.

You also have a circle of friends. Sometimes the friends of you and your partner aren't the same because of being members of different clubs etc. That expands the whole group. On top of this, you also have hobbies. With time, the little family grows with 1 or 2 children and it might be nice to have a pet as well, right? When the kids grow up, they'll need to be taken care off in terms of homework. Most children then have their leisure activities, which you have to drive them to until they are old enough to do it themselves. If you are good then you probably have some kind of volunteer post in a sports club, at church, with the fire brigade etc. But we have forgotten the relatives in all of this – grandparents, siblings etc. They also want to hear something about their lovely grandchildren now and again.

This things gradually increase as the years go on and suddenly you hit 40 and you are caught in a web of jobs, responsibilities, expectations, appointments and your life is dictated by your appointments diary. "We should try and meet with some friends again. Yes, OK. I have 3 hours free on Saturday in 6 weeks. That would work." You rush around to get to your appointments, but if something goes wrong and something takes twice as long as expected, your schedule for everything else is knocked out of kilter and then the stress begins.

And every year, out of the blue, completely unexpected comes Christmas! Then it really starts to get fun.

Sometimes when your parents reach a certain age, you need to start taking care of them and then the emotional and psychological burden doubles for an unlimited time.

At some point we seriously ask ourselves why we suddenly can't take it anymore after having managed for so many years. This situation, however, can be predicted and is unavoidable if you don't reduce the workload, change your priorities or share/delegate jobs (if possible) in good time.

It's like driving a car. If you always drive at top speed, at some point around 60-70,000km you will ruin the car (at least the engine). If you drove more slowly, then you could manage 200-250,000km. So, what's your goal?

Another example would be the gas balloon. You've worked hard on lots of things and you've been trying to transport as much as possible with your balloon. Now you've hit a storm (your burnout) and you've lost some of the gas you needed to carry everything. So what do you do? You throw out unnecessary ballast so that you can get to your destination with only the most important pieces of luggage. It's easy really. If you don't do that, you'll crash land and you won't be able to get off the ground again.

In the end we were surprised what was written in the diagram on the wall, that you can see on the next page:

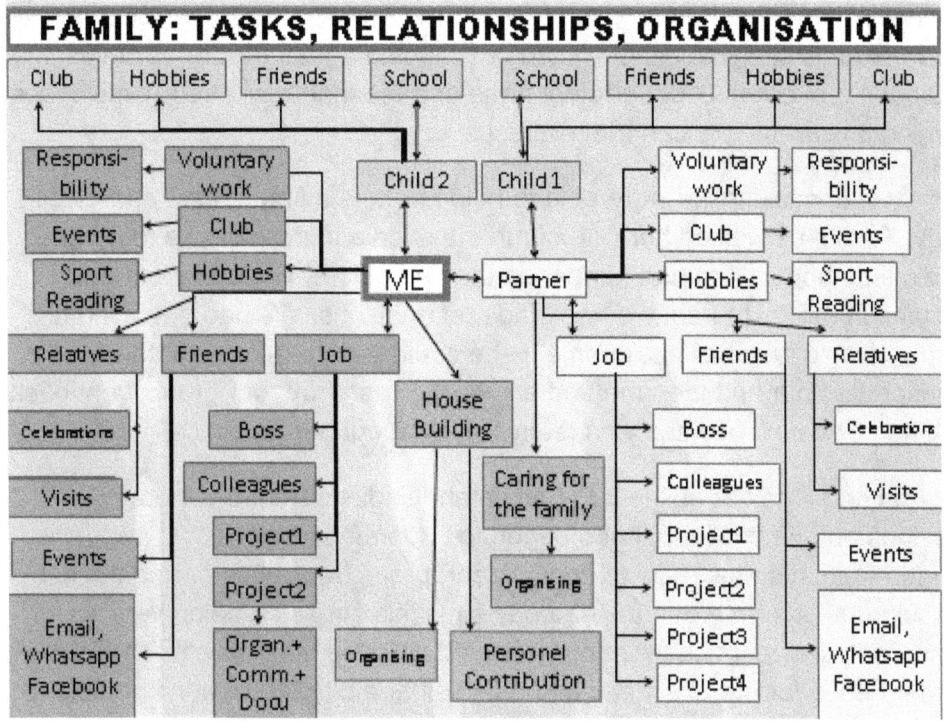

FAMILY: TASKS, RELATIONSHIPS, ORGANISATION

Another example of a woman in her mid 40s:

This woman had a leadership position in her company. She was responsible for around 250 employees and had been working more and more over the previous 10 years. This also meant working at weekends. She devoted herself so much to her work until her body and nerves couldn't take it anymore. She had a breakdown. She could talk to you and you would think that everything was completely fine, but it wasn't easy for her to talk about her situation. Everyday topics of conversation were absolutely fine. By the time she got to rehab, she was afraid of doing anything. Her "safety system" had kicked in permanently due to the huge level of stress. Her situation was similar to mine, but a level higher. She couldn't drive anymore, she didn't like to go out on the street by herself, and she never went out for a drink anymore. She spent most of her time in the clinic. I found out later that the first 2 weeks of her stay this time were spent solely in her bedroom, the dining room and group rooms, but she was never alone. She had to be with someone in case something happened. I could see a lot of parallels between her situation and mine, but like I said, hers was more extreme. At least I could still mix with other people. Her husband brought her to the clinic and at the weekends she was either visited or collected again. Before all of this she had been a successful department head and the manager of 250 employees earning 6 figures! This can really affect everyone.

With a lot of coaxing we were able to help her take a first step at a farewell party. Two of us walked her with her in the middle and we spoke to her the whole time about what had happened the day before. We arrived after 20 minutes at the restaurant we had made reservations. We had promised her that we would take her back home if she could last 15 minutes with us. She managed 1 hour and then me and another woman from our group went back with her. The next day she was really happy about her "success."

After putting together all the information and findings from the therapy sessions and Fear Group, I had begun to understand that both my and this woman's situation had a lot to do with fear, protective behavior and the sub-conscious. For some reason, the body sees this stress as being very dangerous and responds with our inherited defense mechanism. The consequence for me was that I found myself afraid that I wouldn't be able to do what I needed to. I had no idea about the defense mechanism, the adrenalin from Amy and the sympathetic nervous system, and so everything built up to an increase in adrenalin, hyperventilation and heart problems. My protection system had "recognized" this and had tried to avoid all further stressful situations and this meant kicking in even when doing small tasks. This happened subconsciously in my case and couldn't be controlled to start with. In such situations, the best way forward was to work on it in small steps and with lots of patience. If Amy reacts, then I have to be able to control her or use up the energy produced by her colleague Mr. Sympathetic Nervous System until he doesn't have any motivation to recklessly produce adrenalin.

This is how I started my time in rehab – at my lowest point and I was going to stay working on myself for as long as necessary.

My therapist at home had told me that it depended what had happened before the burnout. It depended how bad the breakdown was, how much you could achieve later on.

This was going to be my own personal marathon. I was going to be running it **almost** completely alone. There would be a lot of friends standing on the sidelines cheering me on, but I was the one who had to run. Time wasn't a factor, but the goal was.

That meant the following for me:

Complete training and practicing of all possible relaxation methods, especially those I can use during meetings and which can be practiced in any situation.

You need the courage to continue to take small steps every day. Patience is also necessary. A lot of patience and that needs time. I needed to discipline myself to do things by the book, not to do too much and to say "no". In an emergency I would have to learn to take a step back if I needed to. I didn't want to let myself be emotionally provoked.

It was important to remember where I had come from, how low I had been and who I had gotten to know.

I also needed to be thankful for the second chance and the tools I had been given to make my future better.

I had recognized that nothing is more important than my health and that it shouldn't be taken for granted.

We need to learn to enjoy the small things in life so that we can significantly increase the number of happy moments in our lives.

In order to get through everything, I needed to be physically fit. The first reason for that is that then everything would be easier. Secondly, sport increases the levels of the happiness hormone and thirdly, I would be better prepared for an emergency should things not go to plan so that I would be better able to come through the other side.

Group therapy was sometimes really brutal. You could also see how the others were doing. Suddenly, you don't feel like the outsider, who has let the side down. There were so many others still on the waiting list for therapy. Wow.

Another example: Heiner (Name has been changed):

"I don't know what I'm doing here. It's not doing anything for me. I'm only here because my doctor recommended it. I would much prefer to go home tomorrow. Oh yes, my name is Heiner." This was the gist of what Heiner said when he introduced himself during the morning meeting. Heiner was just about to retire, wasn't motivated to do anything and thought that everything was shit or pointless.

Despite that, Heiner seemed to be a very nice guy if he was talking about something he liked or something he had done previously in his life. Most of the time however, he came across as being very depressed. "Nothing can help me anyway," Most of the time, he sat by himself. Even at lunch he would read a book or newspaper and didn't want to be disturbed. Once we did the creative group together. We were working in a group of 3. We had to agree on a topic and then paint a picture, which we would then have to present to the other groups. This seemed to be a simple task. The problem was that Heiner and the woman in our group couldn't stand each other. It was only about 2 minutes before they were at loggerheads and she started with " You're getting on my nerves with your constant complaining." I had reckoned with 4 minutes.

These weren't really the ideal conditions for group work and painting a picture together. We hadn't even agreed on a topic when the other groups were already getting out the brushes and paints. For some reason, I was still in a good mood on this day.

"Right, listen to me. I have a suggestion: either we go to the therapist and tell her that we can't do this picture together because we prefer to argue with each other instead of doing something productive, or we pull ourselves together and just paint some kind of picture. I don't really care."

Silence

Heiner; "OK. Fine. Let's paint something." The woman: "I don't mind." "Does anyone have an idea about the topic?" I asked. "No", was the answer. "Ok. Well, I have one: A beautiful day. Great, isn't it?" For some reason I was enjoying provoking them. "I don't really think so," said Heiner. "Do you have a better idea?" "No." "Fine, then we'll divide the picture into 3 parts. Who wants to do the top, the middle and the bottom part?" And then we started. Each of us painted our part in silence. I dealt with the river and the meadow. I couldn't really do much more than children's paintings and Disney figures. I don't really have any talent for it. My skills hadn't really developed since kindergarten. The woman had taken the part above the meadow and Heiner bustled around with his ideas of what to put in the meadow and river. He was still quiet. "What are you painting in the river, Heiner?" I asked. "They are flying fish. I always find it funny when I see the fish jumping in the lake or river near my house." Wow! He'd become quite chatty! The woman had painted butterflies and a sun on the paper along with a blue sky. It all fit really well to the topic. Heiner was inspired by the butterflies saying that they were nice and bright and that he liked them, and so painted 2 ladybugs. The picture was finished within the allotted time. It wasn't a van Gogh, but that wasn't the point. The goal had been to work together in a group.

I don't know what Heiner talked about in his one-on-one conversations with the therapist and we weren't together in group therapy because our clinical symptoms were not the same. One morning he spoke to me after the morning meeting and said word for word: "My wife deserves a medal after having to deal with this sourpuss." I grinned slightly to myself and told him: "You should tell her that yourself. Exactly that sentence. I think she would like to hear it." "Do you think?" "Yes, I do." He did and thankfully I had correctly judged his wife.

"Thanks for the tip. We had a really good talk especially after the therapist made a few things clear for me. I was such an asshole."

Heiner developed a very sharp humor often sprinkled with a good dose of irony. We started to get along with each other much better. When he said goodbye in the morning meeting 3 weeks later, he had even made us all a card with a few nice words written inside. I don't think he would've thought that possible 3 weeks beforehand.

Why am I telling you this?

It doesn't have anything to do with burnout, but with how people can change if they want to and if they have the support they need to realize what needs to be done. Heiner had taken a big step for himself and his wife. I think that some things are running a lot differently now, but that things are a lot happier. This had an impact on me and made me determined to work on myself more so that I could reach my own goal.

There were many other people I talked to or with whom I was in different groups. As soon as I realized that I could also get something from these conversations, I tried to find more opportunities to have them. The others felt exactly the same way, even though the topics were normally really difficult. There was this one young guy who had multiple sclerosis and suffered from bullying at work, a young sportsman, who couldn't deal with the constant pressure of being in a successful Bundesliga team, a building authorities manager who had let everything get on top of him, a 65 year old nurse who had had to bury her 40 year old son because he had died of cancer (the stress from being a nurse was already high), a man who cut himself, whose problems I could really understand, but he didn't want to share them (it would be interesting how he is doing today. There are such things as coincidences. Maybe we will bump into each other again one day), a manager of a car company and and and. Burnout is obviously a phenomenon, which affects all industries.

I was pretty sure in the end and I still am now that:

Everything that we worked on in all the therapy sessions and groups was a real heavy-duty work for us. I have huge respect for anybody who sees this through regardless of how things work out for them. You need to have so much courage and strength and even I tried to run away from it all: It's not going to happen to me, I don't need it, I'm strong enough!

We aren't losers leaving rehab. We have only made one mistake, which other people would as well – we just didn't listen when our bodies said, "STOP" because our heads said "IT'S OK. I CAN DO IT."

During the day-to-day routine outside of the relaxation therapy sessions, sport, creative group, one-on-one conversations and exercises, we also had all the other activities, which we organized ourselves and did in our free time, especially at the weekends. Examples of these were:

European Football Championship:

We were allowed to watch the games in the recreation room. It was a nice change and sometimes we also had the fan gear and the catering, just without the alcohol of course! The therapists, who were supervising, often did checks, even when we came back in the evenings from a night out. If you broke the rules, you would be threatened with being asked to leave rehab, be reprimanded or the insurance company wouldn't pay the costs.

Barbeques:

If we wanted, we could go out as a group and use the barbeque in the courtyard of the clinic. Even this had to be done by ourselves. We had to ask the caretaker for the barbeque, ask for permission and agree on a date, set up the tables and ask the kitchen if they could prepare side dishes. We had to organize everything else like food, drinks, coal etc. It wasn't a big deal. It was seen as independent work and you couldn't get an "all inclusive package" from the kitchen.

Of course we had to clean everything up afterwards.

The group of us who sat together at the same dining table decided to organize one of these barbeque afternoons.

We shared the responsibilities so that everyone had something to do.

We were 12 people all together. The weather was nice on that day and everyone was having fun. Doing this meant that we had to have contact with others and take on small responsibilities within the group. It all seemed quite easy, but I kept on thinking back to my situation in front of the dishwasher and with the shopping list back at home. Compared to that, I had taken a big step in the right direction.

4.22) Visit from Marliese, Viky, Sara:

My 3 girls and Viky's boyfriend Stefan drove the 600km and came to visit me twice. That was such a great feeling and it always gave me a boost for the future. The first time, Marliese came with Sara, but all 4 of them came on my birthday. We went on a trip into Chemnitz once and another time we went for a walk in the forest to the lookout tower. We also visited the limestone cave in the area, had a nice coffee and in the evening of my birthday, we went and had dinner in the forester's lodge. I was given so many presents – all 4 of them had made little presents and written greetings cards. They also brought a lot of cards and well wishes from friends at home. It was really nice and I won't forget it. Saying goodbye was really hard as they sat in the car with Viky at the wheel to drive the first part of the way home. It was like when I had driven the first part of the route to St. Peter Ording for the holidays. She had taken over my role.

It was really great to receive the best wishes and encouraging cards from the other patients, who I had gotten to know quite well by this stage. Even though we hadn't known each other for very long, most of the congratulations were very warm.

It was very practical that close relatives could also stay in the clinic for a reasonable price if there was room free. We could then spend the weekends together after breakfast as there was never any official business to do.

Armchair cinema / Allotment bar:

This is something I quickly have to mention. In walking distance from the clinic – around 20 minutes away – there was an old cinema from GDR times. It had been renovated well and at the front there were tables and chairs organized in small groups, but the last 2 rows were red, soft plush armchairs. When you sat down, you would sink into them. There were always 2 armchairs and a table in the middle. Along the back wall there was a bar with drinks, chips, ice cream and sausages. Even during the film, you could go up and get refills. It was so cozy in there. The cinema became the place to be for the patients at CB at the weekends if they couldn't go home or didn't have any visitors. I went there once when "The Intouchables" was playing. I had already seen it, but it was definitely worth seeing it a second time. It was even better watching it in the armchair cinema with a bag of chips and an alcohol free beer.

We also celebrated a party in the last week in a small bar in the allotments around the corner. The weather was beautiful and there were seats outside, the prices were good for small dishes and we often went there for "group talks" so that we could really let out all our frustrations and then make our way back to "Laolabad" (this was the nickname we had thought up) in a calmer state of mind.

Saying goodbye to the table tennis policeman, the colleagues and girls from the arrival group and the priest:

During the 4th and 5th weeks, the goodbyes began because most people had 5 weeks in the clinic. Only I had been able to extend my stay to 7 weeks because of the knee infection and not being allowed to move for 2 weeks. We had the best and funniest evenings when we were the group of people I ate or did sport with – table tennis, volleyball, jogging (when I was allowed). Unfortunately, I couldn't go with them to the reservoir that weekend because of my handicap.

And then there were the "girls" I had arrived with and they left one week later. We hadn't really done anything together in our free time, but we got on very well with each other in the groups and creative activities. Whilst I was on my sick bed, they always tried to give me a boost. I was also persuaded to make a bead ring for our youngest daughter by them. It even worked! Rehab was worth it just for that. Since then we have organized to meet once every year and the first time, we spent a nice weekend in Fulda and enjoyed a barbeque. We've already organized to meet again in 2014. Everyone brings a speciality from his or her home region and then we do a tour of wherever we are before eating. We had a great time and I'm looking forward to the next one.

In hindsight I have to say that I'm really happy that things worked out relatively "mildly" for me despite all that happened. That means that I can lead a relatively normal life with a certain consistency.

I experienced in a short period of time a lot of different people's life situations, feelings and emotions. This has definitely enriched my life. The whole range of emotions and feelings: hate, joy, doubt, love, hope, helplessness, courage, fear, panic, aggression, depression, and harmony. Absolutely everything that you can experience in different life situations. I had the possibility to learn something from it all. Back then, I didn't see things in that way. It was more like additional stress, but you learn to deal with it and build up a safety barrier, which I can still use today.

Feelings are great and valuable if you know how to work with them and have them under control. You have to get to know how they are going to affect you in different situations. That is really hard because who can predict how they are going to react in a certain situation. I would never have been able to do it, but my time in CB has given me experience, which I never would have had before, e.g. the point about expectations, which I have already described.

4 weeks ago, I went on a 4-day skiing trip with a neighbor. A young man and woman were having a conversation in a cable car: "if I had enough money, I would buy myself a Ferrari, awesome clothes and a penthouse apartment. I'm not interested in family. There's so much responsibility, you always have to take care of the kids and you can't just do what you want to. I want to party and do as many crazy things as possible, have a big group of friends and have a lot of pretty girls around me."

I smiled to myself. I had thought exactly the same way 30 years ago apart from the bit about the family. It's OK to party, be free and travel. The kids also need that to a certain extent to set themselves apart, set their own priorities, be able to shut off and get some distance from their parents.

My experience is that a functioning family is irreplaceable. It can't be compared to anything else and can't be compensated for with money or a change to your way of life. There is no such thing as a family or relationship without any conflicts and we all know that. These would very quickly become boring. If you have a difference of opinion, then it's all about how you deal with that and the other person. (Social competence!)

A family normally begins with a relationship. It grows. If the relationship is good, you decide to stay together. If it isn't, the search for the right partner continues. You have to respect your own demands, but be flexible and tolerant. A relationship between 2 people is the first step in practicing a life together, so that you can tackle the question of offspring. Marliese and I are very happy that we have had healthy children. Bringing them up is a wonderful, intensive, emotional and, sometimes of course, very stressful process, which changes as they grow up, but is never boring. Of course there are some times when you would like to throttle them.....but you would never do that. You love your children, but sometimes you have to put your foot down if they go too far, but that's it's called an upbringing.

Our "baby" is now 13 and the eldest is 21. Both of them have provided a lot of variety over the years and have caused a lot of stress, but they have kept us young. We have experienced a lot of emotions during this time and it hasn't always been easy, but we have all gotten used to dealing with it. We get on very well as a family and everyone respects each other, even if sparks fly now and again, but then the eldest will come back and say "sorry. I messed up yesterday". And that does us all good. Sometimes the youngest will take the mickey out of me with a sly and ironic smile in such a way that even I have to smile. These are great moments that I don't want to miss. That's why I would say that the kids and family are a lifelong experience, which are constantly changing and which you can learn from. For the first time I am realizing what kind of meaning this is going to have for Marliese and me as we get older:

1.) We aren't alone. We have children and a family and a strong community around us.

2.) We will have something to do later in life as grandparents, which we can organize as we like. We will be needed even if one us isn't here anymore. The other one won't be alone.

3.) I have a good feeling that what Marliese and I have lived and worked for this whole time hasn't been for nothing. We can pass everything on to our children.

4.) There will be someone there when we are older who will take care of us as well as they can. "Don't worry Dad. We are going to find a care home for you."
And: You aren't alone with your thoughts. A part of you will always be here.

Think of all the experiences we would've missed out on over the last 21 years if we hadn't had children. We've saved our travelling until later in life. OK, there were some highlights just after finishing studying, which you need to be fit for, but we are keeping ourselves in good shape for the future. From today's point of view, I think we would adopt children if we didn't have any of our own. Just because it is such a great experience. Maybe a lot of you will have another point of view, but that's what we experienced and it was great.

So that was a superficial overview of the topics family and the future from my point of view. I've bored you enough with it so let's continue with the end of my stay at CB.

4.23) A difficult goodbye:

Even though I have to say that I felt good in the clinic, the last week seemed to drag on because a lot of the courses had ended apart from the relaxation training and everyone from the various groups, who I had gotten to know were already at home.

This whole thing reads a little bit like a holiday report. We could go out in the evenings. The weekends were free. Visits were no problem. There was a lot of sport, the canteen was OK, no stress. It all sounds really good. You shouldn't forget though: there was a reason why all of us were there "on holiday". Every one of us, without exception, would have preferred to work 3 years longer than be in that clinic for personal reasons. Everyone. Even me.

The 7 weeks were over very quickly. It was like a rollercoaster ride with one loop the loop after the other. I think about how uncertain I was before going in to rehab. I couldn't imagine that I would be able to achieve anything in 7 weeks after failing to do so in 7 months. This wasn't the most crucial point. The crucial point was not when....or how.

The most important thing I had to clear up was WHY. Why did I react so out of control? Why couldn't I cope?

And the WHAT? What can I do to make it better? What do I need to be careful of? What do I need to avoid? What is good for me?

I got all of this information in rehab and could train all the tools I needed there too.

Now I'm working on putting it all into practice. Me and AMY!

So, let's go. Back home and back to work! (But without stress!)

5.) The reintegration

I'm writing this while sitting in a hotel room in Hungary. One of my colleagues on site here was telling me about an hour ago that he has almost the exact same symptoms, but without the heart problems, sweating, stomach problems, diarrhea, insomnia and hyperventilating at the thought of having to go to work.

I'm not sure, but maybe it didn't make any inroads to "Amygdala" or he is just "built" in another way. I know that everybody reacts differently to the same situations. He had needed to take a lot of time off and was only just starting to slowly get back to work. If you broach the subject, you will find so many people, who had a similar situation. It's shocking. Really shocking. It doesn't really seem to matter what profession you look at either. I got to know a priest while I was rehab! You never would think that could be possible, would you? However, even in this area savings have to be made, parishes are being merged, people come to you with their personal problems because you are the minister and everybody in the area knows who you are. That's why the best help at first is being cautious and talking about it. If that doesn't work, then you have to put the brakes on. Getting external help is also important. I definitely only had a good experience with this, even if you think that you don't need it and can manage by yourself.

Oh yes, the reintegration. (RI)

I had a conversation with the counsellor in the clinic as preparation for the RI: "Do you want to go back to your old job?" "Yes, I definitely want to try."

We went through the Hamburg Model for RI together and thought about the different stages: "I think it would be a good idea for you to telephone your manager and the HR Department before I get involved." "I wanted to do that anyway."

I telephoned my boss and the call went very well. The most important thing he said to me was: "Mr. Dietrich, you should arrange the RI in whatever way you think is right. We are all looking forward to you coming back to work." This one sentence gave me the courage I needed and was crucial to hear at that time. THANK YOU!

After this, my counsellor had a much longer telephone conversation and asked me if I was confident that I would be able to deal with a return to

100% of my previous workload. "I'm not that far yet, but I now know how I can achieve that and I'm definitely going to try to be back to full fitness by the end of the RI"

Why a gradual reintegration?

Several people asked me why my return to work was done in stages. I had done everything before it wasn't as if there was anything new so why not just go straight back?

This was a good point, but Amy needed to get used to it first. It was more likely to be successful when taking small steps rather than one big one. The risks are much greater when jumping in the deep end, as I don't know where my new breaking point is. Will I ever be able to be 100% again? It's more likely that I won't because then I run the risk of having another burnout. It would be really stupid not to have learned anything from the whole experience and would also be completely irresponsible in terms of my family and my employer. By going back in stages, I can still add something to the department thanks to my 17 years of experience instead of constantly being away because of being overworked. If things go wrong at one stage, the fear increases that things will never work out. So the answer is small steps. Every step can be seen as a success and, if something does go wrong, it is only a small setback.

The following picture should illustrate this:

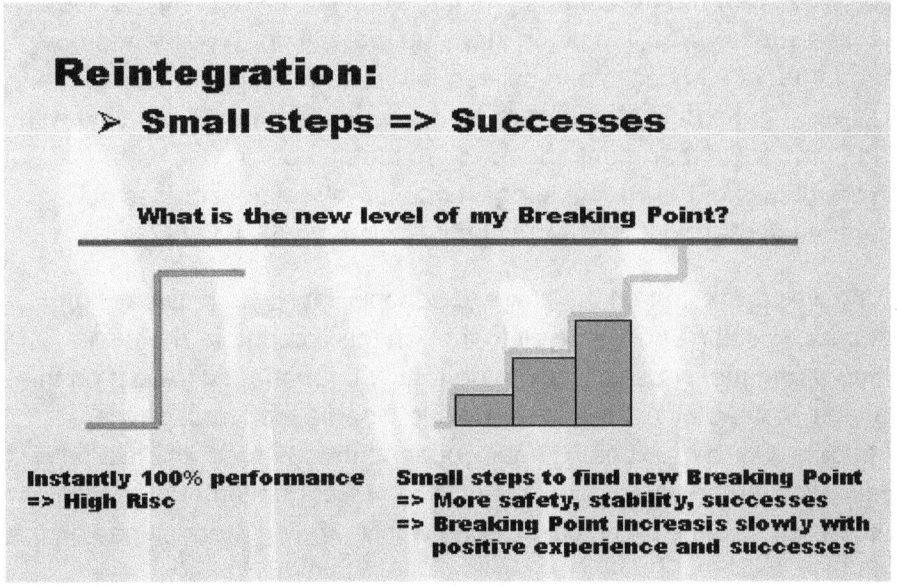

Reintegration:
➤ **Small steps => Successes**

What is the new level of my Breaking Point?

Instantly 100% performance
=> High Risc

Small steps to find new Breaking Point
=> More safety, stability, successes
=> Breaking Point increasis slowly with
    positive experience and successes

I was really looking forward to the reintegration and starting back at the company. We had agreed on a very moderate start: 2 hours in the first week, but that was exactly right for me. After leaving rehab, I had had 2 weeks to get used to being at home again. It's strange. You wouldn't think it were necessary, but, after 7 weeks away, it's a different feeling being back at home. What's more, this is also the first step of the adjustment phase. You concentrate yourself on the courses, your tasks and yourself while in rehab, but when you are home, the family is there and you don't always have peace and quiet when you really want it because maybe the children come home from school with their problems. These are normal things, but I had been shielded from them while in rehab.

The second week went really well. I called the boss at the company now and again and everyone seemed pleased that I would be back in the office the following week.

Monday, 13.08.2012. 8 months and 3 weeks after being taken to the hospital on 23.11.2011 I was standing at the entrance to the company. I was in a great mood. I had managed to make it to this point. I had worked so hard to get here. I was still a long way from where I wanted to be, but I had taken a big step forward. I went slowly through the revolving door at 9am. I lifted my right foot over the first step of the entrance stairs and held it there a moment. On the inside I shouted, "YES"! I put my foot down on that first step and carried on up the rest.

Everyone who knew me greeted me warmly and I got the feeling that they were as pleased as I was. I took the steps up the 4th floor (I wanted to do more sport after all). My boss and colleagues all seemed happy to see me. They had even put a bunch of flowers on my desk. The first RI meeting with the head of the HR department and my boss took place and we went through the details of the RI, the suggestions for my responsibilities during this time and I explained what I would do if something went wrong etc.

Everything was great, but on the first and second days with only having to work 2 hours, I couldn't bring myself to turn on the computer. There was something telling me I wasn't ready to do that yet. I managed to do it on the third day, but instead of looking at my emails, I had a look through the project folders. On the next day, I finally opened the folder for the last project I had been working on when I became ill. It took a certain amount of effort, but as soon as I had the technical drawing with all the different stages on the screen in front of me, it felt like a small success compared to the previous day. It was then that I realized that it would be small steps, which would help me make progress, and some of those would be very small, but would happen every day. I was no longer frustrated about why things weren't progressing faster. I tried things and did what I could at speed I could manage. Step after step. Always in the right direction – towards my goal…

The working time increased to 3 hours, but that was OK for me. After discussing it with me, my boss had given me a new project when I had restarted. It was something that I had done 100 times before, and so it was nothing new and I had enough experience of it (that's what we thought anyway, but things turned out quite differently, but I managed to sort things out). There was enough time to prepare this project and that meant no pressure or panic. The best thing about it was I was able to go through all the phases, step by step, without any time pressure – planning the layout, creating a budget, telephoning with the customer (but still no travelling as that was not expected during the RI), offer specifications and comparisons etc. It was a very good way to work while being within the protective walls of the office, and everything was going wonderfully. I needed longer than I had previously done, but there were no situations where I felt panicked. I very often felt tense and I noticed how my breathing became quicker, especially when it came to discussions on the telephone. I realized at this point that, in the past, before conflicts, discussions or making decisions, a huge amount of pressure would build up. Thanks to permanently training myself and becoming used to the situation, this is no longer the case. If I experienced any physical symptoms (and I sometimes did several times in one day), I did exactly what I had trained myself to do and what I had discussed with my boss: I told him that I was going to the relaxation room so that he knew where I was. There I did some kind of gym exercises or used the skipping rope I had in the cupboard in my office to use up the excess adrenalin and distract myself. After that I did some gentle stretching exercises, tai chi and some breathing exercises. I always managed to get control. Sometimes it was enough just to run up and down the 5 flights of stairs a couple of times. It didn't matter what it was, as long as it worked. And it did. It gave me such a boost and, with time and the training, I felt more and more stable, tension levels reduced and the need to try and deal with the tension became less necessary. It became a part of my routine, just like training for a marathon becomes a routine after some time.

By now I was working 6 hours a day. That was stressful. Despite the breaks I had included during the day (one before lunch and another one about an hour before going home), the long periods of concentration got to me. I had to extend the "6 hour period" by 2 weeks. It was originally planned that this phase would last 2 weeks and then I would move up to 7.5, but I wasn't able to take that step. It was too much. I was actually already doing a lot, except business trips, and I was also occasionally doing some other small things. Everything was working out as I had planned or expected and the 2-week extension wasn't a bad thing. I was sticking to the rules and things were going well. My colleagues' support was perfect. They kept on asking how I was doing and offered me their help. It was like it had always been in our team and it felt good.

Then came the setback.

Thank God it wasn't a total meltdown, but it was a really big setback. I thought I had gotten over the worst, but that wasn't the case.

I had read my name in the list of the projects planned for the next year. It was next to a project, which was almost identical to the one I had been working on when I suffered my burnout. I had realized that that project had only been one of the reasons for my burnout, and it was possible that it wasn't even the main reason for it as it had actually gone quite well. There had been no problems during the project stages, the supplier had done a good job, the cooperation with the colleagues and the works manager on site had been perfect. It had however been time-consuming and I had worked over 6-7 weekends and had planned to take those days off in lieu before Christmas or as another holiday. That was my mistake. On top of that was the planning phase for the projects in the next year.

All of that came back to me like a bolt from the blue. I couldn't do anything about it. Bang! I went to the relaxation room and started my exercises. I was able to get through the rest of the day in the office, but I couldn't get the stupid thoughts out of my head. Even when I was at home, the thoughts kept running through my head. I tried to distract myself with some gardening and that helped for a while. I tried the relaxation technique of thinking about a calming picture and that helped even more. At this time I was still taking a small dose of Mirtazapine. My GP had told me that it was a mild medication that it would help me get to sleep and would allow me 4-6 hours of deep sleep. He said I wouldn't become dependent on it and that there wouldn't be any withdrawal symptoms if I slowly reduced how much I took over 2-3 weeks. I used it to help me get to sleep on this particular evening.

At 4am, the effects of the Mirtazapine had worn off. I had to get up to use the toilet as I normally did. As I went back to bed, the project popped back into my head, Shit! I couldn't switch off. I tried focussing on my relaxing picture, but that didn't work either. It was 5am and I was still awake. There was no chance of any kind of relaxation and I felt totally sleep deprived and anxious like a tiger in a cage. My mind was starting to race. I had always been able to calm myself down so why couldn't I do it now! Would I have to work on this project or is my name only there by accident because I had been planned to work on it before my burnout? Would I be able to do it? Or would it break me? Shit! I started sweating. I thought back to how it all began last time. It was exactly like this. Fear! I didn't want this to happen again. I got up as my therapist had advised: if you can't sleep, change where you are. What's the point of staying in bed? Get up and do something until tiredness sets in and then go back to bed. OK. Tai chi at 5am. Great. Wait a minute. If there is a problem I should talk about it so that I can get it out of my head. My plan was to go and see my boss first thing in the morning.

Unfortunately, I had forgotten that he wasn't in the office on that day. I turned on my PC and felt myself becoming tense. I really had to talk about it with someone right away. I had to get it off my chest and talk with someone in charge. I had to go to the HR Department. The woman there had always taken part in the RI conversations and had experience in the subject of burnout. I spoke to my colleagues and the secretary and went down to HR. She was there and she was happy to take the time to see me. Thank God for that.

She became my therapist and she was very good at it. I poured my heart out to her.

"I don't know why. I can't rationally explain it, but the thought of this project makes me panic. Everything had gone so well up until now. I had worked on almost all the project stages again and it was OK and now this!" She understood and it seemed like she was able to put herself in my position. "We'll sort it out. I know you have been making great progress and you are working on yourself consistently. We aren't going to let things fall apart now. You probably need a little for time for some things (she was totally right. I managed to completely plan the project without any problems a bit later on).

We are not going to risk what you have already achieved." This obvious understanding and the promise of help were exactly what I needed to hear at that moment. I'm sure my wife could hear the load being lifted from my mind back at home! This happened on a Friday. I wrote my boss an email explaining what had happened as he was going to be away on holiday the following week.

The day was over and I was definitely relieved, but pretty exhausted. I went home after lunch and tried to switch off by going jogging. I was totally exhausted by the evening and had to go to bed early. Saturday and Sunday were set aside for relaxation and jogging.

I was able to go to work again on Monday. I felt a little bit unsure the entire week, but was able to get everything done I needed to. I made sure I did a lot of sport by cycling to work, jogging and going for walks at the weekend with my wife. I just had to try and distract myself. The following week when my boss was back, we talked about what had happened. My name was removed from the list for the project and we agreed that I wouldn't have to work on it myself even though I had planned on it. A colleague would be able to take over this part for me.

It was a setback I hadn't expected. Damn it. Of course it would have been too easy to be able to waltz straight through without any problems. I just had to start again from where I was at that moment. At least the problem had been solved. The most important thing was that I hadn't let it eat away at me. I had tackled the problem even though it had been stressful. This was definitely a success and maybe an important step forward: "SAY NO", if it's not OK (yet) and don't lose hope.

The rest of the RI period went as smoothly as before this setback. I worked my way back to 7.5 hours a day and, since the 01.11.2012, that's the number of hours I work.

So, what were the most important things for me during this reintegration phase?

The most important point is that everyone involved has to be aware that burnout is a topic that needs to be accepted as real. Believing "things like that don't happen here", "that won't happen to me" or "that's something for weak people" isn't helpful.

It's extremely important that everyone trusts each other and for me this meant there being trust between the management and the employee. Management needs to be able to rely on their employee and know that he or she will work to the best of their abilities (no slackers!) and won't exploit the relationship with the other employees or manager. The manager also has to show absolute trust in the employee. If the employees need support or understanding because of a stressful or exceptional situation, he or she should receive it and not be exploited, ignored or put under pressure. There shouldn't be any "stop acting like that", "you managed to do it in the past" or "it has to work or do you have another idea what we can do?"

It's also vital that both sides can communicate openly with each other and that there is also mutual respect. There should be absolutely no bullying because that can be deadly. More energy will be used for that than for real work.

This helps a lot to avoid feelings of fear. Fear produces negative pressure and stress and these things, if they continue for a long period of time and depending on personality, can lead to depression.

Understanding and trust, on the other hand, have a positive effect: commitment and a positive attitude at work, which means the employee is motivated to be productive and creative. This in turn leads to increasing the "value" of the employees instead of them just working-to-rule.

I have tried to illustrate this in the following diagram:

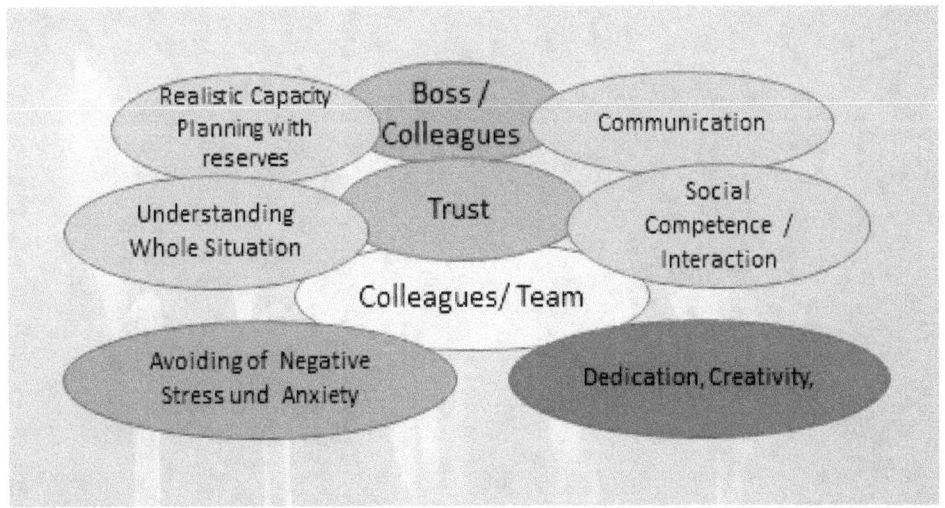

November was also the period of "dual leadership" while the old boss handed things over to the new one in the department. Both of them were on the road a lot during these first 4 weeks. Our old boss celebrated his 60th birthday with a very nice cake and the period before his official retirement seemed to pass quite quickly. The farewell party was quite emotional. We did our best to show our appreciation for everything that he had achieved and the many years of fantastic teamwork.

He still gets in touch with us sometimes. It's not easy to forget 23 years at a company and every now and again, there had been some deep, personal conversations, which went much further than any superficial relationship.

And then there was the "new guy".

6.) Back to work

I've already described how the good relationship with my colleagues and manager helped me in my return to work, but I know that, unfortunately, the same isn't true for all of you.

Even if you are sometimes scared about talking about your problems or situation because you are worried about the possible consequences, it is often better to share them. If you don't, it will just eat you up inside and time won't make it better. Those around you won't know anything about it and will assume that everything is OK. It's important to think about an emergency plan of what to do if a solution, which is good for everyone, can't be found. This will mean that the problem will be out in the open and the internal pressure will be relieved. Of course, it should be normal for both sides to try and look for a solution, but I know that this isn't always easy and that's why there is such a high number of people affected.

Handling Problems e.g. at Work:

> **Verbalize the problem**
> **Discuss the problem with all concerned, (Don't let it eat away at you, overcome the fear)**

Understanding:
>Look for a mutual
 solution

No understanding:
>Try to live with it
>Change behaviour
>Plan B

Today is 11.09.2013.

I'm sitting at the airport in Sweden again and it is 17:30. I'm tired. In fact I'm pretty exhausted, but I'm happy. Very happy.

2 days ago I started a relatively stressful trip to test and start up the picking machines in Stockholm. The first problem was the traffic jam on the highway to Frankfurt. I always plan a 45-minute buffer to be on the safe side. Unfortunately, this buffer was 30 minutes too short this time because of construction work. I had to run from the parking area to check in and security. "My flight will be boarding in 5 minutes. Is there anyway you could help me jump the queue?" Were are you flying?" "Sweden on business. I have a meeting." "Do you have any special luggage?" "No." "Then you can use the VIP lane." "Oh that's great. Thank you." VIP lane: "Do you have a handicap?" I wanted to say I didn't play golf, but the information came from behind me: "he's running late and the Fast Lane won't give him enough time anymore. There's not much going on, so please check him." As I got through security, it was boarding time. I set off to the gate arriving 10 minutes later. All the passengers were still standing there because the plane hadn't been completely checked yet, and so boarding had been delayed. At least I'd made the flight. The first problem had been successfully overcome!

In the plane the flight attendant poured a cup of coffee all over my shirt and trousers. The day had really started wonderfully! He apologized profusely and I was given a Lufthansa shopping voucher worth €25. That was nice of them and at least the coffee stains came out easily later on.

The cherry on top came when I arrived at the branch. There had been a complete breakdown of the conveyor system. The sort buffers for the delivery containers weren't working. There were 1000 of these containers and production wasn't able to continue because the rest of the conveyor system was blocked. Everything had to be sorted and taken to dispatch manually so as to get around the buffers. It was questionable if we would be able to do the tests myself and the delivery company had flown in for that evening. Great.

We had a crisis meeting that afternoon: what were we going to do?

After a lot of discussions and a phone call with the technical management team in Sweden, it was decided to postpone the Go Live, but we were able to carry out our testing that evening and the next day thanks to a few provisional adjustments. Thank goodness for that, otherwise the coffee on the trousers would have been for nothing.

Against all expectations, the tests went really well. They ran from 7pm to midnight after which I went back to the hotel and slept until 11am. I didn't get back to the company until the lunch break, but that didn't matter because during the day, normal operations continue. I concentrated on what I needed to do there, so didn't look at any other mails or make any other calls connected to my other projects. At that moment, my only job was at the branch I was currently visiting. I had enough to do there anyway and I had discussed working like this with my boss. We tested until midnight on the second evening as well and then I took a tablet to help me fall asleep. On the final morning, we had a meeting to discuss the results, next steps and machine checks. At 4pm I went back to the airport. I would be back the following Saturday to start the second testing phase.

And why am I telling you this?

It had been very stressful, but I had been able to cope. I had been able to take the final step towards being able to do all the things I had previously done. I was so unbelievably happy even though I was also tired. I wasn't afraid anymore that things wouldn't work out. I had come so far and I felt good.

It was definitely a lot tougher than it had been before and I don't need to do things like that everyday. I was going to take the next 2 days off to compensate and relax and that was something that I never used to do.

The most important thing was that I had reacted differently to the stress than I had done in the past. I was more in control, calm and confident. It wasn't helpful to get upset about something, which you can't control. When you do, you just end up putting more pressure on everyone around you. It's better to try and clarify the situation and the possible consequences. In the 2 days I have just described, I think I probably had to calm myself using my breathing exercises at least 20 times because I had noticed that Amygdala was starting to make her presence felt. 3 times I had had to run up and down the stairs during the breaks. It definitely hadn't been a critical situation. I had managed to keep my emotions under control much better than before and I hadn't needed to take medication to do it. That was a crucial step.

I knew now that I was able to do pretty much everything I had always been able to do as long as I was careful. It wasn't possible to do such a large number of things, in such a short period of time. I needed to plan breaks and times for relaxation and I would travel the day before a meeting rather than before sunrise on the day it was due to take place. I needed to take timeouts during meetings, but all of this worked for me.

Compared with the feelings of panic I'd experienced standing in front of the dishwasher 18 months early, this was crazy! It had taken a long time, but the hard work and discipline had paid off.

I had to keep this up and continue to improve. This was my goal.

I don't have about 70% of what's on paper at work in my head. Firstly, it's hard to measure, but I had obviously done too much for m and my personal capabilities in the past, otherwise the burnout never would have happened. So how should I measure this 70%? What would've been enough before? Secondly, I can compare what I can do with the skills of the new employees, and can see how important experience is in certain areas. I can avoid making mistakes and can share my experience with the new colleagues, plus I can plan warehouses and conveyance systems and put them into operation without any support from anyone else. That includes creating the drawings and technical contract documents, writing project specifications, comparing offers, getting approvals etc. This saves time and so it's possible that I don't really need longer than anyone else. I try to pass on the knowledge I have as quickly as possible to the new colleagues and that is an advantage for all of us, including the company.

In our department, for example, a new employee needs around 2 years before he can independently and correctly work on a project, but you should also consider the amount of time an experienced employee needs to teach him.

I friend of mine was in hospital to have an operation on his heart. His boss called on the day of his operation saying he urgently needed some information. The man had been prepared for the operation and was given the anaesthetic directly afterwards. His boss asked him to call back as soon as he could after his operation. He didn't wish him good luck or "get well soon" and there was no bunch of flowers for the family or something similar. People like this, who are also mentally ill, can be very useful for their company because they are willing to die for their jobs (and this actually happens now and again). I didn't make up that story. Thank God I don't work for a company like that and I've never experienced something like it.

I'm sitting in an airport bistro in Stockholm, looking out of the window and watching a plane take off until it disappears. I looked up and said "thank you!"

On the following day, I made the next step at a meeting of the Council of Elders.

The next elections for the Council of Elders in the parish were in December 2013. I'd thought long and hard about it because I'd always had a lot of fun doing the work. It wasn't a dry and boring committee. There were a lot of young people, who had volunteered as well. It had begun to take up a lot of time, though, especially because of the church renovations and the tearing down of the parish hall. These were my projects and for the last 6 months, there had been an extra regular meeting every week to discuss the plans and the move out of the old parish hall (which was going to be sold) into its temporary home in the old vicarage. It was all taking too much time and energy and could be something that my family and I could watch from the sidelines. I had to concentrate on the things I could afford to do and, unfortunately, this work wasn't one of them anymore. It wasn't easy to give up because I had built up a lot of social contacts and had invested thousands of hours over the previous 15 years. I wouldn't have done it if I hadn't enjoyed it.

I informed them that evening that I would be standing down from the 2 committees, the Council of Elders and the planning committee, and I wouldn't be available to work after the elections. That gave me some time for the family and free time and it felt good.

One more step forward.

This meant that there weren't as many of the "pressure points" I described at the beginning of the book:

The voluntary work in the parish and the 2 building projects.

If there was something big to do, I could call a professional either in St Peter Ording or Mannheim. That would also mean more time to switch off outside of the office.

But: 20.11.13, department meeting: after 1.5 hours I was experiencing a lot of symptoms. Relaxation techniques during the meeting didn't help and neither did drinking water nor breathing exercises. I had to leave the room and go to the relaxation room. I did 30 push-ups, stomach crunches and squats and then my breathing exercises. I felt better after half an hour, but not perfect. After eating, the symptoms improved. I hadn't expected that. What had I done wrong? Maybe I hadn't taken enough breaks or had had too many things on the go over the last few days. The number of little notes had started to increase again. I had to be more careful of getting a balance. I had been away for work a lot over the weekends and, although I had always taken days off in lieu, I was missing doing sport. I had had a cold for around 6 weeks because of the awful fall weather, and so hadn't been able to cycle to work. The lack of sport was starting to have an effect.

I went home looking forward to a day off the next day and a trip to the sauna. I thought it would also be a good idea to go and see the doctor. I had to make an appointment. I realised that things were not always going to run smoothly. I went to my GP the next day and he signed me off work for one day. I had an extended weekend.

"It could depend on your mood on a certain day, Mr. Dietrich. Forget about that day and what happened. Let yourself switch off for 2 or 3 days and you'll be fine again." He was right. After relaxing over the weekend in the sauna and going for a 1km swim, I felt much better. I made sure I took things more slowly the next week. On the Monday, I met with the new boss to talk: "Mr. Dietrich, it's fine. You don't have to explain yourself. You already spoke to me about it on Thursday and that's fine. You do what's right for you and if I can do anything to help, just let me know. Otherwise, I'm completely satisfied with how you are handling things.

Today is 03.12.13 and I'm sitting in Budapest. Yesterday I managed to do the testings I had to postpone 2 weeks previously. There hadn't been a single incident, which I hadn't been able to cope with. It was just having too many things to do at once (appointments, traveling, project implementation). If you know the cause, you can avoid it happening again.

7.) The old and new boss:

Sunday, 29.09.2013: I'm sitting on a train on the way back to Mannheim for our youngest's birthday. Everything had gone well at the subsidiary with the implementation and changes to the computer system. I'm in a really good mood and I'm looking forward to surprising my daughter because she doesn't know that I'm coming home earlier than planned. I'm sitting in the restaurant car eating a nice salad and an alcohol free beer. So what could I write about now? Right, the old and new bosses…

Why do I want to write about my last two managers? Because both are important people in my life. I worked for 15 years with the first and also pulled off some of the biggest and most complicated projects with him. I also learned a lot from our personal contact while at work. I learned the majority of what I know about project management from him. And who could forget the legendary Christmas parties.

The second, the new one, was a lucky find because he gave me enough time to work back up to working on projects and getting myself stable again. He showed a lot of understanding and good will after the reintegration phase

Of course, I'm explaining what is and was important for me, but that is very subjective.

If anyone in the company deserves anything, then it is our former boss. He dedicated the entire 15 years that I worked with him to the company. It was normal for him to go on business trips with the Board. He helped to evaluate companies, which might be taken over; he worked with yearly budgets of tens of millions of Euros, and so was responsible for the largest expenditure in the company. He very rarely said "no" to something.

He had a very broad knowledge regardless of the different areas our projects were in. He always took an interest in the projects from the beginning, and most of us acquired the majority of our experience in his department. We appreciate him for that. Before him, I had had 8 different managers in 5 different companies. None of them had the level of professional knowledge that he had. At his farewell party he told us: "I always had the incentive to do the work I had been given to the best of my ability."

He was able to highlight all the organizational problems in a distribution center after just ONE look around. He was also able to draw all necessary features of a newly planned subsidiary on an A4 piece of paper, with measurements, after a visit to the location.

His appointments were organized into a very tight schedule and he dictated reports on his way home so that it could be written up as soon as he got back.

We always had a lot of responsibility when working on these projects, the jobs were clearly and equally distributed, but when there were problems and something had been messed up, he would always give us his support. He always wanted to be informed of the current status of the projects and, if something looked like it was going to go off course, he would jump in.

He visited me at home after my stay in hospital and we talked about the future. While I was in the clinic, we telephoned and he gave me the courage to go back to my old job with these words: "Mr. Dietrich you should organize the reintegration phase in such a way that you need and that you think is right for you. We are all looking forward to you coming back and working with us again." At that time, this was really important for me to make the decision to start back at work (as I've already mentioned above). I felt like there was no pressure on me to succeed, and that had been a great relief. This conversation and the support of my colleagues made my mind up to return to my PC. I wanted to be back with the "troops" and I'm very grateful to him for that.

I've already described the reintegration phase in detail in another chapter. I experienced exactly the same problems then as I had during rehab: feelings of being overworked, the fear of failure. I also feared experiencing the same symptoms, hyperventilation, panic attacks etc. and all of these things happened again during the reintegration phase. The only symptom I didn't have again was the heart problems. I couldn't do anything about the panic attacks I had working on one project. Amygdala still needed some training! I had to pull out all the stops and think back to everything I'd done in rehab and also take a day off, but slowly, I managed to deal with it. At the time I'm writing this, I am working on exactly the project, which caused these panic attacks. I did all the detailed planning and created the budget of several million Euros. One of my new colleagues helped me with the work. The fact that I'd overcome my fears was a huge success for me (Thanks AMY!) I used to panic seeing my name on the planning list, but now I could go on site and present our concept myself. This was just unbelievable for me! I'd done it and our new boss had had a lot to do with that!

The new boss started on 01.11.2012.

There was so much uncertainty! What was he going to be like? New brushes clean up the best and I was the one with the biggest handicap (not in golf). The new guy would want to make his mark and I was a hindrance. What would his expectations be? Would we be able to work with each other? Would he be the kind of "top-down" manager or would he be one of us? Would he try to expand the department, and so reduce the pressure, or would he encourage competition between us? Did he have any idea about our work or would he be above such things? No idea. One thing we did know was that he was coming from a Logistics Planning Office and had 3 children. It sounded good. He probably had an idea about what we do and would understand family problems if he had his own children. We would see how it went. I had my back up plan with the loan anyway if something should go wrong. Thank you Mr. Carnegie!

I also had a confirmation that I had a disability degree of 30%. Why didn't I lay it on the table at the start of the reintegration phase? Maybe because I was worried about how the new boss would take it and I didn't want to rely on it from the beginning. The goal was to lead a normal life again, but the disability confirmation would only ever be for emergencies. I would have to ignore that I had it because I wanted to get back on my feet. I would have to be careful and not make the same mistakes I had before. I had to say "no" if I had to, know my limits and prioritize my health and family. Life goes on though and I wanted to make the most out of it. What does a piece of paper matter? It depended on me. If everything went well, I had at least another 30 years ahead of me and I wanted to travel the world, enjoy my grandchildren, walk along the beach on the North Sea with Marliese, admire the 234th sunset and then take my zimmer frame and go back into our holiday house. There were so many other possibilities as well. Maybe I could read at the kindergarten or become the oldest student at university studying who knows what. It doesn't matter as long as I'm having fun and fun doesn't stop at 70% of what's on paper. I learned that from the film "the Intouchables". Why has it become such a cult film? Of course because of the jokes that were included, but for me, it was about the will to live, the way of living, the humor and the positive attitude of the actor, who was reliant on a wheelchair and the interaction with his carer. It was fantastic.

So, the day finally came when the new boss arrived.

The first day wasn't actually too bad because he wasn't actually there just like during the first 4 weeks of the hand over period. Both old and new boss were traveling most of the time to the various subsidiaries and distribution centers in Europe to get to know the different contact partners, Boards of Directors, and Logistic Directors. It was a busy schedule. The new guy appeared maybe 3 times in those 4 weeks in the office, when he greeted us all and waved through our office windows, but then he was back collecting air miles.

On one of the few days he was actually in the office, I formally introduced myself to him: resume, background, marital status, important projects, goals etc. The usual stuff. In the back of my mind though, I had he thought: things are gong to change, that's normal. We are going to have to increase the number of employees we have and also tackle new areas of work.

Briefly on the subject of employee motivation: "every employee is naturally motivated, otherwise he wouldn't do any kind of work."

The day our old boss left was quite moving and we gave him a great send off. A lot of people, including some who had worked with him in the past, came. Of course there was a speech prepared by the Board. We had a departmental breakfast, gave gifts including a picture book of the last 23 years of projects and, at the end, he left us with some moving words, thanking everyone for trusting in him, but most importantly, thanking us, his employees, for our hard work implementing the projects. I think at that moment he felt that he would miss us. This feeling made the goodbyes very emotional. A week later, he wrote a personal letter to all of us.

So, the old guy was gone and with him went our secretary (she had retired). She was the second strong woman behind the man, who had led the department for 23 years. She was as solid as a rock and we could totally rely on her. Everybody liked her and this was also a very big change. She organized us all very well and was also a huge support, but it wasn't as if her job was stress free. She had left before our boss and we also had had a lovely leaving party for her, but to help her successor, she was brought back out of retirement. Together with the person who sometimes filled in for her (and who still works part time for us), she managed the handover wonderfully.

And then the new guy finally started!

His first task was to have one-on-one conversations with all of us. We had to make an appointment with the secretaries and plan 2-3 hours for it. We had 2 weeks to do it. In the following 4 weeks, we could select an out of house appointment, project presentation or on site meeting, which he came with us to. "You prepare the appointment. I'll just be listening in the background. It'll be like I'm not there."

My one-on-one conversation was very open. He told me about himself and then it was my turn. Family, background, focus, what I would like to continue doing. I was quite tense, but he told me later that he hadn't noticed. And then came the 64K dollar question. I had decided to talk about it as openly as I could. "I wanted to tell you, that even though I am back working my normal number of hours, my burnout and time out last year means I'm not completely able to deal with everything I used to be able to and I can't tell you right now how much that will change."

"That's good and very honest of you to talk about it. The HR Department and my predecessor have told me about it. I think you are very brave. I'm going to make a suggestion: I'm going to give you a year to get back to a level that you think is acceptable. Then we can talk again about the situation. If it's OK for you, I would find it great if you could regularly let me know how you are. If you need a timeout for whatever reason, call me or send me an email and that'll be fine. Otherwise you can organize your work how you like. I don't know what you are capable of at the moment. Only you know that. I'll be able to see what the results are.

This all sounded pretty good. I had expected a lot more pressure from a new manager. So, we would just see how things went.

I prepared myself intensively for our joint presentation appointment 2 weeks later on the 12th December. I wanted to be sure because I was going to have to give the presentation in English for the first time since coming back and, in the afternoon, I was going to be one of the Chairs of a meeting with the suppliers. Due to this, the presentation documents were quite detailed so that I had a good outline for my lecture and I had had some good documents for the colleagues on site to read as well.

I had worked with the Logistics Director and employees on site on previous projects. We all got on really well and they all knew what had happened to me and accepted that I was working on this particular project. In the breaks, they asked now and again how I was. I had told them beforehand that it could be that I would have to interrupt the meeting now and again, but that I just needed a timeout, it wasn't terrible, but my boss would be there should we need him. Everybody knew and everyone was OK with it. I began the presentation by standing up and formally introducing myself. I thought back to the first morning meeting in CB and the lump I had in my throat. I found my flow after a couple of sentences and moved on to the second slide. I was looking at it with my back to the meeting room. No one could see my face. I felt good. This was my chance. There were no obstacles; only chances and I wanted to use them! I grinned to myself. "Come on Amy, let's dance," I said to her and she took my hand. (I know it's corny, but it was a great moment!)

The atmosphere was relaxed and easy. The 3-hour presentation went well. I even dealt with the questions at the end without any problems. I was able to answer directly or sketch on the flipchart. I felt euphoric, like I had succeeded and this spurred me on, but I had to be careful. I could feel the tension increasing and I was talking faster and starting to make mistakes. I consciously made the effort to talk and breathe more slowly. When I wasn't talking, I took 3 deep breaths in and out. Nobody noticed, but I needed to take a break. I couldn't mess things up now! I allowed myself to take a break after 1.5 hours and everyone was fine with it, especially the smokers. The room was aired, coffee served and 20 minutes later, after 7 rounds of tai chi out on the terrace, we carried on. It was a great feeling. I remained calm and didn't allow myself to get stressed. When there were several questions at the same time, I sometimes had to ask for quiet so that I could order my answers, but it worked. Whatever else was going to happen, I had made a good start. Yes!

Everyone was happy with the meeting and the information I had given them. We then had lunch and I was able to enjoy every single bite. It was great. The conversation with the supplier that afternoon was of secondary importance.

There were another 3 hours of work in the afternoon. The new boss jumped in for me now and again, but that was fine for me.

We were all satisfied that evening. He asked me: "How was it for you today?" "I'm really happy with how it went. I was able to use my relaxation "tools" well and I don't think there were any big differences between that and a normal meeting. It went very well even though I'm going to have to take a short timeout before dinner." He answered: "I found it to be a completely normal meeting. I couldn't see any difference at all. You were well prepared.

That was a relief. A huge relief....

Next step:

3 months before I had had a blackout because I had seen my name on the planning list next to a certain project, which was exactly the same as the one I had been working on when I had my breakdown.

Boss: "Mr. Dietrich. It's now the middle of December. By the end of February, we should organize a trip where we can both visit the old subsidiary, which was modified by you and the new one, which is still using the old system. We'll need 2 days with travel. I have only been to them briefly and I would like to see in detail what has been done."

OK. I still had a bit of time until then, I thought.

In January I felt good after the holiday. His schedule was already pretty full, but I found an appointment that worked for both of us.

First of all, we went to the subsidiary, which had already been modified. Everything was running well. I was able to see it completed for the first time as well. My colleagues had taken over the work for me.

We were both enjoying a beer that evening when he said: "I think it's great how you are coping by using your methods and taking breaks. And Mr. Dietrich, to be perfectly honest, if you can work, you should do so to benefit the company. It doesn't matter if you need to take a break now and again or even go a little bit earlier. It'll be ten times more expensive if you are signed off for a long period of time and can't work for weeks. You should take time off if you need it. As I said before, just let me know and then it's OK. I've seen how you prepared for your trip to Sweden and how you gave your presentation. I know that you aren't exploiting us. I trust you."

I would have to be crazy to exploit or endanger this trust in anyway. I wouldn't make such a big mistake. I had to continue, taking small steps forward. That was the most useful for me.

On the second day of our trip, we visited the subsidiary, which still needed to be modified. The project next to which my name had stood, which caused my panic attack. I was there, but I wasn't worried anymore. I felt a little tense when it came to a couple of new, tricky points we hadn't had previously. I wasn't going to be afraid of this project anymore. I had managed to do it by myself. I had used the time I had been given by my boss and that was the right thing to do. After the trip, a colleague and I worked on 3 changes to the plan and there were no problems anymore.

Of course, not everything ran smoothly at the beginning. Things didn't quite go as planned during a meeting in March. I had once again planned about 40 pages for a presentation. I hadn't been to this particular subsidiary for about 10 years and the manager there wasn't really happy with our planning and strategy. The discussion became heated. "The planning was bad 12 years ago. We had to straighten everything out. Have you already built something like what is drawn on this piece of paper?" "Yes, twice." "That's not going to work here especially not during daily operations." There was a lot of tension. We looked each other in the eye. Neither of us backed down. I started speaking more slowly and clearly. There was no trust there and it wouldn't be possible to execute a project when we had that as a foundation, especially not during normal operations. I was going to have to save myself before the end of the presentation. "If you see some problems, we are happy to rework those points or you could give us some suggestions for alternatives." In this way, I was able to win some time and postpone that discussion until the end of the presentation.

We went back home without having found a mutual solution. The good thing for me on this day was that I had stood my ground. I had worked with Amy to try and keep my adrenalin levels under control. I had pulled out all the stops to control my emotions with what I had learned in rehab while my boss was talking: relax, breathe in slowly, relax, and breathe out slowly. Nobody noticed and we were a group of 6 people. The only thing they noticed was that I had begun to speak more slowly and clearly. It worked.

Our new boss liked to hand out books about technical things ("You don't have to learn it by heart, but you should know what's in it so that you can find something if you need it.") There were books about psychological studies, management styles, motivation etc. One book I found particularly interesting was about leading employees. (It was a small book. I thought I might be able to read it after having given the first 3 back unread. I'm quite lazy when it comes to reading!)

"The Minute Manager": It wasn't really up-to-date, was written quite simply and some sections repeated themselves so that a lot of things remained in my mind. It was all about how it is possible to motivate employees with clear rules and giving them bearable responsibilities, so that they can be self dependent, efficient and successful, creating a good working environment. (According to the forward, many readers recommended this!)

My first performance appraisal was also an important development for me in terms of my job. It happened after 6 months and is standard in our company. After 10 minutes of the appraisal with my new boss, we had come to an agreement. In terms of an evaluation of my personal qualities, I did quite well. Of course, in terms of being able to work under pressure, I was a little behind my other colleagues. The conclusion was that I was still an employee, who could support the department and its work. That was fantastic and I had no objections. I still had the confirmation in my pocket that I had a degree of disability of 30%, which I had been keeping to myself for almost a year. My goal had been to see for myself to what extent I could still do my job. How would he react to it?

I brought it up at the end of the appraisal and asked how we should deal with it. "Mr. Dietrich, that's no problem. I'll discuss it with HR. Don't worry about it. Why didn't you tell me about it before?" "I would definitely have given it to you, don't worry. You have it now. I just wanted to see for myself what I was capable of and how I would be able to use the methods I've learned without having to wave this confirmation at people. I did it on purpose and if it hadn't worked out, I would have come to you sooner."

"OK, but you have to realize that I have a duty of care to my employees and I don't want you to do too much because then I'll be really angry. If you have problems, we'll find a solution, but I have to know what they are otherwise I can't help. I'll get back to you after I've spoken to HR."

The response when it came was very positive.

There are no limitations to the work you do. I can still entrust you with everything if you feel up to it. I also managed to clarify something else. You've told me and I can see from your hard work that you want to continue working in this department. If for any reason that changes (I know you don't want that, but anyway), there will always be a suitable position with suitable responsibilities in another department in this company for you."

Thank you! That meant I didn't have to worry about my job and there were no more questions about what would happen next etc. I had done everything right. Everything that had happened before had been worth it. It had been the correct decision to come back and I would carry on as best I could. I had already come so far.

Without this promise, I probably never would have written this book.

I had to do without a lot of things during this time, apart from normal health and my normal activities: a friend's wedding in the USA, which we had accepted an invitation to; various holidays, which we had always taken (skiing, summer holiday etc.); 2 x 50th birthday parties of good friends; but the biggest thing had been the high school graduation of our eldest daughter. My wife and kids had shown me the photos in rehab, but it was still a shame. I had to wait 5 years before the next graduation of our youngest. I don't want to complain though. Other people are much worse off.

I had a very personal and special goal. I want to win over a very special friend with this book. Maybe it'll work and if it does, it will be the last thing to be ticked of my list of things to do I had written in Carolabad.

I should say that the head physician at CB had agreed to read the draft of this book and give me some feedback. Her answer encouraged my to get it published!

This is a good point to end on, isn't it? I love happy endings (corny, but true. No film!)

I wish every reader and the best and thank you for your support.

8.) Letter to a friend

I wrote this letter to a very good friend of mine after he had an operation. He agreed to it being published in this book.

Hello dear friend,

What are you up to?

I should say first of all that I'm really sorry to hear about your heart attack and I hope that you will be back on your feet soon after your operations. You are in our prayers every evening and I think the guy upstairs will take care of everything.

At least He hasn't taken you from us yet. He could've done, so I think He still has some plans for you.

I found out by accident what had happened to you. I was riding home from work when I met your daughter on the street. She gave me a hug and burst into tears and she told us a few things about what had happened.

It's not possible to change what has already happened and I'm annoyed with myself that we didn't talk more about the situation because it seems the causes are quite similar to what happened to me.

Of course you can't undo things, but you HAVE TO learn from it and take necessary steps. You need to reprioritize because the doctors can't always step in in time to help.

I'm just going to write what I think and about some of the things that I HAD TO do to make sure that I got back on track and that I'm still here enjoying life with my girls (we have the same family set up anyway). I've already started writing some things about the start of my burnout and the time in rehab for myself. I've included some if it for you. Maybe there is something interesting there for you. If not, then just throw it away.

It was really hard at the beginning for me to admit that maybe I wasn't quite myself anymore. I had made the mistake of ignoring the signs my body was giving me. They were telling me to stop, to change something, that it was too much. I didn't want to be a failure. I didn't want to be the one in the department, who couldn't cope anymore. I didn't want to let the others down. I didn't want to risk my standard of living. I wanted to grit my teeth and battle on because everything had been OK in the past. I had tried to suppress the problems at work that wouldn't let me sleep. The things that meant I woke up at night, sweating, and saw me buying a notebook so that I could write down what I had on my mind. I thought about the people, who would lose their jobs because of my plans and I couldn't get out of this cycle of fear: what's going to happen if I lose my job?

At some point, enough was enough. My body couldn't take it anymore: "If you don't want to listen, then you are going to feel it." And that's what happened, just like with you.

After that, I spent 7 months fighting for a place in rehab. First of all I was declined and then there was a new assessor, then the waiting time, then the DRV misplacing the assessment etc.

But then there was the rehab. They asked me a few basic, but essential questions, which I had to answer for myself. I don't remember all of them, but the most important question was:

WHAT'S THE MOST IMPORTANT THING IN YOUR LIFE?

Answer (It's simple and sounds trivial, but you have to think about it first): YOURSELF.

Why is that? Because if you aren't around anymore, it doesn't look good for your life, does it! And think about what you mean to other people? That creates a massive problem. I was pretty shocked.

My situation was different at that time to how it had been before.

I had always wanted to stay healthy and use my life insurance with Marliese to go travelling etc. YOU know when you are getting ill, but there is always some great medicine from the doctor and everything is OK again. You can insure yourself against damaging property and everything is fine so why can't a person live to be 100 years old? That's how it used to be, but since my breakdown, things have changed. SHIT!

At the time, the doctor at the hospital told me that the problem with my heart could reoccur if I weren't careful. If I was really unlucky, my heart problems could lead to clots, which in turn could lead to a stroke. WONDERFUL! Just what I had always wanted. It was like winning the jackpot!

It was only when I thought about this that I understood the answer to the question.

It doesn't matter what job I do.

It doesn't matter how much money I earn.

It doesn't matter what other people think about me.

It doesn't matter if I live in our house or in a 3-room apartment.

There is one thing I want: to LIVE with MY GIRLS!!

They shouldn't have to stand over my grave in tears just because I was too stubborn.

I'm not going to ignore probable consequences because only one thing is important: MY LIFE.

Marliese and I have made a plan for the WORST CASE scenario:

Sell the holiday apartment, move to a 3-room apartment, rent out my parents' house, rent out our house, Marliese works part time, no more holidays, only 1 car and take the bus and hopefully give our daughter her grant to study and finish Sara's training. These were the new conditions. I still remember my mother going cleaning for me so that I could go to school. If she can do it, so can I.

I would also work part time and not travel for either my old employer or in a new job. Before rehab, I didn't feel I could cope with all the demands placed on me. The fear of losing my job was probably unfounded, but at that time I wasn't in a position to work and I didn't know why. I wanted to give up my voluntary work for the parish because it took up so much time and the renovation project was also becoming quite stressful. (I'm definitely going to do that this November before the elections. I'm not going to stand and I'm also going to step down from the council planning the rebuild. Why should I take responsibility for something, which is actually someone else's job? Especially when I'm not up to it from a health point of view? I've done it for long enough. Please keep it to yourself until I can let the Council of Elders know). There are no taboos when it comes to our emergency plan. There is just one goal.

Social services in rehab were very willing to help and also very consistent. So many of the patients there needed 3-6 months of further treatment and they were advised to find a new job. They had enough time to look for something.

One of the patients there was 60 years old and he was worried about the following years until he became 63. The therapist helped him understand that there could be a way for him to retire earlier and the time in between could be filled with courses recommended by the Job Center. He could also find something that he finds fun and then the time would pass even more quickly.

In my folder, I have a piece of paper and on it is written: degree of disability 30/100. That means that, according to this medical certificate, I am 30% disabled with regard to my mental toughness. At first I thought, SHIT, SHIT! How am I supposed to be able to do my job? What if they throw me out? I'll never be able to find work anywhere else.

Due to that, Marliese and I pieced together the emergency plan I wrote about before. The basis was: THE MOST IMPORTANT THING IS ME AND THAT MY GIRLS DON'T HAVE TO STAND AT MY GRAVE.

THIS IS MY RESPONSIBILTY! AND I'M GOING TO MAKE SURE IT DOESN'T HAPPEN. I'M GOING TO MAKE SURE I BECOME AS OLD AS I POSSIBLY CAN, BUT STILL HAVE AS MUCH FUN AS I CAN WITH MY GIRLS.

The emergency plan showed us that I would get by with less than 50% of my money.

Most people saw the happy Bodo, because I learnt in rehab to be happy about the small things that happen everyday – a day when I wake up in a good mood with the sun shining and being able to go out with Marliese in the evening. A day on which I went out cycling with Marliese etc. Movement is really important. It doesn't have to be a 10 km run, but it is a good distraction and is just as good as swimming or going to the sauna. For me, going to the sauna is like hitting the reset button in my head so that all the odds and ends in my mind are erased.

I also had a strict plan if things didn't work out at work anymore.

It was a really important step to create this emergency plan and do you know why? I didn't fear the "worst case" anymore. I could sleep at night and get some rest instead of constantly worrying about "what would happen if...." And these thoughts going round and round in my head until I was so exhausted I would fall asleep. Of course, I still felt a bit uneasy, but I had a realistic way out. Since that point, I was able to build up some strength and try and start again.

Thank God (and I mean that literally) everything at work worked out well, I could get control of any fears I had about becoming overworked again and the new boss totally understood. Together we planned a strategy, which means I can still work well, but at the end of the day, I still do a lot more than the new boy.

I now also have a new goal, which I'm currently working towards: MY QUALITY OF LIFE NEEDS TO BE BETTER THAN IT WAS BEFORE!!

That isn't possible? Yes it is and I know it. A person can control a lot of things. I'm happy about the small things in life, which I always used to overlook. If something goes wrong, then that's life. You sometimes realize later on that it wasn't as bad as you thought or you find another way to get something positive out of the situation.

My new boss told me: "Mr. Dietrich, if you are signed off in the long-term, it will cost the company three times as much as if you are missing for one day because you need a timeout. If you need a holiday, plan it in and organize the project appointments according to your holiday if possible. If it isn't possible, we'll find a solution."

Your "engine" has been repaired as well as possible. That means you are back in the race (at least with some limitations and some medical check-ups now and again), with other people with pacemakers.

Your 2 girls are getting old enough and becoming more independent and if you were to ask them what is important to them, they would probably say your health.

You have to be careful. There isn't any other alternative! I have to be as well - stick to my breaks, do as much sport as my doctor allows, no cigarettes etc.

I have a few more IMPORTANT points/suggestions for you:

Take everything you possibly can from rehab – information, courses, relaxation techniques, advice from the counsellor, therapeutic tips etc.

Request an assessment of your degree of disability. If you are lucky, it will be a kind of safeguard for you and your family and I think that is something positive. It doesn't matter what's written on the paper. It's only important what's going on in your head. You will still be able to have fun, take part in life and enjoy every day with your wife and family. If I can do it, so can you.

You have worked for over 30 years, so there is no reason for you to feel bad about it.

And there's something else: don't let things eat away at you. Talk to your girls if you have a problem. It's always good if you can get things off your chest. You can call me if you like. I know how much good it can do to do that.

You have the right to worry about yourself without thinking about other people because you have reached a point where it is crunch time. It's just about you and your family.

Think about what your problems are at work or somewhere else. Think about acceptable changes/solutions. Talk about them with your therapist and the counsellor because they can help you. Think about what's good for you not for your employer. If you want to work from home (maybe because of a long commute), then discuss it. It could be a solution. Maybe it's also a good idea to reduce the number of hours you work. That's what I plan to do in the medium term.

If the job itself is stressful, ask for support. Are there other departments you could move to? Is there a branch in Mannheim you could work in instead of making the long commute to Frankfurt? Could you commute on the train? Do you have business trips? Can you reduce them or even stop them? There is sometimes the possibility of telephone conferences.

I know, it sounds really easy and some things will be unrealistic in your case, but I want to show you that we have similar experiences and the same questions.

The only important thing for your 3 girls is that you get back on your feet. This is your responsibility. Nothing else. Everything else can be managed. I know this letter is a little direct and provoking. I'm sorry if it was too direct and I hope you aren't angry. If you would like to talk, I'd be glad to. Just call. I hope that you are back to full fitness soon and things improve afterwards.

I'm only an engineer, but I still think Him upstairs can straighten things out. As I said, he could've just let you go. He has enough to do after all. So be happy and do something with it!

I hope your rehab goes well. See you soon.

Bodo

9.) My Therapist

This was really a coincidence or an emergency solution. The result of my desperate conversation with the doctor of Psychology and Neurology was that he gave me the business card of my future therapist. I was supposed to try it out after I had spent 2 weeks unsuccessfully telephoning around and being rejected. It is possible to visit several therapists for up to 5 hours each to find out if there is any chemistry. This definitely wasn't the case with the first 2 ladies. I've already described the first visit!

Why did I choose a behavioral therapist and not psychological support? Behavioral therapy examines the thoughts and feelings of a person in a variety of situations. It applies to the current time period and current behavior, and so can be successful relatively quickly. In the course of the therapy, it is also possible to discover and analyze the causes of the various behaviors.

Psychoanalysis can take longer because the causes are the most important factor: childhood, parent-child relationship, key experiences in childhood/adolescence etc. You get closer to your problems and questions by thinking about the past.

I already knew the reason why I always try to avoid direct confrontations, mostly act as the intermediary in a conversation and try and find solutions. It was more than likely that it was because of the relationship with my parents before their divorce as I witnessed their arguments and felt as if I was made the mediator by both sides, even though I was still a child. ("Tell your father..... Tell your mother.......")

I think this age is very important for the education and character building of a child. Laughing a lot, playing, having time, and reading all make an impression on a child in the future. Sometimes these things aren't possible, though because both parents have to work in order to survive. Where should they find the time?

Everything was great with this one therapist from the first conversation. I could get everything off my chest and I felt like I was understood especially when it came to my insecurities and helplessness when it came to my recovery progress. The care I received while I was waiting for my place in rehab was extremely important especially when I wasn't making any progress and it seemed that everything would fall apart.

He always listened to my frustrations and gave me some tips on how to behave, e.g. changing the subject when I started to feel uneasy, changing my location, getting out in to the fresh air, breathing techniques to relax and movement. That helped very often to find someone to talk to and then release the pressure through sport or conversation.

When I couldn't sleep or woke up soaked in sweat:

"Why stay in bed if you are awake? You can't sleep anyway and your thoughts are just going around in your head, aren't they? If your body is tired enough, it will normally want to sleep. You should distract yourself first – get up, drink some water, read the newspaper so that you can switch off from those thoughts, which won't let you sleep. Do some relaxation exercises. It doesn't matter what time it is. A healthy person can survive on an average of 6 hours sleep without problems if he has to." That's then exactly what I did during several nights even though 6 hours sleep weren't enough for me.

Something else that was very important for me was his experience as a senior physician in a clinic. He was able to tell me about a lot of similar cases to mine, and so the conversation wasn't only theoretical or straight from a textbook, but authentic cases from which I could learn something.

I have these sentences from the conversations in rehab still in my head:

"It's not inconceivable that you won't be able to get back to a level that you were at before. That doesn't mean the same performance or the same surroundings because that would mean there being the same danger of being overworked as you before. There is of course the possibility that you can overcome your inhibitions, which your body has implemented for "safety reasons"."

The goal of therapy and rehab isn't to learn how to avoid tense situations, but how to deal with the tension and the physical reactions in those situations, channel them and relieve yourself of them" (Confrontation therapy). "What's more, it is just as important to figure out and accept your limitations and to be able to say "no" when faced with a situation which could cause stress.

He tested how I would react before I went to rehab to see if I would be able to cope with its demands and those of the therapy sessions. That's how I interpreted it anyway. It was totally unexpected. He brought me into a situation where there was no way out and left me there. It was during a therapy session and I flipped out. I paced up and down the room, felt incredibly tense, heard myself getting louder and even started on him. I went to the window, opened it and took a few deep breaths to calm down. I ended our session early and left. He made sure that everything was OK and asked if I needed help. "No, It's fine. I just need some fresh air. It's a nice day, so I'm going to the Water Tower to sit in the sun." "If you need something, you have my mobile number, OK?" "Yes, fine." We discussed and cleared up the problem within the first 5 minutes of the next session. It was a test for me.

After the reintegration phase, things steadily continued to improve. In the end, we extended the time between sessions from 1 week, to 2 weeks to 3 weeks.

I'm sitting at the airport in Budapest. It is 9:35 am. It is 03.12.2013 and today I'm going to have my final session with my therapist and my wife. We want to give him a small gift to thank him for all the help he gave us to make sure our family got back to leading a normal, happy life.

There is only one thing left to say: THANK YOU and BEST WISHES to you and your family!

10.) Return to the Rehabilitation Clinic 21 months after 11.06.2012:

The group of us, who arrived on the 11.06.2012 met again in April 2013 in Fulda. It was a really nice weekend. We had chosen Fulda so that each of us had a similar distance to travel. One person organized the accommodation and everyone brought some typical food or drink from their region. We did a tour of Fulda and then had a barbeque in the evening.

Everyone spoke about how they had been since leaving RC. Everyone had different experiences, but the majority of them were positive. RC had definitely helped us all to cope, even though we had experienced setbacks. We wanted to remember what we had learned there and that is exactly what we did.

Today is the 06.04.14 and we have just said goodbye to each other after our second annual meeting in Heidelberg. Meeting is good for us. We all have fun, of course, but we've also become a small community. A community that doesn't just meet once a year, but which is interested in each other because everyone knows that they are understood by the others due to shared experiences. We don't just talk about our problems. We meet in the same way a skittles club or handballers do when they have club outings. You can tell there's more to it because we have travelled from all corners of Germany to be there. One has travelled from the North Sea, another has shortened a seminar so that he can be there and a third has planned to arrive late in the evening so that he can be there for at least one of the days. We try and meet every year near to where one of our group members lives.

We had a great time in Heidelberg this year and next year, we will be going to Berlin.

We also stay in contact during the year. It doesn't have to be that you finish at the clinic and just go home!

I'd like to thank the group. All 9 members. Everybody knows who is meant.

Return to Carolabad:

Appointment in Gotha:

After the last of my 3 appointments on a business trip to Gotha, I took one day holiday. We finished on time and, instead of driving home, I had time that afternoon to drive the rest of the distance to RC.

The core of the table tennis team had agreed to meet.

After a 2-hour drive, I parked the car in front of the clinic. I felt satisfied with myself. 21 months previously I had started the journey back home and back to my life. That was a good feeling.

I visited the clinic briefly that evening and the young lady at reception still remembered me. "I don't remember your name anymore, but you stayed with us." We were both thrilled. I was really enjoying being back there. That evening I tried to recall as much as I could from my time there.

I walked to the tower on the hill above the forester's lodge, taking an alcohol free wheat beer with me. I took the route to the viewing platform on the hill and there I made a toast to all the people at the clinic, recalling the time I had spent there. I wanted to say that I was thinking about them and THANK them for all their help. Could it get better? I repeated it at sunset!

After that I went back as quickly as possible. I really wanted to repeat as much as I could. I went to the brewery, in which we had celebrated the leaving parties, for dinner. Then I went to the old GDR cinema with the red, plush armchairs and the small tables. I didn't care what was being shown. The price was the same as before – "4 Euros please". "The Wolf of Wall Street" was playing. The first 2 thirds of the film were good, up until the party when they were throwing dwarves. That was enough for me then. It was clear how it was going to end anyway and it was getting late, so I left for my hotel.

The next morning I went back to the clinic. The young woman greeted me just as warmly as the caretaker. "I lent you the projector that once for the pictures", he recalled.

I met several therapists in the corridor between courses and lectures and was able to quickly say hello. We spoke a little bit and they all wished me all the best and continued good health. Even the head physician took the time to speak to me. She was on her way to another appointment, but encouraged me to keep working on my book. I was delighted. I could also talk with the sports occupational therapists. Then one of the ladies from the medical center told me that she still had my Mickey Mouse picture hanging in the recreation room. I spent 3 hours there, soaking up as much as possible. It had been a short time, but the most important part of my life.

Then I had an idea.

I looked at my watch and saw that I still had another 2 hours until I met with the 2 table tennis guys. That could work….

I made a decision:

I drove to the children's hospital and looked for the picture I had painted and donated 20 months previously. The receptionist was happy to describe the way. It was only 20 minutes away, so I jumped in the car and set off.

As I was looking for somewhere to park at the hospital, I realized that it was as big as the city hospital in Mannheim. It was like its own little town! I went to the information desk and asked for the oncology department. I felt a little bit uneasy about what those children were going through. After wandering around a couple of hundred meters of corridors, I found the department and was welcomed by one of the nurses: "How can I help?"

I explained why I was there. "Yes, I remember that picture, but we've just renovated this floor and I don't know what happened to the picture. Maybe it's hanging somewhere else."

Oh well, it was worth a try. I walked slowly down the stairs from the second to the first floor. I thought I would have a quick look on the first floor and, as I opened the door, there it was! All three pictures on a long wall. I hadn't wasted my time painting them! They aren't real works of art and never will be, just as I'm not an artist and never will be. Somehow these pictures looked funny and colourful and would cheer up a patient in this department, who probably wouldn't have so much to be cheery about otherwise. I felt satisfied with that.

The nurse on the first floor came over and asked: "Can I help you?" "Yes you can. Could you take a picture of me in front of those pictures". "Why?" "Because I painted them." "Well, if that's the case I will definitely do it for you."

Some things are meant to be and others aren't. I had actually already given up hope. It wouldn't have been a disaster if hadn't found the pictures, but now I'd managed to draw a line under everything that had happened.

As I walked back to my car, I looked up at the clear blue sky: thank you!

The picture that I painted for the Children's Hospital in Chemnitz while in rehab.

I jumped in the car and drove to meet my two table tennis friends. If I had tried to plan all of these things in 1.5 days, something is bound to have gone wrong! I had just gone with the flow and everything had gone really well.

So, the day had started off well and at 1pm, I met with my table tennis partners. It had worked out perfectly. On the motorway to our meeting place, I took the wrong exit and had to call to get directions. I had to turn around, but still arrived punctually at 1pm at Gasthof Hirsch. We were both happy to see each other. He had organized a B&B for me to stay in, so I quickly checked in before driving back to his place to wait for the third member of the group. It was so great that we were all together again. The sun was shining, the weather couldn't be better and we were sitting in the garden with a beer. Each of us talked about how things were going and what had happened and then we went to the Automobile Museum in Zwickau. That was really interesting. It had a lot of well-restored vintage cars and somehow it was like a metaphor for us. The museum presented the complete history of the car, plus the development of the manufacturers Horch, Audi and Sachsenring Motorenwerke, from their founding until the end of the GDR. I could still remember some of the names from the Top Trumps cards I had as a child.

After the museum, we went for a short walk around the city and then we went for dinner. We get on really well with each other and that evening we could enjoy a relaxed atmosphere and the old stories from Carolabad. We agreed that we should call a fourth person from our group. You could tell even over the phone that he was so surprised that he almost fell off his chair! After an extremely successful day and a wonderful reunion, we said our goodbyes and I drove home the following day.

The trip was more than worth it. Thank you so much to both of you!

11.) What have I changed?

On our holiday to Namibia this summer, we experienced something very simple, but very interesting. One day in the capital, Windhoek, we drove through a township. The staff of the guesthouse we were staying in all lived in this township. These were poor, mostly black people, who were just happy to have a job they could live from. In some cases, they could also afford to send their children to the township school. The owner of the guesthouse supported her staff by sometimes giving donations. It was possible to talk to these people directly as they mostly spoke English, and there was a possibility to do a tour through the township called Katutura. We booked to go because we wanted to see another side of the city, which was about the same size as "our" part of town.

The woman showed us where she lived, where she went shopping at the little market and the "Main Street" in Katutura. The translation of Katutura is: The place nobody wants to live. We visited a soup kitchen for children, which feeds 600 children everyday and we also saw the mobile medical service with 2 treatment rooms and a never-ending line of parents with their children. This one truck comes once a month.

The people living here have almost nothing. It's just like you see on the TV – corrugated iron huts with one room for the entire family and a pit latrine in front. Everything is dry and water comes from a tanker or from one of the few wells that are easy to spot due to the long lines of people. They have enough to survive. When we got to the market we got out of the car with our "tour guide" and had a look around. She showed us the stands she often buys things from. To be on the safe side we were a little reserved, but the people were very friendly, even though we didn't buy anything. Of course you shouldn't walk through there in the evening wearing gold chains, just like you wouldn't in some parts of our towns and cities. It's something quite different to be confronted with how people in other countries live. It reminded me of what my mother and my grandfather (who lived through both world wars) told me about the period after the war. The people back then also had nothing.

We were most impressed by our visit to a private organization, which supports children, the BNC. A Canadian woman has been working there for 8 years, looking after children after school, helping them with their homework, keeping them busy by playing games and doing some work in the garden. She also gives them something to eat in the afternoon. She does all of this for 160 children on a voluntary basis, relying on donations and the help of 2.4 other volunteers. She lives in Katutura herself and is well-respected because of the work she does. This is a person, who has spent 10 years of her life taking care of other people's children in an area of poverty, without earning a single cent or saving anything for her own future, but who enjoys everything she does. Isn't that crazy? In our eyes, maybe yes, but not in the eyes of Mary B. She has drawn so much optimism, happiness and energy from the children, who are happy because they have found someone to take care of them, they aren't alone, they don't have to steal to survive, they have things to do, they can learn, have fun with the ball and few donated games they have and they have something to wear. All the children do all the domestic work themselves. We hadn't been there very long before several 7-10 year olds asking questions surrounded Sara: "Where are you from?" "What's your name?" "Where do you go to school?" "Which language do you speak?" "How old are you?" "Do you have any sisters or brothers?" Etc. Then they gave her a private tour of the rooms, the "Secret Garden", the herb garden and everything else they have there. They didn't know each other at all, came from completely different countries and cultures and were poor and "rich". They both had to use a foreign language to make themselves understood, but they understood each other straight away and had a lot of fun. It was so impressive how happy these children were, even though they had hardly anything. You could see in their eyes that they were happy and also in the way they played with each other, greeted us and showed us around.

We live in such luxury!

We made a donation, which was enough for us to buy peanut butter for a month, but Mary B. was delighted and so were we. We thought about how we could support Mary from Germany. It would be worth the effort, that's for sure. In Mannheim, we make donations to the church and the Jose Carreras Gala evening for children with leukaemia. In the case of the slum, it would be possible to achieve a lot with very little and that was the great thing about it. Especially as this was just about Mary. In her organization, money wouldn't be wasted on paperwork, administration or additional work. Everything donated would go straight to the children.

Marliese and I thought about a new hobby.

We collect "childhood years" By that I mean a donation to support a child for 1 year. 1€ per day = 365€ per year. It somehow fits to our "theme" We celebrated our joint 50th birthday together and we wanted to do the same with our joint 100th. (It's going to be hard, but we are working on it. Let's see how it goes. You never know, I might get run over by a bus tomorrow!) I want to do 100 push-ups, sit ups and squats (3x33 or 5x20. At least, I started to do that!) We could also collect "childhood years". We have been sponsoring a child in India for the last 6 years. It costs €1 a day. Together with some friends, we donated a "year" to Katutura in Windhoek (If you like, you can Google "BNC Windhoek" and Mary B. It's very interesting.) That means we have 6 years already. Let's see how many we get before we are 100 years old. Maybe we'll even manage 100 "childhood years." That would be great. We could just not buy a new TV or a laptop for a generation and then we already have 3 "years". It seems quite easy.

One of our past acquaintances is a woman who was around 45 years old. She suffered from an incurable illness. She had to inject herself with medication 3 times a week. "If I don't do it, there is a risk of an unpredictable relapse. That could mean many things – I could be paralysed, go blind or have problems speaking. I've had this illness for 30 years already and it means I have to be very disciplined when it comes to nutrition. I also have to do some consistent sport. This illness is inherited, and that means that I won't be able to have any children, even though I've always wanted some. I think it's too much of a risk to adopt as well. It wouldn't be very responsible. The thing is, I won't gain anything from being negative all the time. I've been doing my job for 25 years and can work normally. I just have to be very strict with myself for the rest of my life. I still enjoy my life despite these things. I take what I can and I'll be happy as long as I can continue doing what I want."

That is courage, the will to live, strength and a sense of responsibility. Good for her! Respect!

My story about donations is incidental in comparison!

I wrote at the beginning: we assume so often that things are going to run smoothly. Someone we know ended up in hospital with intestinal polyps. The treatment should have been routine - remove a part of the intestine. No risk of cancer and no metastases. He is a policeman and as fit as a fiddle. The operation went well, but the wound didn't heal and he contracted the hospital virus MRSA. Shit! He has been battling with it for several years now. He had another operation in autumn and has been in intensive care for 8 weeks in a life threatening condition. He has a wife and 2 children. Bullseye! This is all because of a lack of hygiene and a misdiagnosis at the hospital. He was promised an appointment at the hospital on a Tuesday after being treated by an on call doctor at the weekend for a badly swollen abdomen. His stomach burst on the Monday and he ended up in a coma. If we have a parish fete and don't have a cover over the cakes to protect them, the health authorities can close us down. I know 5 people, who have been sent home from hospital with wound infections. 2 of them have died since then. No joke! I read a report in our daily newspaper last week about patient data, which shows that 19,000 people died in Germany 8 years ago because of incorrect treatment and/or unsatisfactory hygiene. How can the doctors and nurses do their jobs properly when the number 1 priority is cost effectiveness, especially if a nurse has to take care of 40-50 patients during a night shift, or a doctor has to operate for 36 hours? You hardly get any information about that though.

Despite these statistics we are counted as one of the "good" countries. In the USA for example, hardly anyone can afford to stay in hospital. A friend told me recently that it is standard in many companies to let people go if they have been off sick for 2-3 weeks. Great! And this is the land of opportunity! This is only indirectly connected to my topic, but I met quite a few nurses in rehab who couldn't deal with the stress anymore.

This happened to a 13-year-old girl: her legs became numb because a tumor had grown on her spine and was pressing on the nerves in her spinal canal. She had an emergency operation to prevent paralysis, but it was partially inoperable. This happened 2 days before Christmas. Think back to Michael Schumacher - everyone was shocked. A professional sportsman, extremely fit and a role model for a lot of people. He was careless once, had a skiing accident and was in a coma for months. Hopefully he will survive. I'm sure he would pay €100 million to turn back the clock, but he can't.

All of these experiences showed me that I should be more satisfied with what we have as a family. A bike for short trips or to get to work is OK. We don't always have to have the newest TV or the best cell phone. It's also not necessary to completely change the contents of the wardrobe every season. We are also quite healthy in comparison with other people.

What does this experience mean for me? The same as before. If I can be happier with less, I will have less stress trying to maintain my "high standard of living". If I am happier with less, I can be happier more often and have more periods of satisfaction, because I have the time to enjoy these "fewer" things. I want to treat myself to the luxury of time. The luxury of being able to turn off my phone in my free time so that no one can reach me.

Things can change from one day to the next and it may or may not be your own fault. You have to be able to take that in before you know how valuable it is to just be healthy. That's why people should focus more on that.

My priorities have fundamentally changed.

Health, family, fun, friends, work.

The assessment of my situation is that I am now a lot more relaxed about things without taking them less seriously, I don't worry about consequences as much, and so can think more clearly.

We have done the same with our daughter at school and seen success: The school system is very demanding on the kids, but I don't want to rant about the excessive timetables here. She takes her grades and subjects very seriously and everything is going relatively well and she is quite good at organizing herself now. As always though, maths isn't the best. The teacher likes to set difficult assignments. Of course, it has to be someone's fault! She once got a Grade E, but we told her: "You are good at all other subjects. You are learning two foreign languages at the moment. Why are you worrying so much about 1 subject out of 10? Even if you have to repeat a year, it's not like someone has died. In fact, sometimes it's really helpful because things become easier to understand. As things stand right now, you'll be able to do your final year exams later on. We'll learn maths together and we'll just take things as they come, no matter what your grades are on that day. The result was her grades improved from an E to a C because the pressure to do well and the worry were both gone, but the motivation and dedication were still there. This was enough of a confirmation for me.

I can be happy about the little things because now I know what things can be like.

I don't grumble like I used to about a problem. I first think whether or not it is a top priority. If not, then I push it to the back of my mind so that I can think about something more important. I come back to the problem when I have time for it. If I have too much work, I organize it in a way, which means I can handle it and if I can't, then things can be postponed. I am enjoying the freedom. At the moment I am working on the planning phase of a project worth several million Euros. If there is a mistake in the concept, it will cost a lot of money later on, and so it's better to look at something like this to the best of your ability now. This has really helped me, plus I have also stepped back from certain things (See volunteer work in the parish, private pressure points etc.)

Dealing with mistakes:

A mistake can be motivating.

You can learn from mistakes.

If I can rectify or avoid a mistake, I can be pleased.

A mistake can have consequences.

The consequences of a mistake can cause fear.

Fear can paralyze a person.

Fear can lead to physical symptoms.

Fear can change behavior.

Fear can influence the psyche.

Constant fear can be destructive.

And the moral is: avoid mistakes and be happy. Period.

A boss once told me (One of the 8 I mentioned before): "Mr. Dietrich, you should work to the best of your ability and then you won't make any mistakes." Rubbish, I thought. Everyone makes mistakes, every day. Me, him, ever one of us. You can't avoid it. It's normal.

I hadn't interpreted his comment correctly, though. Of course everyone makes mistakes, but we only recognize them after they have been made or things develop differently to how we planned. Maybe we have overlooked something or we have assumed something, which isn't correct. We have to make thousands of decisions everyday, some of which we make automatically as a reflex. Things often work out as expected when it comes to these small, everyday things. It often doesn't make a difference whether I turn left or right and then arrive at my destination 10 minutes earlier or later (unless I miss a flight or my wife has the dinner on the table!)

You can never be totally sure how things are going to work out. We normally do our level best when it comes to making important decisions. We make them based on what we know at that moment, taking into account all possible outcomes as far as it is possible. We act to the best of our knowledge, either alone or in a group. At this point, we think we haven't made any mistakes, but in hindsight it can turn out that that wasn't the case. Bad luck. You then have to do something about it. Maybe you have already thought about potential problems and have a Plan B in order to react to them. This means: A person who acts according to his/her best knowledge and doesn't just thoughtlessly tick-off jobs "doesn't make mistakes". Most of the time, if something should really go wrong, we look for one person to blame, but I know that, in reality, things are not often that simple.

What does this new attitude "I don't make mistakes" mean for me? (I know it sounds quite arrogant and superficial.) The answer is simple: I don't worry when presented with a new task. If the boss knows that you will do the job with care and will discuss with him or the colleagues if there are any problems and then things go wrong, he won't blame you but will work with you together to find a solution. Afterwards, you can sit down and talk about what could be done better the next time and what has been learned. This information can be passed on to the other colleagues and that is it. No one guilty party, no passing of the buck, there is no pressure, you can sleep well at night and there is no fear about the job in hand. You think about solutions and don't have your head filled with worrying about what will happen if things go wrong. If you do think about it or you imagine there could be a risk (risk analysis), you will try and look for a Plan B.

The best thing is to do our jobs well and then everything is fine. We are always wiser afterwards and there will always be know-it-alls (Again, this is nothing new, but I think there is a good connection to what I want to say.) With this attitude; I was able to better deal with the teething problems of my first projects of the reintegration phase.

My demands aren't as high as they used to be and I don't take things for granted either, e.g. health.

What about my expectations of other people? In rehab, the behavioral therapist told us very simply that we couldn't expect people to react in a particular way to our behavior. What was that supposed to mean?! I expect thanks if I've helped a person or after I have asked for some advice or the way. I can expect that my wife is thrilled about an expensive necklace. After all, I've worked hard for the money! I can expect that the dinner is on the table when I come home from work. I can expect that my children help around the house. It's part of a good upbringing.

Yes, I can expect everything. If it doesn't happen, how would I normally react? That's right, I am annoyed, but I have a reason to be! My expectations hadn't been fulfilled.

I have recently tried to deal with things differently. If I help someone or I give a gift to my family or friends, I don't expect anything in return. Nothing. They might give me a gift or they might invite us somewhere, but there is no obligation. I'm just happy about being able to do something for someone else. Maybe it was fun preparing it! As I said before, I've had my fun and enjoyed giving the gift or making the invitation. There are no obligations and no pressure when it comes to the appointment, the size of the present etc. Things will work out as well as you expect them to. If there is some kind of positive reaction to what's been done, that's even better. The reaction should be an honest one, which can also mean hearing "hey, I can't be bothered today", or "I really don't like the present". I can handle that. It also takes away some of the pressure from everyday life: "We have to meet with the Meiers again soon, but I don't know what to cook because they are vegetarian." Or: "How much did Aunt Trude's present cost? We don't want to give her anything cheap." It doesn't matter. Good friends can have fun without any of this stress.

Right now I can think of 3 situations when I set my expectations too high: I was having problems, real problems and I assumed that a good friend of mine would help me out. We got on very well with each other when it came to partying, but this time, I heard nothing at all. "Yes, I'll call you, but I have a lot to do right now." Nothing. We bumped into each other: "Sorry, I hadn't forgotten about you, but you know what it's like with work and everything...." Again, I heard nothing, no call up until today. I had wanted that he had time for me. I didn't really know him in tricky situations, though, only from celebrations. Back then, I was angry, but I'm not anymore. It's not his fault I just made an incorrect assumption about him. I had been disappointed because I had been wrong. So I just want to say to him, don't worry about me, I'm fine. I don't expect any help from anyone, but I'm happy when I get something back.

In another situation I put a lot of effort into making a personal present for someone that couldn't just be bought in a shop. I thought it would be perfect, but no, it was a total disaster. Why? I had made a mistake by misjudging her. I didn't really know her so well. It was a special situation, which we hadn't experienced together before, so the mistake was on my side. The present just didn't fit to her. As soon as I had understood that, I wasn't disappointed anymore. Today when I look back, it's completely OK for me.

I have a third example and then I will be finished with this topic: I worked for over 15 years on a steering committee. We all got on with each other, and we still do. We sometimes get invited to birthday celebrations and we were a great group and I had a lot of fun. Due to my burnout, I had to stand down, but everybody understood and we had a farewell party just before Christmas. A colleague and I organized the drinks and everything was great. When we had had farewell parties for other colleagues in the past, we had given a small gift to thank them for all their work and cooperation. However, nothing like this happened for me. Everyone wished me all the best and verbally thanked me, but there wasn't any kind of present like a group photo, which everyone had signed. All I got was a thank you for the last 15 years. The group leadership had changed 1.5 years previously and the successor gave myself and the 2 others, who were also leaving, a card with "best wishes and thank you". I thought it was strange as this was from the person who knew me for the shortest time. There was nothing from the rest of the group, even though I made sure I collected all the documentation related to what I had been working on and handed them over before leaving. This time, however, it didn't feel like such a big deal. Hey, I had my fun during this time, but it's over now. I had to draw a line under it and remember the good times. I still have valuable contacts from this time and I'm pleased about that. Why should I get annoyed about it?

So, the question is, what's the point of all of these examples? It just shows how my relationships with my friends are now much more relaxed. There isn't any "Oh, I just have to…" and no frustration about any unfulfilled expectations or any other underlying stress. I now have more time for things that are good for me, but it took a while to get to that point because I needed to work on my basic attitude first. It sounds quite superficial, but it isn't, and anyway, if it's good for me, what's the problem? It's all about me being able to cope better with things without turning into a nasty piece of work.

Humor:

This is a delicate subject. You can achieve a lot with humor. If the chemistry between 2 people is right and you have the same sense of humor, almost nothing can go wrong. If you can make a joke of a bad situation, this can bring some relief and gives you time to take a deep breathe and that is good for you. What's more, it's been proven that laughing releases endorphins, which make you happy (you can Google it!) There are even relaxation courses using laughing exercises and training. It's good for you! Sometimes if I feel tense and recognize that AMY is making herself felt again, I try to think about something funny and try to make myself laugh. I mean really laugh. It relaxes and makes it easier to manipulate yourself. Am I playing the fool? No, and even if I was, nobody sees it, and so it doesn't matter. The most important thing is that it helps and I don't need to take any medication.

You do have to know how different people deal with and react to humor or if they will be easily offended. Humor only works if you are able to give and receive criticism.

Satisfaction: I read a nice proverb about this.

If I have a bowl, which is big enough to hold everything that I want, I am satisfied with all those things. When someone adds something else and the bowl is full, I am pleased and happy. If it over flows, I can give the things to other people.

If I make my bowl smaller, I will be happier much more quickly and more often. I will also feel more satisfied with little things and will also pass things on to others more often. That makes me feel good as well.

I could also want more and more and keep on making my bowl bigger, but then I would never be really happy anymore and I also wouldn't pass anything on to others, and this could make me an outsider and leave me all alone even though I keep taking more from the people around me.

Is it bad to change yourself after experiencing such a low in your life?

No, absolutely not.

It is NECESSARY.

Why are the numbers of burnout cases increasing so much?

As I said, I'm not a doctor, sociologist or an employment specialist, and so I can't really answer this question knowledgably or completely. Dr. Schell already discussed this topic in the foreward, but the following probably shouldn't be dismissed out of hand.

Psychological pressure can build due to the ever-increasing demands to perform well in a shorter period of time. The effect of much faster methods of communication should also be considered as it adds to the amount of information we have to take in and process at work and also in our free time. Everyone can be reached at anytime and nobody wants to miss anything.

We have successfully made our processes, production and living environment much faster and more profitable with the help of computers and technology. Everything is fine and can raise our standard of living as long as we can keep up! We have to be much faster than we used to be because in the meantime, we have become a part of the process, and so we don't treat ourselves to any kind of time out. Computers and machines can be set to work at different performance levels and humans are slowly becoming a weak point when it comes to our work processes.

Then we come to our free time: if you don't do anything in your free time, you are boring, but most people want to experience new things and spend their time sensibly.

There is a huge difference to the past because we never used to have such a wide range of possibilities. As a child, it was a highlight to be allowed to go on holiday with my aunt every 3-4 years.

If you consider how a child develops into an adult, it's clear to see that humans are very adaptive. Just look at the complexity of learning a language, which a child can do before starting school without being able to read or write single letters. And then there is the learning of motor and musical abilities. I'm not sure if our ancestors evolved with football and piano playing in mind. There's also the process of thinking and combining knowledge and information, which a baby is incapable of doing. We can see with our children how difficult it can be to perform to the best of their ability in the time up to their exams, even though they are normally perfectly capable of dealing with their subjects. It's just the fact that there is so much to learn in such a short period of time.

Why are even young people complaining about excessive demands? Later in life, work is all about growth rates and increasing profits and performance.

The magazine "Der Spiegel" reported about this in an article on 01.09.2014. It would be a relief if someone invented something to make activities faster and simpler. The only problem is that we would increase the number of activities we have by so much that there wouldn't be any kind of time saving or relief at the end of the day.

It could be that we have quite simply arrived at our "biological performance limit" in our newly created living environment, which was created for us by evolution or by God.

As I said, having time is becoming more of a luxury.

Communication / Media Changes:

> **Letter**
> **Telephone**
> **TV**
> **Pocket Calculator**
> **Computer**
> **Videos**
> **Internet, Network,**
> **Mobile Phone**
> **Smartphone, iPad,**
> **Facebook, Whatsapp**

Everybody can see the difference. In the past I came home after work. If the telephone didn't ring, that meant there was peace and time for the family and yourself. Today the first thing you do is check your private emails and have a look at the 30 or so messages you have on Facebook. You don't know which of those are important, so you check them all. When you are out and about, how many people do you see on their iPhones and other smartphones? They are always available. I think the majority of personal communication is unnecessary, but we have the possibility to tell everyone everything immediately. It's logical that you'll become inundated.

12.) My personal conclusion:

What would I pay attention to today? What will I do differently? How would I behave today?

1. I will listen to my body and the signals it gives me. When something comes up, which I can't deal with in the long run without there being some consequences for my health, I know I will have to change something. I haven't experienced such a situation since I reduced what I do in my free time. I can do everything I used to be able to at work, just not the same amount. Any questions I got about voluntary work I have politely refused.

2. I have to talk to everyone involved about the problems I have and what is causing me stress. You have to talk about your problems and not let them eat away at you. I wasn't crazy, but there was the risk that I could have become permanently depressed if I hadn't been open about what was going on.

3. I have to work together with the others involved to try and find a solution. Sometimes a partial solution is also enough as long as it leads to having enough energy to deal with what's left. You have to learn to prioritize.

4. If this doesn't work for whatever reason, I have to have a Plan B of how to change my life so that I can get by. This can affect several things depending on the situation. There should be no taboos as I have already discussed. This is not necessary at the moment because I can deal with the current level of demands placed on me.

5. I have to define changes and the ways I can achieve them. This has to be realistic and attainable for me.

6. I have to have the courage to take certain steps, which could be difficult, but in the end, it's all about being able to get back on my feet.

7. It could be that you discover new and positive things, which you hadn't been able to see before, just like this book.

8. Important: The most important thing you can do is pay attention to physical health and fitness. That doesn't have to mean elite sport, but regular endurance exercises and going to the sauna helped me. It's good for the body, releases endorphins, improves resilience, frees your mind and even means that the alcohol free beer you drink

afterwards tastes twice as good. Sport also extends life expectancy by 10 years and that isn't 10 years of using a walker, but using a bike! If you have a car, you change the oil, clean it, wash it and have it checked, so why not do it for yourself? Everybody knows these things as your doctor always tells you. Do you do it? What do you mean, no time? It's all about your health and 10 good years of your life. Make time! This is a luxury you can afford.

9. When it comes to eating I take care that I don't drink too much coffee or alcohol. I recognized that both of these have an effect on me – too much caffeine and I become nervous, hectic and I can feel tingling and tension, so it's better not to consume it. The same goes for alcohol. 1 beer is ok, but after that I only drink alcohol free.

10. I know that I had created a very good framework with AMY over time. I had to change some things about myself and my hobbies, but there were a lot of people and things to support me in doing this. I know that this is more difficult for a lot of you, but sometimes it's necessary to climb a mountain to be able to leave the fear behind. That's exactly how things started with me. You will only be able to reach your goal if you take the first steps along the road. Sometimes the way is the goal.

11. These days I need to take more breaks during the day. I can plan those as I like and could mean 10 minutes at work when I don't have to concentrate on anything or breathing exercises during a meeting, which nobody notices. It's at this point that I realize that it's possible to become very tense without really noticing. Breathing out slowly makes me feel like I'm unwinding from my neck, down my spine into my legs. It also feels like the tension is leaving my body.

12. I listen to other people much more closely when they talk about burnout and stress. I take them seriously because I can learn something from them.

13. I look forward to every day. Everybody knows the line from the famous film about the big ship: "because every day counts."

The following is taken from a letter by an elderly lady:

(http://www.zeitzuleben.de/2846-aus-dem-brief-einer-alteren-dame/)

"If I could live my life again, then the next time I would risk making more mistakes. I would relax and be more laid-back and funnier than this time. There are very few things I would take seriously.

I would travel more and be a little bit crazier. I'd climb more mountains, swim in more rivers and see more sunsets. I'd go walking more and just enjoy everything more. I would eat more ice cream and fewer beans.

I would only have "real" problems not puffed up ones. If I could do it all again, I would just try to live life from one moment to the next rather than planning every day years in advance.

If I could start again, I would get around much more, but travel with less luggage. I would learn to play the piano. If I could live my life again, I would walk around barefoot much longer in the spring and autumn. I would skip school more often.

I wouldn't work hard for high positions unless they came up coincidentally.

I would go on more rides at the fairground and would also pick more daisies."

(Nadine Stair, from: The Robbins Power Principle by Anthony Robbins, page 533)

We had a very interesting encounter last week. A woman in her mid-70s was sitting in the Anna Chapel in Burrweiler, next to a table of jam. We had a short break in the church and thought about buying a jar of jam from her to make her day. She had some interesting flavors, which you can't buy in a supermarket.

We started to have a conversation and suddenly this little old lady with her wrinkled face and thick glasses turned into sales manager: "I sell homemade jam during the year and use the money I make to support a nurse in Tanzania, who is still taking care of children and preparing 80 meals a day despite being 76 years old. I make a bout 2-3,000€ a year selling jam and doing other arts and crafts! I also take care of the pilgrimages here. The largest is in the summer when the Bishop comes and consecrates the donations and gifts. I also have 4-500 loaves of bread baked and write to all the vintners and famers in the area and they donate wine, fruit and vegetables. About 100 people come to the service led by the Bishop and, at the end they can all take something from the gifts in return for a donation. We make another 3-4000€ in this way and we can support the nurse in Tanzania very well. It means she can help the children and keep her hospital open. I'd prefer to do something like that than be idle in front of my TV. It's not like it's stressful. I'm working with people and it's doing good for others."

Wow. Here was an old mother who, at the age of 75, was sitting on a wobbly church chair, doing more for social issues than I have done or probably ever will. Hats off to her! This is how you do it. It's not for everyone, of course, but it's a great example.

So, if you ever find yourself in St. Anne's Chapel and you see a grandmother selling jam, there's only one thing I can say – it tastes exquisite!

Recently, my wife drew my attention to an article in a drugstore's magazine. Every month, Professor Götz W. Werner, who works on the advisory board of the store, writes a column. In the August 2014 edition he wrote about courage and humility in connection with success. In a nutshell, if you want to achieve something, you need a certain amount of courage, but you shouldn't be too cocky and overestimate what you can do otherwise you could lose sight of your goal. He quotes the American George Washington Carver, who was born as a slave, but later honored by President Roosevelt and Henry Ford for his achievements. Despite this new-found prestige, George talks with humility:

"How far you come in life depends on how tender you are with the young, how compassionate you are with the elderly, how sympathetic you are to people who make an effort and how patient you are with the weak and strong. One day, you will be all of these things."

This quote impressed me, especially because a successful company manager was able to talk about humility.

This was just a small digression to discuss a fleeting meeting while out for a walk and a newspaper article.

Today, 15 months after the end of the reintegration phase, I can do almost everything I could before. I have been able to do every one of my previous tasks at work once again e.g. layout planning, data analysis, project presentations, comparing offers, conversations with suppliers, business trips and even starting up systems. I have managed to do everything and so I can continue to earn my money!

I am so happy and thankful about that.

I still have to take breaks and also have days off in lieu of business trips. I still need the possibility to arrive the afternoon before an all day meeting and then leave the following day. If I can't meet a certain deadline because I'm busy, I tell someone. It's better than agreeing to do something and then everyone being unhappy when it doesn't work out. It's important and I make the most of being able to say no because there is mutual respect and understanding between my colleagues, my boss and me.

I've also changed my private life and priorities. I take more time for my family or myself. I've given up responsibility for the parish and there isn't any renovation work to do by myself any more because someone else can do it. I have more free time to do sport, to go to the sauna with Marliese, to paint a picture or just lie on the couch and relax.

All in all, taking everything into account, my performance levels are a little bit lower than before my burnout, but it's still enough to be able to do my job and still have fun.

If there comes a point when I'm not able to deal with the demands of the job anymore, then it won't be the end of the world. I'll just try and find a solution or alternative with the company. If there is a will, there is a way!

Every change can be a new chance.

I will always try my best to be consistent. If everything works out and the "boss" upstairs is happy, I can still do a lot in the next 30 years and hopefully make many people and children laugh. It doesn't hurt, it's easy, doesn't cost much and is a lot of fun.

My therapist would say that I have been able to come to terms with my experiences a little bit more because of this book, and that's true. I see things differently now and have also changed my behavior in certain situations. I have said goodbye to a lot of "ballast".

A manager in one of my previous companies once told me: "Mr. Dietrich, you are too soft."

I'd hit rock bottom - I'd looked after my mother for 2 years, raised 2 children, executed projects worth 6 digits, built 2 houses, worked voluntarily for 15 years for the parish and sponsored a child, but I was at rock bottom. I managed to pull myself back up after rehab – I got to know new people, from whom I learned what real problems are (mine were small problems, but I was happy I didn't have those of some of the other people), I managed to achieve everything I could in 7 weeks of rehab, I have returned to my old job despite alternatives, I work in all areas I used to and I have written this book.

I'm quite pleased with myself!

I have changed myself and a new period of my life is beginning:

NOW!!

This is the experience I would like to share with you. Everyone is different. Take what you can use from this book and do something with it. It's your life and you only have one of them! Good luck and remember: commitment is good and so is positive stress, but be careful when it comes to your health!

Today is 31.12.2013 and it's been a good end to the year:

- I'm just finishing the basic concept for this book. I'm going to send it to the head physician at CB to be corrected and approved. She has replied to me and given me the courage to do this and that's a great feeling!! ☺☺
- 2 days ago we had a family get together with relatives we haven't seen for a vey long time.
- I don't have any responsibility for the parish anymore.
- Our new cat, Momo, is house trained! The cat litter tray is empty! ☺

I'm looking forward to 2014 with my family and AMY! ☺   ☺   ☺

13.) What do I have to do with God?

I'm a technician so what do I have to do with God? It's possible to explain the Big Bang using physics, mathematics, chemistry and biology and we can even recreate some of these processes in a particle accelerator.

Wow. The things we have researched and learned! If we can't comprehend something, we build ourselves tools, use sensors, measure invisible waves and radiation, look into space with telescopes, fly to the moon, start wars and spy on each other. We can cure so many things using medicine, transplant organs and have even created new viruses we can no longer treat (MRSA). With today's computer technology, we can do almost anything.

If we can't see something, then it doesn't exist. We can prove or explain everything, or so we think. So why do we need God? We are God, aren't we? At least that's how we treat the Earth and not favorably either. Despite all our knowledge, progress and technology, we don't behave any better or more cleverly than a swarm of locusts, which eats up everything around and keeps on reproducing until they starve because there isn't enough to go round. You could also say this in a more refined way, but this just came into my head as I was writing.

There are so many things that happen without us knowing about it and which we can't plan for. "If I had known, I would've reacted differently." We say this is coincidence. Maybe. Maybe not. I don't know.

I have dedicated 16 years of my life to working voluntarily for the parish. For the main, it was a lot of fun at the beginning, but in the last 6 years it became more stressful because even the churches have to save.

The whole work was more of a hobby. I was working with friends and nice people, celebrated together, helped during church services and took responsibility for the church leadership. On a social level, this was a lot of fun and still is, even without the Council of Elders.

Now suddenly you are in a do or die situation. This at least is how I felt and the doctors and therapists confirmed it. You can't cope without other people's help anymore. It's about your life, but the situation seems to be hopeless, but then you remember God. The one you often turn to ask for help for other people. The one your mother and grandfather prayed to during the bombing raids over Mannheim. The one you talk to when you can't understand something anymore, it can't be explained with technology or you are in need. The one who is always there when you are in trouble and don't know what to do next.

The doctors tell you that "mechanically" you are healthy, but you feel miserable.

In this situation, I prayed for help for myself for the first time. I didn't know what else to do. Should I have got more information for myself? Maybe, but I couldn't imagine what links there were. I didn't know where I should start. I expected some kind of trade off. I had made a deal in my head between God and myself. I know you can't make deals with Him. You can't demand things from Him. You can only ask him for things and then do what you can. You have to open your eyes and try and see the positive in most things. I was able to draw strength from doing this and have the following summary:

1.) I'm still alive (if what the doctor in the Emergency Department told me was true, things could've been so much different)

2.) I don't have any permanent damage to my health apart from being slightly less resilient.

3.) My family stuck with me through thick and thin.

4.) A lot of my friends and colleagues gave me courage.

5.) I went to exactly the right Rehabilitation Clinic. They gave me the support I needed to start on the road to recovery and I had very good doctors there.

6.) After 7 months of waiting, I was given the information and tools I needed to find my way again.

7.) Having the infection meant that I started painting again.

8.) Once I had worked out what I wanted to do, I changed myself to be better than I was before so that I could achieve my goal, enjoy life as much as I can and to help others. I'm now working towards this.

9.) I had a very good therapist at home.

10.) I had a boss, who gave me the courage to come back to work and I still have contact with him.

11.) The new boss has been a perfect support.

So why, after everything that has happened, shouldn't I start believing in God? It's all coincidence? Not for me! You can all make your own decisions abut that. It's true that things could've turned out differently, but it didn't and I am going to make the most out of that. I'm also working on keeping my side of the "deal".

I'm going to turn around what I wrote before about needing science to prove something: as long as nobody can conclusively prove that God doesn't exist, I will believe that He does, despite all the contradictions, thanks to my personal experiences

I still have the question that I had at the beginning. Why did I suffer from burnout?

In hindsight I have to say that it was my fault. All the signs were there, but I ignored them. I hadn't reckoned that it would get so bad until it was too late. I just couldn't see it happening to me. I was afraid of the consequences of making changes, which would have come in the wake of the decisions I made. Today I would do things differently. Of course, we are always much more clever after the event...

The question: "Why do all these terrible accidents and tragic things happen?" (I'm sure you hear that from your group of friends as often as we do.)

Unfortunately I don't have an answer, but should I have one? I'm only talking about my personal situation - my small family and me. I know we aren't anything special. We're just trying to do our thing, that's all.

He isn't there when things go wrong (because of our actions) to put everything right. We could do things better or stop others from happening if we wanted. In a church service to remember the dead, the priest said that God wasn't there to help us avoid suffering, but to help us get through it if we let Him. He offers some kind of solace.

Does it really matter if God plays a role or not?

It doesn't hurt to believe in God. Maybe He is only some kind of comfort for us, but it worked for me. In the end it's only important how you live your life before you end up in your box:

Did I have fun or not?

Did I live at the expense of others or not?

Was I a good parent and did I take care of my family or not?

Was I prepared to help (as much as possible) or not?

How will people remember me?

Did I ever mislead people?

Was I selfish and did I always look for the advantages in a situation for myself? Etc.

In the movie "The Bucket List" with Jack Nicholson and Morgan Freeman (both have cancer and know that they will die within the next 6 months), the character played by Morgan Freeman asks the question: "When you die and are standing at the gates of heaven and you are asked: "did you enjoy your life? Did you try and please other people? What are going to say?" (Egyptian proverb).

It's very unlikely that I don't have enough air miles to get an entrance ticket, but as I said, the experiences I have had getting to know the happy children in Katutura, Namibia; my friends and those people in rehab really impressed me. All they need to make them smile is food, clothes, a ball and someone to take care of them. If it is fun for me to give the children a reason to smile, then why shouldn't I do it? Other people enjoy their stamp collection, their new iPhone, car or X-Box. The therapists are happy when they manage to get someone back on track. Everyone has their own hobbies and experiences.

If you enjoy helping children and other people and they smile and thank you, then what is so bad about that? I think it's absolutely fantastic!

Am I a wimp because of that? I think I've already answered that question.

So, thanks up there for all the help and I'm sorry if I caused any problems. I'm trying my best not to mess up my side of the bargain.

I believe in God and I'm going to fulfil my side of the deal and this book is the beginning.

Welcoming Committee at home:

14.) Thanks:

We tend to say thank you too rarely for so many things because we take them for granted. So many things have become trivial.

We take for granted,

that we'll wake up healthy in the morning,

that we'll have enough to eat,

that our children will grow up and not die before us,

that the illnesses we get will be treatable,

that we won't have an accident,

that we can always do our hobbies

that we will get old but stay healthy,

that we will have our life insurance paid out,

that one partner won't die before the other,

that we can enjoy our old age together,

that we have friends, who will stick by us,

that we have a job that we enjoy,

that work and projects run well,

that we can afford things,

that food in a restaurant tastes good,

that the bread in the bakery will always be fresh,

that the car will start in the morning,

that the buses and trains will always be punctual,

etc.

All of these things can change from one day to the next within the space a few moments.

You only want one thing: TO LIVE! Nothing else, just live and you'd do anything for that to be possible. If your own child were dying, nothing else would matter: not money, the house or the car. Just living!

I'm thankful when I wake up in the morning in good health and can enjoy the day, as well as when I can look forward to something, someone cheers me up, I succeed in something, I have time for my hobby and if my wife and children are well etc.

Nothing is 100% certain just because it always happened and you can't assume that it will stay that way.

I have a lot of people to thank:

My wife Marliese. She stuck by me and gave me the courage not to give up. She took over the work I had at home and always made sure I was free of obligations so that I had the time I needed and still need today.

My children Viktoria und Sara. They encouraged me and held me. They visited me in rehab along with Stefan and that gave me a big boost. Thank you to Sara for the relaxing piano playing and to Viktoria for supporting my wife.

My late mother. I learned from her that you shouldn't give up and about how important family and children are.

Heidi, Dieter, Matthias and Olga, who have been there for the last 52 years when we needed them regardless of the time of day. That says a lot.

Robert and Ute, who always asked after me and were there for Marliese in an emergency. I often poured out my heart to Robert while running.

Arthur and Marianne, Hiltrud and Klaus and the children, who belong to the family and were also at the ready in case of emergency.

My uncle, who always helped Marliese with the garden and so relieved her of the work.

Ralf, Lydia and Stefan for their understanding, encouragement and humor.

The **"Graz 4"** for the more than 40 years of friendship, which is deeper than any other and who somehow belong to the family despite the distance.

Ilona and Wolfgang, who gave me a lot of tips before going into rehab and always gave me encouragement.

Reiner and Gabi for their information and sharing their experiences after their own 4-year burnout.

Uwe and Beate for renewing our friendship and reminding me of the good old times.

The Schuff, Pietschke and Sittinger families, who are like a second home for our children and who always gave me a boost.

Anke and Ralf for the emotional support from Luxemburg

My GP, who reached out to me at the critical moment to tried and alleviate my fear and in whose hands my family and I are still in.

My therapists, without whom nothing would have worked out and I wouldn't have written this book.

The doctors and therapists at the clinic in Carolabad:

My therapist and the management of the clinic for motivating me to finish this book, the head physician, the leader of the creative and social competence groups, the group therapy and problem solving doctors, the doctor who treated my infection, my colleagues from social and nutritional services and the sports teams as well as the ladies from the medical center, reception and the 2 facility managers. I would like to thank everyone else I might have inadvertently forgotten to mention already. They all gave me the keys and the tools to understand my situation and my reactions so that I could get back on my feet. I wouldn't have managed it without all of them. THANK YOU!

The colleagues from the Council of Elders for the great time we had and for their constructive cooperation in the last, difficult years and their friendship.

My previous boss, who visited me at home and encouraged me to return to the department. For everything I learned from him and his help towards a successful reintegration. For his personal letter before his retirement and for always asking after me, as well as for his good advice and his improvement for suggestions after reading this manuscript.

My work colleagues and the secretaries:

It was never a question for them if I still belonged to the team or not. They always took/take my situation into consideration when necessary. Without them, I wouldn't be there anymore.

My new boss, who trusted me and had a lot of understanding for my situation from the beginning and who always showed me support and gave me advice in private conversations. These things aren't a matter of course. He gave all the time and freedom I needed to find my way back into the job. I managed to do that to the best of my ability and I'm still quietly working on it. Now that my therapy has been completed, he told me "now we are doing it on our own," OK, let's go then! Do your best to get more out of me…!

The Director and the Dean of the evangelical church, Mannheim for their help with the church conversion after I returned from rehab.

Our company's external architect for this: "impatience is a very bad counsel", which I always have in my mind and who sometimes helped me to remain objective. In the end, he was right. The most important part of the reintegration phase was being patient and being able to see the small steps as being positive.

Renate, for her great picture, which she gave us for our joint 100th birthday. It's hanging in our living room above the TV. I've probably looked at it at least 1000 times and was able to relax thanks to its vibes.

The former priests in Martin and the parents for both of the encouraging letters while I was in rehab.

My co-patients, with some of whom I'm still in contact and without whose help I wouldn't have got so far in rehab:

The ladies and the guys I played table tennis with from the groups 1-10.

The team from my dining table group and the people in the morning meeting. All of them. You will know who you are if you read this book.

Rich, Patty, Kathy, Randy, Lizzy and John for the encouraging emails from the USA.

And all the other neighbors, acquaintances and friends, who I may have inadvertently forgotten here.

Everyone who encouraged me while writing and who has given valuable advice.

And of course **Jenny**, who helped me a lot translating that book from German into English. I am sure she did a good job.

Oh yes and shouldn't forget:

GOD! Without Him, I wouldn't be here any more and I never would've written this book. That's how I see it anyway, even though there probably isn't any reason for that. Maybe He and his helpers had nothing else to do at that time. "Look at that Dietrich guy moaning. It won't take long. He just needs a little push at the right time. Just don't spend too much time on him. We've got more important things to do". Whatever. I'm happy about it!

Thanks BOSS!

Herzlichen Dank für Deine Hilfe, alles Gute,
Gesundheit, Gottes Segen
und werde 100 Jahre alt
Bodo

Thank you very much for your help.Wishing you all luck, health and God's blessings and the hope you become 100 years old, Bodo

A small thank you to all helpers and readers. I painted this picture in rehab and used it as a farewell.

15.) List of references:

- Own drawings from the work groups in the clinic

- The Dale Carnegie book: "How to Stop Worrying and Start Living" (Fischer)

- "Simplify Your Life" by Werner Tiki Küstenmacher. (Knaur)

- "Gelassen und sicher im Stress" by Professor Dr. Gert Kaluza, (Springer) (In my opinion, highly recommended) Recommended to my by my therapist in Carolabad.

- The book: "ALDI: einfach billig" by Andreas Straub, (rororo paperback)

- Collection of sayings from post cards and the internet (see appendix)

- We compiled the pictures and diagrams in the work groups in Carolabad. I reconstructed the charts from my notes, but they can be found in more detail on the Internet.

- The first and cover picture illustrate my personal situation at the time of my burnout.

- Wikipedia regarding the topic of suicide and the suicide rates.

- "Burnout: avoidance, recognition, understanding, action."
Dr. Stefan Poppelreuter, TÜV Rheinland Consulting GmbH and "Psychological pressures at work: causes, effects and possible actions" (Poppelreuter/Mierke) Very detailed analysis with practical examples and solutions.

- Paper by Business und Management Coach Mrs. Ramona Meinhardt: "Burnout Prevention is better than a cure."

16.) Appendix:

In the clinic we always exchanged encouraging poems and sayings. It might sound sentimental or cheesy, but it can be very helpful if you have really hit a low. A helpful word from a friend has never hurt anyone.

It was also very helpful to hear stories, read sayings from post cards and also biographies of well-known people, who had managed to find their way again after being so low. Hearing these gave us all a boost.

Here is a collection/bullet points of things you can Google:

- Abraham Lincoln never gave up: Short biography of Abraham Lincoln – very interesting how far up a person can work himself after a nervous breakdown. It's an example, but you don't have to become President! (Wikipedia)
- A very good poem by Charlie Chaplin: "As I began to love myself" can be viewed here: http://www.youtube.com/watch?v=-ZQ4ZliCDBM

- "What's really important is…"

  A Professor of Philosophy stood in front of his class having set up a small experiment: a very big jam jar and 3 closed boxes. When the class began, he opened the first box and took out some golf balls, which he put in the jam jar.

  He asked the students if the glass was full.
  They answered yes.

  He then opened the second box. It contained M&Ms. He poured these on top of the golf balls in the jar. He moved it around so that the M&Ms could fill the spaces between the golf balls. Then he asked the students again if the jar was full. They agreed it was.

  The professor then opened the third box, which contained sand. He poured this into the jar as well, shaking it as he did so. Logically, the sand filled up the remaining spaces. He then asked for a third time if the jar was full and all the students answered "yes."

  He then pulled two cans of beer out from under the desk, opened them and poured the contents into the jar, filling up all the remaining space between the grains of sand.

The students laughed.

Once the laughing had stopped, the professor said, "I want you to see this jam jar as your life.

The golf balls are the important things: your family, children, health, friends, the preferred or passionate aspects of your life, which would fulfil you even if you lost everything else you had."

He continued: "The M&Ms symbolize the other things such as your job, house and car. The sand is all the little things.

If you put the sand in the glass first, there won't be enough room for the M&Ms or the golf balls. The same is true for your life. If you invest all your time and energy in the little things, you'll never have space for the important things. Pay attention to the golf balls, the things that are really important. Prioritize.

The rest is just sand."

One of the students raised his hand and asked what the beer represented.

The professor grinned: "I'm glad you asked. That shows you that regardless of how difficult your life might be, there's always space for one or two beers."

- The soul feeds off the things that make you happy.
- A friend is like a lighthouse, who always has an overview even if we can't see anything anymore.
- Humor is the spice of life and if you have humor, you'll go far.
- If you can also be happy about the little things, you can be happy everywhere and always.
- Give everyday the chance to become the best day of your life.
- Be yourself. There are enough "other" people.
- Hope isn't being convinced that something will go well, but the knowledge that there is a reason for it if it doesn't.

- People who can spread a little joy and lust for life are people you should be fond of.
- Every journey begins with a first step, even if it is very small.
- A smile is the shortest way to another person's heart.
- In life, it's not about having luck, but being happy.
- You need courage to throw yourself into the currents if you want to reach the other side. (Lothar Zabler)
- It's better to light one small candle than to curse the darkness. (Confucius)
- Paths cross, paths drift apart, paths are justifiable, paths go up and down, but only you will find your own path.
- As long as you can move your feet and your light is on, let it shine and don´t run to be the best, but dance, sing and enjoy your life to the full.
- Happiness, laughter and joy are not a matter of money, but of your heart.

- As I have already mentioned, the background information regarding the following psychological topics was essential for the positive development of the required behavior, necessary to find a way back to a normal life

  - Fear in connection to growing strain, pressure and stress,
  - What is fear? How does it come about and what is it for?
  - Strategies for dealing with fear.
  - The same questions regarding stress.

There is a lot of literature for a personal, informative introduction to the topics. This cannot replace the professional help offered by therapists and doctors.

www.ingramcontent.com/pod-product-compliance
Lightning Source LLC
Chambersburg PA
CBHW081345280526
45788CB00009B/2777